Schooled to Order

Schooled to Order

A Social History of Public Schooling in the United States

DAVID NASAW

OXFORD UNIVERSITY PRESS

Oxford   New York   Toronto   Melbourne

Oxford University Press
Oxford   London   Glasgow
New York   Toronto   Melbourne   Wellington
Nairobi   Dar es Salaam   Cape Town
Kuala Lumpur   Singapore   Jakarta   Hong Kong   Tokyo
Delhi   Bombay   Calcutta   Madras   Karachi

Copyright © 1979 by Oxford University Press, Inc.

First published by Oxford University Press, New York, 1979

First issued as an Oxford University Press paperback, 1981

Library of Congress Cataloging in Publication Data

Nasaw, David.
Schooled to order.

Bibliography: p.
Includes index.
1.   Public schools—United States—History.
2.   Educational sociology—United States—History.
I.   Title.
LA217.N35   371'.01'0973   78-10216
ISBN 0-19-502529-6
ISBN 0-19-502892-9 pbk.

printing, last digit: 10 9 8 7

Printed in the United States of America

For Dinitia

Acknowledgments

I began work on this project at the suggestion of Stanley Arono-witz. Stanley, Rosalyn Baxandall, Elizabeth Ewen, Joel Kovel, Carol Lopate, and Richard Drinnon read parts of an earlier draft. I benefited from Stuart Ewen's commentary on an early draft of Part One and from Daniel Coleman's and Dinitia Smith's careful reading of the final completed draft. Colin Greer has read—and generously criticized—the manuscript at each stage of completion.

I have profited from discussions in class and out with my students at the College of Staten Island.

I want to thank Susan Rabiner, my editor at Oxford University Press, for her unflagging support and Parke Puterbaugh and Joellyn Ausanka for their diligent copy editing.

Jacob Conrad assisted me in the preparation of the bibliography. Florence Macy Stickney helped ready the manuscript for the final stages of production.

My mother, Beatrice Nasaw, contributed to the book through her confidence in me and her lifelong interest as parent and public school teacher in the questions I am raising.

I am grateful to the College of Staten Island of the City University of New York for a summer research grant.

Contents

Schooled to Order

Introduction

A history of American public schooling reduced to graphs would tell a simple story of almost continuous growth. In every category, the graphs would incline upwards, recording a steady rise in the number of students in school, the time they spent there, the teachers who taught them, the schools that housed them, and the dollars expended. The upward trend would continue unbroken from the 1820s until the 1970s. We cannot, at this time, chart the downward course that has commenced (if only temporarily) in the mid-1970s. We know only that that part of the American public that votes on school bond issues and makes its opinions known to professional pollsters is no longer willing to spend as much money or place as much trust in public schooling as it once was.[1]

It is too soon to predict the future course of public schooling in America, but a good time to reconsider the past. To understand why Americans have grown disillusioned with their public schools we must look beyond the immediate present to the larger history of the United States and its public schools.

The public schools of this country—elementary, secondary, and higher—were not conceived full-blown. They have a history, and it is the social history of the United States. This essay will not attempt to present that history in its entirety but will

focus instead on three specific periods decisive for the social
history of this society and its public schools: the decades before
the Civil War, in which the elementary or "common schools"
were reformed; the decades surrounding the turn of the twentieth century, in which the secondary schools "welcomed" the
"children of the plain people"; and the post-World War II
decades, which found the public colleges and universities
"overwhelmed" by a "tidal wave" of "non-traditional" students—those traditionally excluded from higher education by
sex, race, and class.[2]

In each of these periods, the quantitative expansion of the
student population was matched by a qualitative transformation
of the enlarged institutions. The common schools of the mid-
1800s were charged with re-forming the moral character of the
children of failed artisans and farmers from both sides of the
Atlantic; the expanded high schools at the turn of the century
with preparing their poor, working-class, and immigrant adolescents for future lives in city and factory; the "open-access"
public institutions in the postwar period with moving their
students off the unemployment lines and into lower-level
white-collar and paraprofessional positions.

The common schools, the high schools, the colleges and universities—all in their own times—were expanded and transformed so that they might better maintain social order and increase material productivity. But no matter how enlarged or
reformed, they could not do the jobs expected of them: they
could not solve the economic, social, and human problems generated by uncontrolled urbanization and industrialization
within the context of the private property system.

In the long run, the schooling reforms succeeded only in
shifting the locus of discussion and action from the social and
productive system to the people who were now held responsible for not fitting into it. But even in this role as distorting mir-
rors for the society at large, their utility was limited. As public
schooling became integral to the maintenance of the American
way of life, it became more and more suffused with the contradictions of American society, ultimately reflecting but not capable of resolving the primary tensions between the rhetoric of
democracy and the reality of a class-divided society.

I
The Common Schools
1835–1855

1

The New World and the Old

The children

The European visitors had much to marvel at in the New World they visited in the second quarter of the nineteenth century. Not least among the oddities encountered was what appeared to be a new breed of children.

Mrs. Trollope, among the first to report on the situation, was not at all pleased with what she found. American children seemed to her a dirty, noisy, misbehaved, undisciplined, disrespectful lot. She confided to her readers that she was not the only gentlewoman who had come to this conclusion: "I have conversed with many American ladies on the total want of discipline and subjection which I observed universally among children of all ages, and I never found any who did not both acknowledge and deplore the truth of the remark." [1]

The "ladies" may have "deplored" their children's behavior, but most Americans did not. In fact, what seems to have disturbed the visitors even more than the children's lack of manners was the parents' lack of concern.

Eneas MacKenzie was amazed that children were seated and served their tea with dirty faces, uncombed hair, and "evidently untaught" dispositions. He reported that all members of the American family "from the boy of six years up to the owner . . . of the house appeared independent of each other." [2]

A British naval officer reported the following scene he claimed to have overheard in 1837:

> "Johnny, my dear, come here," says his mama.
> "I won't," cries Johnny.
> "You must, my love, you are all wet, and you'll catch cold."
> "I won't," replies Johnny.
> "Come, my sweet, and I've something for you."
> "I won't."
> "Oh! Mr. ———, do, pray make Johnny come in."
> "Come in, Johnny," says the father.
> "I won't."
> "I tell you, come in directly, sir—do you hear?"
> "I won't," replies the urchin, taking to his heels.
> "A sturdy republican, sir," says his father to me, smiling at the boy's resolute disobedience. [3]

The young were, it seemed, doing no more, nor less than was expected of them. Their parents seemed pleased at their children's independence, even to the point of condoning their disobedience. Self-reliance had become a virtue, perhaps the premier virtue in the New World. There were no servants or nursemaids to coddle children into adulthood. They had to learn to care and fend for themselves, even to feed themselves at an early age. As the foreign visitors watched, the children of the New World performed feats of daring unimaginable across the Atlantic. Mrs. Mary Duncan reported firsthand from the New World that "little creatures feed themselves very neatly and are trusted with cups of glass and china, which they grasp firmly, carry about the room carefully, and deposit, unbroken at an age when, in our country mamma or nurse would be rushing after them to save the vessels from destruction." [4]

Harriet Martineau was delighted by scenes such as these. She ventured the opinion that the European visitors, instead of remonstrating against such behavior, should begin to understand it. It was, she believed, an inevitable by-product of republican life. The Americans were simply endeavoring to bring up their children as good republicans. This necessitated a different kind of child-rearing than was customary in the Old World. [5]

Parents and children were on more familiar terms in America. In the Old World, according to Tocqueville: "The style of family correspondence [was] always correct, ceremonious, stiff, and so cold that the natural warmth of the heart can hardly be felt in the language. In democratic countries, on the contrary, the language addressed by a son to his father is always marked by mingled freedom, familiarity, and affection, which at once show that new relations have sprung up in the bosom of the family."

The encouragement of independence was strong among girls as well as boys. Tocqueville, the French aristocrat, in a rare display of candor confessed that he had been "almost frightened at the singular address and happy boldness with which young women in America contrive to manage their thoughts and their language."[6]

Though both boys and girls were, from the perspective of the Europeans, allowed excessive freedom as children, their paths sharply diverged as they approached adulthood. The boys continued on their trajectory towards absolute independence. More often than not that path led far away from the household in which they had grown up. In the Old World the young men had stayed at home or settled close by; in the New World, they set off in search of their own land and their own fortunes as soon as they were able.

If adulthood meant independence for boys, the opposite was true for their sisters. Young girls were expected to surrender their former independence on reaching adult life.

> The independence of woman is irrecoverably lost in the bonds of matrimony. If an unmarried woman is less constrained [in America] than elsewhere, a wife is subjected to stricter obligations. The former makes her father's house an abode of freedom and of pleasure; the latter lives in the home of her husband as if it were a cloister.[6]

Wives had been tied to the household in part because the older children were so free to abandon it. The early departure of the young men made it imperative that the wife become a full-time worker in the household. In law and custom she was the "servant" of the household. She could not vote, nor could she

own property. Divorce, separation, or even temporary disobedience were forbidden.[7]

The household, though often without the older children who
added to its support in the Old World, remained in the New
World the basic unit of social organization. It was home, workplace, church, and school all rolled into one. It was within the
household that the young learned to obey their elders and the
law; to work hard and without complaint; to respect the other's
belongings as beyond their reach; to say their prayers and fear
the worst if they neglected them; and to worship the Founding
Fathers, the Constitution they had drafted, and the state they
had established.

The household was expected to teach the young their letters
and at least enough ciphering to avoid being cheated. The children could be taught at home or, if the adults desired, they
could be sent to school to learn their "rudiments." Only in New
England were there laws mandating communities to provide
schools for their children. But even these laws merely ratified
social custom. They were never enforced seriously enough to
force a community without a school to establish one. Schooling,
when available, was considered a supplement, not a substitute
for the household, which remained the primary agency of
child-rearing, education, and socialization.[8]

There were exceptions to the primacy of the family in child-
rearing matters. Almost from the time of the foundation of the
New World, state and church authorities had been empowered
to remove children from their natural parents if it could be demonstrated that they were not being properly cared for. Throughout the seventeenth and eighteenth centuries, such "neglected"
children were "placed out,"—apprenticed to households that,
in return for their unpaid labor, taught them their manners,
their letters, and, if possible, a trade.[9]

Not unexpectedly, it was the poor families of town and city
who were most often singled out for such extraordinary treatment. It was presumed—and without need of proof or opportunity for rebuttal—that those who had not the "moral character"
to raise themselves out of poverty similarly lacked the qualities
needed to rear their children.

Those households possessed of the necessary capital, skills, or property to support themselves adequately could take delight in the spirit of independence and self-reliance their children exhibited. But these virtues, a source of pride in some children, were a sign of character disorder in others. Children born to poverty were not supposed to look out for themselves. Those who did were accused of being actual or potential criminals, vagrants, or delinquents.

Poor children were adjudged as *a priori* ill-raised, ill-mannered, and undisciplined. Fortunately for them, however, parental "neglect" was not irremediable. Poor children could be saved from poverty by a rigorous injection of the moral qualities their parents lacked. They had only to be trained with sufficient self-discipline, and they too would be prepared for respectable and responsible adult lives.[10]

The first step in the character retraining was removal of the children from their natural parents. Poor children, orphans, and suspected or convicted "delinquents" were throughout the 1820s removed from their homes to be placed in newly established institutions: asylums, reform schools, and orphanages, where they would be isolated from their parents and placed under twenty-four-hour institutional control.[11]

These institutions were intended for the most extreme examples of childhood indiscipline. There were thousands of poor children not committed, poor children who, though not yet criminal, were still considered a potential burden on their more prosperous neighbors. These children received a different kind of special treatment. In the towns and rural districts, only the declared paupers were allowed to send their children to school for free. Children who worked in factories or mills were not only provided with gratis schooling but such schooling was mandated by special legislation that required employers to establish factory schools and release their child workers to attend them. The state legislatures and local communities who took such extraordinary measures were not especially concerned for the well-being of the poor and oblivious to that of more materially fortunate children. Rather, they went out of their way to school the poor because they were convinced that no one else, neither parents nor employers, was providing these children with the moral training they needed.[12]

The poor should not have been a problem in the New World. Indeed, as the foreign visitors implied and the natives affirmed, there was no reason for poverty to rear its head on this side of the Atlantic. The New World had no barriers obstructing the road to riches: no landed aristocracy, no feudal crown or court to rob a family of the fruits of its labor. Hard work would be rewarded directly not only because nature was beneficent and land available but because the social order protected and paid homage to those who worked to accumulate property.

And yet, despite the abundance of land out West and the beneficent social laws and customs, the poor grew in number and visibility throughout the nineteenth century.[13]

There had, of course, always been dependent classes: those who could not work and those who worked but could not earn enough to support themselves. Through the second quarter of the nineteenth century, not only did this "poor and dependent" population not go away, it multiplied with the inflow of thousands upon thousands of newly impoverished adults and children. As the frontier moved West, so did the center of food production. The older, established New England farmers found themselves competing with frontier farmers who—with larger arable acreage and land less exhausted by generations of overuse—could produce more food and at a cheaper price.[14]

These family farmers did not abandon their livelihoods without a struggle. Some tried to supplement their dwindling farming income by "taking-in" work from local jobbers. By supplying town merchants, rural storekeepers, and emerging capitalist entrepreneurs with finished or semifinished goods for sale and distribution, they earned enough to keep the farm solvent through the bad times and slightly ahead through the good.

Though many farm families were able to supplement their farming incomes to the point where they could continue on the land, many more could not. The rural-to-urban migration in the four decades preceding the Civil War changed the face of the New World. In 1790 there had been not one American city with more than 50,000 people. By 1830 almost half a million lived in cities that size. Through the next decades the movement would only accelerate.[15]

The growth of the cities was not greeted with equanimity by Americans of property, most of whom were well aware that the English experience had not been a reassuring one. The population explosion that had already begun in the Old World was generated almost entirely by an increase in the poor population. The process of urbanization seemed to feed on itself. Once rooted, there was no stopping or controlling it. Not only did the rural poor flood the cities, but once resident there, they exhibited an astounding rate of natural increase that rapidly expanded their proportion of the total population. Manchester in the center of industrial England had exploded in size from a town of 17,000 in 1770 to over 70,000 in 1801 to almost 150,000 in 1831.

The American cities were growing rapidly, if not yet as spectacularly as the English ones. Still, even into the second quarter of the new century this was not considered a serious problem. As the mayor of New York City explained in 1819, the situation of the New World "is not, and cannot be for ages, similar to that of England." In the Old World, those born to poverty were condemned to adult lives of squalor, destitution, and dependence because of the absence of democratic mores, republican virtue, and fertile land. In the New World there was, on the contrary, a social and geographical environment that encouraged—indeed, almost guaranteed—economic independence for all who sought it. Or at least so the mayor and the thousands of propertied and prosperous Americans he spoke for wanted to believe.[16]

The numbers and variety of the urban poor continued to increase through the middle decades of the nineteenth century. These poor people were not spontaneously generated; neither were they the victims of an epidemic of improper child-rearing. They were rather the inevitable by-product of the economic progress that consumed the nation in the antebellum decades.

The impetus for economic growth was the expansion of the cotton trade and the geometrical increase in profits. As the English textile mills (and to a lesser extent, those of New England) devoured as much raw cotton as could be delivered to them, the value of cotton exports almost tripled in just six years—from $25 million in 1830 to $70 million in 1836. By 1840 raw cotton represented 63 percent of the nation's total export sales.

Much of the income from this trade went directly to the Northeastern merchant/financiers who, through providing loans to the plantation owners as well as the capital necessary to crate, cart, ship, market, and insure the cotton, guaranteed themselves a healthy percentage of the profits. The profits were further invested—to the benefit of the Northeastern merchants—in Northern textile mills and manufactories and in canals, turnpikes, and, later, railroads that linked the Northeast and the Middle West.[17]

Improvements in transportation made it possible to ship products from town to town, even from region to region. As food moved east through the canals, turnpikes, and later railroad routes, textiles, clothing, shoes, boots, and iron goods were shipped in the other direction. The same class of merchants who had organized the putting-out systems in the countryside now spent large amounts of capital in town and city to purchase raw materials, organize production, and transport and market the final products. As these merchant capitalists expanded their control of the interregional and local markets, they began to hire unemployed journeymen and youth at rates well under those charged by the skilled craftsmen and artisans. Though warned by the craftsmen, the journeymen and apprentices accepted the work offered at the rates and conditions of employment set by their employers.

These journeymen and so-called apprentices were becoming in fact, though not yet in name, that permanent industrial proletariat once thought endemic only to the European factory towns. They worked for minimal wages or piece-rates, received little or no training, did not own their own tools or workshops, and had no chance whatsoever of achieving the skills and accumulating the capital to go into business for themselves.[18]

The craftsmen, journeymen, and some of the apprentices did not stand by idly and watch their futures disappear. They formed political parties and unions to protect their craft and their finances from the increasing power of merchant capitalists, bankers, and their agents in local and state government.[19]

The independent craftsmen were becoming a dying breed. Unable to compete with the larger-scale enterprises that were employing unskilled or "apprentice" labor, the craftsmen were forced to alter their work conditions, or stop working altogether. More and more, they found themselves transformed against their will into "wage slaves" beholden to outsiders for their work and their subsistence.

In times past, only the manual, unskilled day laborer had received "wages." As Norman Ware has written, the extension of the term and the practice of wagework to those previously self-employed denoted more than a change in the form of payment:

> The old term for the remuneration of the mechanic was "price." It referred to his product rather than to his labor, for it was his product that he sold. When the producer, whether master or journeyman, sold his product, he retained his person. But when he came to sell his labor he sold himself.[20]

The unemployment that grew out of (but did not disappear with) the Panic of '37 coupled with the decline of real wages through the forties intensified the problems of urban poverty. By 1844 G. H. Evans of *The Working Man's Advocate* was already looking back on the good old days of thirty years before when "the number of paupers in the whole United States was estimated at 29,166, or one in three hundred. The pauperism of New York City now [in 1844] amounts to 51,600, or one in every seven of the population."[21]

The poor population increased through each decade of the nineteenth century. The foreign visitors of the 1840s and 1850s were as perplexed by the persistence of New World poverty as earlier visitors had been delighted by its absence. "They could not understand, nor could Horace Greeley and many of the [American] philanthropists of the period understand, why a new country could show so many signs of congestion and pauperism like that of England."[22]

The spread of indiscipline

The paupers and poor had, in the past, been feared because of their suspected criminality. It was a foregone conclusion on the part of the more prosperous that poor children, if not rescued early enough, would grow up to be prostitutes or criminals. Through the middle decades of the nineteenth century, these historic fears were exacerbated by another one specific to the New World and its political institutions. The suffrage had been won by all white men, regardless of property-holding, schooling, or moral worth. The vote of the poor worker had become as significant as that of his more substantial neighbors—and there were many more of the former than the latter.

The era of the "common man" had been officially inaugurated with the election in 1828 of Andrew Jackson, not exactly a "common man" himself, but still the first president to come from the backwoods rather than the old established families of Virginia and Massachusetts.

Not only had King Mob replaced the well-born and well-bred Adams with an Indian fighter, but once established in the White House, that Indian fighter proclaimed it a republican principle that any man was as capable as any other in matters of governance: "In a country where offices are created solely for the benefit of the people no one man has any more intrinsic right to official station than another." [23]

For the first half-century of the Republic, the "better" people had owned not just the wealth and property of the New World but the White House and the elected and appointed offices of local, state, and federal governments. Now the newly installed president of the common man was claiming that the "people" would no longer defer to their social "betters" in matters of governance.

It was not only in national electoral politics that the common man was flexing his muscles and, if even in fantasy, exploring the possibilities to be won from his newly secured political power. In the states, too, questions were being raised about such common practices of Old World and New as imprisonment for debt, special charters for closed corporations, and a banking and currency system removed from the control of the electorate.

For the prosperous and propertied, older established families of town and city, the potential power of the urban masses was dangerous in the extreme. That men with the vote had offered it to an Indian fighter was evidence of a lack of wisdom and, worse, a lack of discipline. Well brought-up, disciplined working men would have voted for the boorish but eminently respectable Adams without a word of protest.[24]

The spread of indiscipline among the working people—their refusal to accept their place within the established social hierarchy, their continued agitation at workplace and poll—were traced back to the households in which they had been (improperly) raised. Moralists, reformers, and assorted experts on the family and its children were convinced that this breakdown of the household was, in part, the consequence of urbanization. Fathers who in the country had worked within sight and sound of their homes and children were, in town and city, obliged to leave home to reach their workplace. Child-rearing had, by default, been left entirely to the women who, the experts decreed, were by temperament possessed of too much soft-hearted gentility, tenderness, and affection to do a proper job.[25]

Not all women were considered equally incapable of raising their children in the men's absence. The more prosperous could well afford tutors and servants to provide the steady hand they themselves might lack. Such women were also more likely to be in contact with the church, a fountainhead of advice and information in such matters.

Again, it was the poor and working families that were considered the problem. Not only did their men abandon the households at dawn six days a week only to return at dusk, but the women left behind were not seeking out those who might have provided them with the guidance it was believed they required.

After 1830 a new generation of child-guidance books was written and published to remedy this problem. In earlier decades such books had been written almost exclusively by English clergy and had read much more like religious tracts than "how to" child-rearing books. The new American guidebooks were not as crudely "hell fire and damnation" Calvinist as their predecessors. It was no longer stated in unequivocal terms that

children had to have the devil beaten out of them before good
sense could be beaten in. Tenderness, kindness, gentleness
were given a place in the child-rearing regimen, though only in
moderation and as a reward for obedience.

It was obedience and respect for authority that were emphasized and reemphasized in all the guidebooks. Only the child
who had learned from birth to obey would internalize the self-
discipline necessary to withstand the temptations of the modern
world.

> The foundation of all excellence of character, declared Ar-
> temas Muzzey in his widely read book, *The Fireside,* "consists
> in obedience. . . . It becomes important that we learn this les-
> son in our earliest childhood. The fact should be impressed on
> the very infant, that he has no alternative but obedience."
>
> A collection of open letters to young mothers by Ann Porter
> reiterated this theme. "The first, the second, and the third
> requisite in family government," declared Porter, "is obe-
> dience. This must be secured; it is the helm to guide the
> ship." [26]

Though the child-guidance books addressed both parents,
they spoke to the mothers directly on the assumption that the
fathers were occupied with making a living and already knew
how to manage their young. The child-rearing literature, without noticing the contradiction, was simultaneously charging the
mother with complete responsibility for the children's future
and declaring that she was by temperament incapable of doing
the task properly. The mother had become a convenient scapegoat for the society as a whole. She was now held at fault for the
spread of indiscipline, which, it was believed, was eating away
at the heart of the Republic. [27]

Charity schools

Through the first decades of the nineteenth century, the merchant and financial elites of every Northeastern city founded
their own philanthropic agencies. With the support and assistance of church authorities and lay reformers, they established

charity institutions in order to rehabilitate, if possible, and remove from the community, if not, the actually or potentially un-
ruly children of poor parents. These problem children were, for
the most part, the offspring of the most recent migrants to the
city: the failed family farmers of the Northeast. Later in the century, the special treatment afforded them would be extended to
encompass other "problem" groups, most notably the Irish.

It was left to the more prosperous families of town and city—
the merchant, financial, and professional community—to take
on the task of rehabilitating the children before they became
poor and dangerous adults. This was not considered an extra
burden as much as a responsibility those better off had towards
their poor.[28]

It was believed at the time that if the church had exercised a
greater hold on the poor, dependent, and laborer population,
the propertied and prosperous would not have had to fear the
growing numbers of poor children in their midst. But the con-
gregations were not up to the job. The proportion of steady
churchgoers among the entire population, not to mention its
poorer elements, appeared to be declining. One urban mis-
sionary was shocked and distressed to find in 1817 that in New
York City not only were the poor not attending church but over
half the families did not even own a Bible.[29]

In New York City the most prosperous merchants and financiers contributed to asylums through the Society for the Prevention of Poverty and to schools through the Free School Society.
The list of contributors to the latter society reads like a Who's
Who of New York wealth in the early nineteenth century. Its
president was De Witt Clinton, and among the trustees were
"five Motts, four Ogdens, five Underhills, two Van Rensselaers,
three Palmers, and other notables such as Robert Cornell, Peter
Jay, James Roosevelt, and Hamilton Fish."[30]

The guiding force behind the New York City Free School Society was Thomas Eddy, a wealthy Quaker acquainted with
philanthropists on both sides of the Atlantic. Eddy recognized
that if schooling were to be given to all the poor children of the
city, either much more money would have to be raised or a more
economic schooling process developed. From a correspondent

in London, Eddy received news of the Lancasterian system, named for its designer, Joseph Lancaster, who, through the utilization of older students as unpaid teachers and a scientific rearrangement of the classroom, had increased the enrollment in one-teacher schools from sixty to one thousand students. Here was the godsend the philanthropists had been praying for. No matter that the system as such appeared to violate every norm of democratic and republican social life. It was cheap, efficient, and apparently effective.[31]

The Lancasterian schoolrooms were arranged in strictly hierarchical fashion, more appropriate to a feudal kingdom than a New World republic. The teacher sat far above his students and assistants on a raised platform or stage. The assistants or monitors, themselves older unpaid students, marched up and down the long rows of younger students conveying the instructions of the teacher and maintaining absolute order. Students were punished for

> talking, playing, inattention, out of seats; being disobedient or saucy to a monitor; snatching books, slates, etc., from each other; moving after the bell rings for silence; stopping to play, or making a noise in the street on going home from school; staring at persons who may come into the room; blotting or soiling books; having dirty face or hands; throwing stones; calling ill names; coming to school late; playing truant; fighting; making a noise before school hours; scratching or cutting the desks.

Students and monitors were arranged hierarchically. Every day, every lesson, students were moved forward or backward according to their performance. Monitors were also ranked. The head monitor was the only one in direct communication with the teacher while the assistant monitors were informed through the "head" of the commands of the teacher.

The primary teaching technique in the Lancasterian schools was called "dictation":

> The monitor in charge of dictation . . . appropriately called the "dictator" would move from form to form, giving each

class a syllable or word on its level of ability. The monitor of each form would repeat the word for his pupils, who then wrote it on their slates. After the dictator gave each form six words or syllables, he would then order all . . . classes to prepare for inspection; at that signal, each boy would put his hands behind his back, and the class monitors would inspect their pupils' work. The dictator would then give an order to clean slates, the monitors would check again to see that the slates were indeed clean, and the process of dictation would begin again.[32]

De Witt Clinton, president of the Free School Society, described Lancaster's system as a "blessing": both economical and effective because it achieved for schooling the same standards of efficiency that labor-saving machinery had pioneered in the production of factory goods. Lancasterian schooling was so efficient in imparting discipline to its students that, according to Lancaster himself, classroom order was maintained whether the instructor was or was not in the classroom.

In a [traditional] school the authority of the master is personal and the rod is his sceptre. . . . His absence is an immediate signal for confusion. But in a school conducted on my plan, when the master leaves the school, the business will go on as well in his absence as in his presence, because the authority is not personal.[33]

Here was the perfect system of disciplinary training, one which compelled the internalization of respect for authority to such a degree that it no longer mattered whether the authority figure was present.

Word of the system spread rapidly through philanthropic circles. In 1818, at the invitation of the Philadelphia Board of Governors, Lancaster himself came to the New World to start a model school.

He was received with acclaim. In fact, his visits to the cities took on somewhat the appearance of a triumphal tour. In Washington, Clay yielded him the Speaker's Chair. Many cities in all parts of the United States followed the lead of New

York in establishing Lancasterian schools and societies. Statesmen, including governors and congressmen, urged the general adoption of the plan.[34]

These Lancasterian schools were, for the most part, intended only for pauper boys. Because boys and girls were not allowed in the same classroom, often not in the same school, schooling both sexes required a great deal more funding than schooling just the boys. Though it was argued that poor girls needed schooling to supplement the deficient moral upbringing they too were receiving at home, the philanthropists who funded the schools did not consider such schooling important enough to allocate the additional money.[35]

The Lancasterian schools, though the most grandiose, were not the only philanthropic attempts to bring order to the lives of poor children. In many Northeastern cities and towns, philanthropists established infant schools for the same purpose. The infant schools were designed for children much younger than those enrolled in the Lancasterian schools. The instruction these infants received was also different from that of the Lancasterian system. In part because their students ranged in age from eighteen months to six years, the disciplined dictation approach had to be tempered with an extra dose of gentility.

The *raison d'etre* of the infant schools appeared to be the removal of poor children at the youngest age possible from their poor parents. "Officers of the Boston Infant School Society believed that by reveling in ignorance and vice the parents of poor children set only bad examples for their offspring. 'To counteract the bad influence of home,' infant schools placed children under the care of a pious and intelligent teacher."[36]

These "pious and intelligent teachers" were supposed to gently but firmly undo the damage visited on the children by "careless" and "fond" parents. As an 1828 article from Hartford makes clear, it was the behavior of the young, their manners and "minding," that was most carefully watched over in the infant schools:

The perfect order and harmony manifested among the little pupils, their happy countenances, and the readiness with

which they obeyed every movement of the hand of the
teacher, Miss Emmons, did her much credit. They entered the
room marching in procession, singing the addition table, and
keeping time by clapping their hands. After taking their seats
on the stage, all joined in a prayer suited in language and sen-
timent to their capacities. Then they sang a hymn very
sweetly.[37]

Such behavior as exhibited by Miss Emmons's pupils was not
only aesthetically pleasing to the society patrons who supported
these schools, it was also proof that the children had been set
on the road to prosperity. Good manners were the outward
manifestation of a disciplined and moral character. It could be
presumed that the child who behaved well in school had internalized the necessary character traits for success in adulthood. As an article in a New Haven newspaper reminded its
readers, the infant schools had to be supported not only because they were good for the children but because they were
good for the larger society.

The charities, in aid of the education of the poor, are not only
an individual but a public blessing. Poverty does not always
teach good lessons; she may be the "mother of invention,"
but her inventions are, too often, the craft of wickedness. The
child, brought up, or rather left, in idleness, will not form
good habits, except under very rare circumstances. It is a
duty, which the community owes to itself, to guard against
the vices of its members. . . . It is easier to train than to correct the mind. It is easier to inculcate virtue than to eradicate
vice. And it becomes a community, regardful of its moral and
intellectual character, to guard, with the utmost solicitude,
against the introduction of evil principles and habits.[38]

The Sunday schools were another institutional attempt to
save the poor from poverty and the propertied from social disorder. Like the Lancasterian schools, Sunday schools were im-
ported from England and supported almost entirely by the
wealthy and established urban residents. The Boston Society for
the Moral and Religious Instruction of the Poor, which established Sunday schools in that city, listed among its founders

"a group of prominent citizens—including William Thurston, a wealthy lawyer; Pliny Cutler, merchant and manufacturer; Samuel Armstrong, printer, publisher and bookseller; Charles Cleveland, a businessman specializing in brokerage and exchange services; and Henry Homes, son of one of the leading members of the Old South Congregational Church." The New York Society contained as prominent and propertied a collection of gentlemen.

The Sunday schools, though Protestant, were neither church affiliated nor intended for the children of any specific congregation. They were all-purpose institutions designed to stuff as much Protestant civilization into poor children as was possible on that one day a week. Volunteer teachers, distinguished by abundant goodwill and a total lack of experience or training, taught some reading, writing, and arithmetic, and a good deal more manners, morals, and religious precepts.[39]

In the many newspaper reports that praised the Lancasterian, infant, and Sunday schools and solicited funds, what was emphasized time and time again was not what the children learned but their clean and orderly appearance, the precision with which they marched into and out of school and classroom, the readiness with which they obeyed their teachers, the "solemnity" with which they knelt and said their prayers, the "correctness of time, tone, and melody . . . with which they sang their "delightful, devotional exercises," the rapid improvement in their morals, "docility and gentleness," the number of their "young immortal souls . . . put in a state of discipline for the enjoyment of celestial glory," the habits of industry, of regularity, and of obedience which they imbibed, "the peculiar correctness and propriety with which they read (out loud) and spoke." If the children learned to read, write, and figure, so much the better. But they were being sent to school for more important reasons: to learn how to become church-going, God-fearing, law-abiding, private property-respecting citizens and workers.[40]

By 1830 Lancasterian, infant, and Sunday schools had been established throughout the Northeast and were receiving not only philanthropic but public monies to support their civilizing mission. Outside the Northeast, however, there were few such institutions.

This is not to say that the other regions were without their poor populations—and their civilizing missions. Blacks in the South and Indians in the West were no doubt as economically deprived as the Northeastern poor. But because their poverty was considered to be of an essentially different character, so too was the quality of the institutional rehabilitation provided for them.

Nineteenth-century paupers were white and Anglo-Saxon; they were, if not practicing, then potential church members. Their children were eminently "rehabilitable." Given remedial attention, they could be cured of the character defects that had consigned their parents to poverty. This was *not* considered the case with the blacks and Indians, who were not white, Anglo-Saxon, or Protestant, and were incapable of becoming such.

Schooling for blacks was, from the 1830s on, proscribed by law in the South and "custom and popular prejudice" elsewhere. In 1830 the fine for teaching blacks—free or slave—was increased to $100 in Virginia. South Carolina had the same fine, but supplemented it with six months' imprisonment. Georgia's fine was $500 and imprisonment. North Carolina's was from $100 to $200; Alabama's, up to $500. For freed blacks who attempted to teach slaves the penalties were of course much harsher, almost invariably including whipping.[41]

The Western and Northern states were as opposed to the schooling of blacks as were the Southern ones. Ohio, Illinois, and Oregon had laws forbidding freed blacks to even enter the state. The Northern states did not have explicit laws forbidding the teaching of blacks. But then they did not need these laws. Most public schools were simply out-of-bounds for black children. In New England and the Middle Atlantic states, those blacks of school age who were admitted were sent to segregated institutions. In the newer states of the Middle West, there were not even these segregated and underfunded schools available.[42]

The expansion of schooling that occurred in the second quarter of the nineteenth century was not intended for blacks, slave or free, Northern or Southern. This is not to say that all

blacks remained uneducated. There were still those who secured an education but without the aid of those philanthropic
and public agencies that had taken upon themselves the task of
schooling the poor white children.[43]

In the period under discussion, most blacks were confined to
plantations, and the laws, customs, and mores dictated that this
was where they belonged. The situation of the Indians was different. They had not yet been confined to "total institutions"
like plantations or reservations, though this appeared to be the
direction in which the authorities were heading.

Those missionaries who traveled west to bring Protestantism
and civilization to the Indians believed that for their own good
all Indian children had to be institutionalized. Institu-
tionalization was the only means of guaranteeing their total
isolation from the pernicious influence of family and tribe. The
Indian Mission School was designed as a "self contained community in the wilderness . . . a totally controlled environment," located as far as possible from the tribal home. Not only
were parents, siblings, and relatives forbidden to visit the children, but it was frequently deemed necessary to surround the
whole school with a fence to keep out intruders whose savage
ways might induce backsliding in the Indian students.[44]

For poor white children, some evidence of degeneracy was
needed before the cure of the total institution was prescribed.
The asylum approach was only considered for those who had
demonstrated their incapacity to join the social order by being
born orphans or being convicted (or likely to be convicted) of
vagrancy or delinquency. For Indian children no such proof was
required. The fact of their birth as nonwhites was evidence
enough of their essential degeneracy to have them confined—
for their own good—to the sanitized, "rehabilitative" isolation
of the mission school.

The charity schools and asylums of the early nineteenth century could not, and did not, work the magic expected of them.
They were obviously too much of an Old World transplant to
succeed in a New World still self-consciously republican.[45]

It was in the long run the poor themselves who did most to

seal the fate of the charity institutions by avoiding them whenever and wherever possible. The charity institutions had been designed for the poor as a uniform class of people, all suffering from the same characterological defects, all in need of the same cure. But, as the poor themselves knew better than anyone, they were not all morally deprived or depraved and would not be treated as such.

As Joseph Tuckerman, Unitarian minister to the poor, reported to the Massachusetts Assembly, the poor were a "very mixed class." There were those who were idle out of choice or incapacitated by drink, but there were more who were poor because they could not find work or when they did, received less than subsistence wages for their labor.[46]

For many the problem of poverty was the direct consequence of a lack of capital and work. Schooling their children would do them no good unless their children, unlike themselves, were provided as adults with work or with the capital to set themselves up in business.

It was these poor people—working, underemployed, and unemployed—who had placed themselves beyond the reach of the charity institutions. They could perceive no greater humiliation than delivering their children to such charity. They would rear their children as best they could without asking for or accepting help from the philanthropists or their agents.

In New York City when the Free School Society became aware that the poor were avoiding their free schools, they changed their name and their charter. As the Public School Society, they tried to camouflage their charity by inviting the more prosperous—for a nominal fee—to send their children to the public schools. The strategy failed. There was no disguising the charity schools, no matter what they were called or who was invited to attend.[47]

The charity schools had been a first attempt to establish institutions *in loco parentis* or, more accurately, *in loco matris*. That they had failed to do the job demanded did not discredit the institutional approach in general. If anything, the perceived effects of antebellum industrialization and urbanization strengthened the position of those who argued for further institutional intervention into the lives of poor children. If the charity schools and asylums were considered improper and inadequate, then more proper and republican institutional forms of child-rearing, socialization, and disciplinary training would have to be devised in their place. Under no circumstances could the children of the poor be abandoned to the exclusive care of their parents.

2

The Ultimate Reform:
The Common Schools

The myths of America, though tested by the Panic of '37, by the political and workplace agitation of the working people, by the addition of layer after layer of urban poor, were not abandoned. Those who had succeeded and those who aspired to material success continued to argue that in the New World the absence of aristocratic barriers to profit-making and property-holding, combined with abundant land out West and expanding cities and towns in the Northeast, created a social situation in which opportunity was available to all.

The stories of "self-made men" who through hard work and inner discipline pushed their way to success were publicized everywhere and, in times of business prosperity, with added emphasis. The success of the prosperous was the sign that virtue was rewarded in this best of all social worlds. That this was not yet the land of milk and honey, that there were poor people in the New World, did not invalidate the myths. If the promise of the New World had not yet been realized for everyone, that only demonstrated that not everyone had the character necessary to convert opportunity to material success. Poverty could be remedied by simply providing the poor with those character traits which they lacked.[1]

The reformers

Among the foremost believers and most effective proselytizers of the myths of America were those men and women who led the campaign for an expanded and extended public school network in the decades preceding the Civil War. These school reformers chose as their institutional model not the Lancasterian or infant schools, which—as charity institutions—had repelled those for whom they had been designed, but the New England "district" or common schools, which were as republican and American as the charity schools were aristocratic and Old World.

These district schools were open to all the children of the community. They were supported by district taxes, state funds, and by "rates"—tuition—paid by parents. Those who could not afford their rates could apply for rate exemptions.[2]

The common schools were primary schools. They taught the rudiments to all who needed such instruction. Achievement, not age, was the criterion for entrance. The youngest pupils might be seven or eight; the oldest could be in their early twenties.[3]

Each town, city, and rural county had its common school promoters—men and women of wealth, property, and social standing. They included churchmen, professionals, older established merchants and bankers, newly arrived manufacturers and entrepreneuring lawyers; all were dedicated to establishing common schools where there were none and expanding them where they already existed. The reformers at the local level were connected to one another and to the common cause by reformers with statewide, regional, and national reputations.[4]

Though it is always risky to generalize, we are on firm ground in using Horace Mann to represent this generation of school reformers. Like Mann, most of these reformers (later to become state superintendents of common schools) had been raised on Northeastern family farms that, though far from prosperous, never failed to provide their young with food, shelter, and abundant moral precepts. Most had, prior to joining the cause of the common schools, been active in other branches of nineteenth century reform, either as practicing minister/missionaries or (Whig) lawyer/politicians. All were true believers in the American dream of unlimited material progress for the society at large, of upward mobility for all its people.[5]

For Mann, hard work was the key to the kingdom of riches, power, and personal glory because that had been his own experience. When it came time to write his autobiography, Mann could not remember a time when he had not been working. As soon as he was old enough to walk, he had become part of the household unit, contributing to its material well-being.[6]

Mann had been born into the small family farm at precisely the moment in which it was entering its period of terminal decline. But the Mann family, especially Horace and his older brother Stanley, had not passively mourned its disappearance. They had rather followed the example of their elders, adjusting their life and work plans to the requirements of the changing economic situation. In Horace's village, several of the older women had discovered a way of supplementing the household income by braiding oat straw into strands that could be woven into straw hats. When a local manufactory was built nearby with machines to convert the braided strands into straw hats, the demand for braids expanded almost geometrically. It became more profitable to braid straw for cash to purchase store bought goods than to produce those goods in the first place.[7]

The household economy was transformed from near self-sufficiency to dependence on the straw market and the general store, but the transition left the family with more material goods than ever before. Mann's brother Stanley saw the road ahead and invested his inheritance in a textile mill. Horace himself, though unwilling to follow his brother directly, was even less willing to stay on the family farm. As soon as possible, he left home for college and then law school. With his new expertise and credentials, he found his own way to cash in on the opportunities opened by the industrialization of New England.[8]

As the market expanded, formerly self-subsistent rural households became dependent on the merchants who now supplied them with goods they could no longer afford to make themselves. These merchants, frequently from Boston or the larger New England towns, needed the assistance of young "rural solicitors" to collect the debts incurred by the farmer households that had fallen on bad times. Through hard work on behalf of these merchants, Mann built himself a law practice and accumulated enough capital to become his brother's partner in the manufacturing business.[9]

Mann had, in his own professional way, seized the opportunities opened by the industrial progress achieved in Massachusetts. He had made himself a name and a living. Still, he realized that his success had not been entirely his own doing. He owed his good fortune to his family and the upbringing that, he believed, had prepared him for the transition from family farm to urban community. The family farm as such no longer existed, but the moral training, the discipline of hard work and delayed gratification, and the respect and obedience to authority that had been internalized there could be reproduced under other conditions. What he, Horace Mann, had been blessed with, others could be provided.

The reformers took for granted the changes at the base of the social turmoil. Industrialization, urbanization, the rise of merchant and manufacturing capitalism, the decline of the self-sufficient family farm and craftsmen's workshops were not to blame for the social discontent and suffering. Poverty and pauperism were not caused by capitalists and industrialization but by the lack of character of those who became impoverished when their livelihoods were threatened. Reform of the people and not the productive order was believed the solution to all problems.[10]

Horace Mann and Henry Barnard, probably the most influential of this generation of school reformers, both began their reform careers as Whig legislators. Mann, in Massachusetts, had been instrumental in the establishment of a state hospital for the insane and legislation licensing liquor retailers. He was also an active and influential member of a Boston society for the prevention of pauperism and the Prison Discipline Society. Barnard, in Connecticut, was just as active and omnipresent a reformer. According to Merle Curti, he had in a brief legislative career sponsored "legislation designed to improve the condition of all sorts of unfortunate groups—the blind and the deaf, the insane, and the inmates of jails and prisons, as well as degraded paupers." [11]

Mann was the first of the two to devote his reform efforts exclusively to the cause of the common schools. A decade of work as all-purpose reformer had brought him to the uncomfortable conclusion that he had been wasting his time trying to work miracles on individuals too far corrupted to be rehabilitated. As he himself put it, he had shifted his focus from the already corrupted parents to their children because "men are cast-iron; but children are wax. Strength expended upon the latter may be effectual, which would make no impression upon the former." School reform, as "preventive" rather than "curative," was, for Mann and others, the ultimate reform. If it were successful, no other would be necessary. [12]

The problem
with the (unreformed) schools

Horace Mann, like those reformers already at work and those to come, entered the common school campaign assuming that American schooling was failing American society. Curiously enough, while he and other reformers were decrying the decline and fall of American schooling, foreign visitors were celebrating its achievements. Tocqueville stated quite directly that he knew "of no people who [had] established schools so numerous and efficacious." [13]

Mrs. Trollope, who had heard Americans boast about their schools while still in England, discovered during her visit that though the quality of instruction was not as high in the New World as in the Old, there were indeed a great many schools on this side of the Atlantic. [14]

Michel Chevalier was impressed not only with the number of schools but with the American passion for building new ones. On the frontier, every new town began erecting a school just as soon as the church was completed. In Cincinnati, still a new

town in 1833, there were already eighteen public schools and
nearly as many private ones.[15]

Through the Northeast and further west, American parents
and communities were establishing schools for their children—
public, private, and church schools. There was at the time no
strict demarcation between the public and the private: most
public schools required the parents to pay some tuition (their
rates); many private schools received state or local funds. There
was also no absolute class differentiation between the private
and the public school populations. Though it could be taken for
granted that the private schools contained no paupers and the
public ones no aristocrats, both types of schools enrolled children from both prosperous and poor families.[16]

Only in New York City and Philadelphia were the public
schools attended almost exclusively by paupers and "charity"
cases. But there were also, in these cities, a great variety of
private schools, some grand enough to call themselves "academies," others so small they easily fit into the living room of the
"dame" who taught them. A few of these, like the General Society of Mechanics and Tradesmen School, took in enough money
in tuition and contributions to admit without charge the children of poorer artisans and orphans. Through the middle 1830s,
these pay schools accommodated those city residents unwilling to send their children to the public schools.[17]

In New York City almost 60 percent of those children aged
five to fifteen attending school were enrolled in private pay
schools. The proportion of children attending such schools was
probably smaller but still significant in New England. Henry
Barnard, surveying the state of the schools in Connecticut in
1841, discovered to his dismay that almost every district in the
state contained a private school in direct competition with the
public one.[18]

At the time the reformers began their crusade, there were
numerous schools, public and private, and the percentage of the
school-age population attending them was so large that twenty
years of reformer agitation would not significantly increase it.
The problem with the schools then, as the reformers perceived
it, was not a simple lack of enrollment. There were plenty of

students going to school. The problem was rather that it was those who most needed the schooling who were not enrolled.[19]

As we have seen—and as the reformers were most aware—the structure of social life and work was being "industrially revolutionized" in mid-century America. The cities and towns of the Northeast and, with a time lag, the Middle West, were filling with rural migrants and their descendents who, without property, capital, or skills worth much in the urban marketplace, posed a potential danger to the peace and prosperity of the New World. It was the children of these migrants from farms or failed workshops that the reformers felt obliged to rescue. The "manufacturing villages" and "densely populated sections of large cities" in which they congregated were their special targets.[20]

Henry Barnard, in his *Sixth Annual Report* to the Connecticut General Assembly, stated clearly, if somewhat melodramatically, the special circumstances that made it imperative that the state—through the common schools—intervene in the lives of these children.

> No one at all familiar with the deficient household arrangements and deranged machinery of domestic life, of the extreme poor and ignorant, to say nothing of the intemperate—of the examples of rude manners, impure and profane language and all the vicious habits of low-bred idleness, which abound in certain sections of all populous districts— can doubt that it is better for children to be removed as early and as long as possible from such scenes and such examples and placed in an infant or primary school.

Barnard warned the Connecticut legislators to pay special attention to the "manufacturing population," which was, he claimed, rapidly overtaking the agricultural population. Though the present generation of factory workers was uncivilized enough, their children would be even worse. The parents had at least come "from the country . . . bringing with them the fixed habits, the strong family attachments, and elevated domestic education, which have ever characterized the country homes of New England." Their children would grow to adulthood with none of these advantages: from birth to death they would be town or city dwellers.[21]

It was these children of poor and working people recently arrived in the urban environment that the reformers were most worried about—and for a number of reasons. The route to economic independence was very different in mid-century America from what it had been earlier. The poor, if they were going to succeed, had to internalize as young as possible the character traits necessary for success as modern, urban wageworkers. They needed to be socialized not only to the basic requirements of communal life—respect for one's elders, for the law, for the church, and for the Republic—but to the new standards of discipline required in the urban workplace.

The farmer and independent craftsmen had worked long hours, but they had determined their own work schedule. In the countryside, it was the sun, the crops, and the season that set the tempo of the workday. In the towns and cities also the rhythm of work was set by the season, the day of the week, the amount of orders accepted, and the desires of the craftsmen/artisans. "Blue Mondays," long meal breaks, time off for electioneering, family festivities, and public and church holidays were not a sign of bad work habits as much as of a distinct style of work.

In the new urban workshop and factory, this had to change, and it did. The employer and his paid agents alone set the work hours, the work tempo, and work rules according to the logic of productive efficiency. The decision-making process was two steps removed from the worker. The machine dictated to the employer who arranged work patterns and conditions according to its requirements. Punctuality was important—workers had to be on time to feed the machinery. Accuracy was crucial—the machine had to be tended properly. Order was necessary—the machine dictated how work must be performed. Diligence was essential—an hour wasted by the worker was an idle hour for the machinery and a profitless one for the employer. Perseverance was required—expensive machinery had to be run from dawn to dusk to pay off its costs with profits.[22]

The reformers saw wage work not as the permanent destiny

of the poor and working people but almost as a moral testing ground, a challenge that if met would mean economic independence in the future. The common schools were to be the institutions in which the poor would receive the character training necessary for success: first as wageworkers, then as independent farmers or self-employed artisans. Those youth who learned the virtues of hard work, frugality, and temperance in the common schools would never forget them. As Mann put it, "Train up a child in the way he should go, and when he is old he will not depart from it." [23]

The reformers were not the first to believe that universal schooling would bring social harmony. But they were the first to envision the possibilities and benefits to be derived from providing such universal schooling through common schools. What the reformers were proposing was not simply schooling every segment of the population but schooling them together in the same public school classrooms, rich and poor, side-by-side.

As Samuel Lewis of Ohio explained in 1837, the common schools would in the long run prove to be the best antidote to social strife precisely because they were "common":

> Take fifty lads in a neighborhood, including rich and poor—
> send them in childhood to the same school—let them join in
> the same sports, read and spell in the same classes, until their
> different circumstances fix their business for life: some go to
> the field, some to the mechanic's shop, some to merchandize:
> one becomes eminent at the bar, another in the pulpit: some
> become wealthy; the majority live on with a mere compe-
> tency—a few are reduced to beggary! But let the most eloquent
> orator, that ever mounted a western stump, attempt to preju-
> dice the minds of one part against the other—and so far from
> succeeding, the poorest of the whole would consider himself
> insulted, and from his own knowledge stand up in defence of
> his more fortunate schoolmate. [24]

All would profit from the mixture of the classes in the common schools. The rich man's son would come away a better man by learning firsthand as a child "that it is by a rough contest with the rougher members of society, that he is to work his way through life." The poor would profit even more. They would be "excited to emulate the cleanliness, decorum, and mental improvement of those in better circumstances." They would learn directly from the more prosperous, if not how to be prosperous themselves, at least how to act like it. As Mann himself wrote with his subtle mixture of disdain and diplomacy:

> The lower classes in a school have no abstract standards of excellence, and seldom aim at higher attainments than such as they daily witness. All children, like all men, rise easily to the common level. There, the mass stop; strong minds only ascend higher. But raise the standard, and, by a spontaneous movement, the mass will rise again and reach it.[25]

Note the way Mann associated the "lower classes" with the weaker minds. He assumed, as did the other reformers, that not only did the lower classes lack discipline, they also lacked "stronger minds." In both cases, their schooling could only be benefited by sitting next to the better bred, better disciplined, "stronger-minded" children of the more prosperous classes.

The reformers had discovered a republican solution to a universal problem. Their faith was enormous and contagious. The common schools could, if properly run, protect "society against the giant vices which now invade and torment it;—against intemperance, avarice, war, slavery, bigotry, the woes of want and the wickedness of waste. . ." That they were not yet achieving these aims, even in New England, where the percentage of children enrolled was already well over 50 percent, was, the reformers believed, not the fault of the institution but of those who were responsible for its day-to-day functioning.[26]

The common people of town, city, and rural county did not, according to the reformers, understand the promise of universal common schooling. More concerned with their tax bills than with their schools, they had, the reformers charged, allowed these institutions to deteriorate to the point where they were near worthless as agencies of civilization. The problem was not only that not enough children were attending but that those who did attend were not being properly schooled.

They were, in the first place, crowded into schoolhouses unfit for habitation, buildings characterized by Mann as so poorly constructed that there was "more physical suffering endured by our children in them, than by prisoners in our jails and prisons." The reformers reported with horror of schoolhouses without outhouses, or with outhouses so situated that they afforded not the minimal degree of modesty essential for civilized life.[27]

If the schoolhouses were bad, the schoolmasters were worse. Each reformer had his own particular story to tell about the lack of education, breeding, morals, character, or the total lack of sobriety of a certain teacher. If proof of such dissolution were required, it could be found in those outhouses which, when available, were uniformly scarred by obscenities too blasphemous even to be hinted at in polite company.[28]

Given the present state of the common schools—as presented by the reformers—it was self-evident (at least to them) that these schools were not capable of performing the tasks assigned them; it was as evident that, if reformed and energized, they could and would work miracles. The reformers were not simply exercising their talent for hyperbole when they proclaimed that the common schools, once "improved and energized" could "become the most effective and benignant of all forces of civilization." Their logic was inexorable. If, as Mann had put it, children were as docile as the "lithe sapling or the tender germ," then by applying the proper pressure in the proper places, the twigs could be bent to the desired shapes. All that was necessary was that the reformers, or like-minded citizens of town and country, be allowed to transform the schools as they were into the institutions they could and should become.[29]

The reformers had the answer to all social ills. Their problem was getting others to listen to them, follow their advice, and spend their tax dollars accordingly.

A "common" republicanism; a "common" Protestantism

It was not coincidental that the campaign for the common schools was launched in the aftermath of the Jacksonian vic-

tories; nor was it coincidental that the most prominent and influential of reformers were anti-Jacksonian Whigs.

The common schools had for a good fifteen years before the
campaign been promoted as the best available property insurance, the best antidote to the social turmoil generated by universal male suffrage, Jacksonian democracy, and a restive population of urban laborers.

A common school education would be a moral education. By
making the population more moral, the common schools would
also make it more docile, more tractable, less given to social dis-
cord, disruption and disobedience. The young would be taught
to vote right and to pray right, to distinguish the responsible
citizen from the demagogue, the false from the true, in matters
of state and of church.[30]

Political education would be a primary and explicit function
of the reformed common schools. Now that all white men had
won the right to vote, regardless of property, birth, or social
background, some way had to be found to assure that they
would exercise their franchise properly. It was, as Mann put it,
"an easy thing to make a Republic; but it is a very laborious
thing to make Republicans." The common school by "making"
the latter would ensure the security of the former.[31]

The common school classroom was to be sacrosanct ground
where only the doctrine and principles of republicanism were to
be preached. Common school teachers were to avoid all subjects
of political controversy. They would teach from the texts, never
deviating from the consensus view they were supposed to represent.[32]

Whether intentional or not, the reformers' call for teacher
neutrality in political education guaranteed that the only instruction in politics and republicanism would come direct and
undiluted from the texts. The vast majority of common school
teachers were neither prepared nor expected to do more than
follow the text, correcting students when they veered from it.
For teacher or student to question or criticize it was unthinkable.[33]

Political principles were introduced into the common school
classrooms not only through the history and geography texts

but in the readers and spellers, primary and advanced, that formed the core of every curriculum. These books exalted America and its political institutions, proclaiming the inherent virtues of the New World and its white, male, Protestant, and Anglo-Saxon population. That the nation contained others was a fact conveniently ignored.[34]

Not unpredictably, these texts, though American through and through, were not as benignly "republican" as the reformers claimed. The republicanism represented was in fact no more or less than the Whiggism preached and practiced by the reformers themselves: it was a republicanism that emphasized the need for public obedience rather than public participation, a republicanism sharply distinguished from the democracy preached by the followers of Jefferson and Jackson. The children of the poor and working people who were the special target of the reformers had to be taught greater respect for the republic as it was, for the sanctity of private property, for the inherent authority of their social betters. Democratic doctrine did precisely the opposite. By preaching overly much about the equality of Americans, by emphasizing the commonality of all at a time when the poor and working people had to be more securely locked into their places in the social hierarchy, democracy was bad politics, but even worse pedagogy.[35]

As party politicians, many of the reformers had spoken clearly and forcibly from the side of those who had opposed and resisted the democratic movement that had brought Jackson and his party into the White House. Now as school reformers, they continued to speak politically through the textbooks found in every common school classroom. Ruth Miller Elson, who has meticulously studied more than a thousand nineteenth century texts, has found not unexpectedly that Whig prejudices color the presentation of most issues. On the subject of national heroes, these biases are perhaps most pronounced. Jefferson and Jackson are, for example, conspicuous by their absence. When Jefferson is mentioned at all, it is usually in the form of some veiled criticism: he was too rich, too much a party man, and had shown poor judgment in his support for the French revolutionaries. Jackson is almost never mentioned. When he is, he is identified simply as a soldier who was also a president.[36]

The great Federalist and Whig statesmen/politicians take up the space left by the exclusion of the democrats. According to Elson, in almost "all of these books, George Washington bears more resemblance to Jesus Christ than to any human being," Hamilton's death (at the hands of a renegade Jeffersonian) is presented as a national tragedy of the first order, and Webster's speeches are quoted abundantly.[37]

Not only was the textbook pantheon of republican heroes filled with Whigs and Federalists to the exclusion of their political opponents, but the catalogue of republican/American virtues sounded curiously like a Whig one. The American Revolution was a conservative revolution led not by "rebels" but by men of law and order. To revolt against tyranny is just, but to revolt against a just government is a crime against humanity. "To rebel against the American government is the greatest crime, because almost by definition the United States represents liberty and cannot be tyrannical." The republic that had survived into mid-century was sacrosanct in form and function. The Constitution was the law of the land, and would always be so. That it could be amended, that one of the Founding Fathers had even recommended continual amendment as not only possible but desirable was a fact not often mentioned.[38]

The reformers did not emphasize the pedagogical advantages of Whiggish textbooks. They argued instead, on purely pragmatic grounds, that political education should be left to the texts, not the teachers. Party politics, if brought into the classroom, would destroy the institution. Those belonging to parties different from that of the teacher would withdraw their children, leaving the public schools far from "common."[39]

The reformer rationale for barring denominational religion from the common schools was identical to that for barring party politics. The common schools, it was claimed, if they did not abjure "denominationalism" would drive away families of denominations other than the teacher's.[40]

As long as it was left to the district itself to define what was meant by nondenominational Protestantism, the principle itself was not in dispute. In fact, there had been almost no opposition to the Massachusetts Law of 1827, which prohibited the use or purchase of school books "which are calculated to favour any particular religious sect or tenet."[41]

Congregationalists and Unitarians, the orthodox and the liberal, had lived with this law for over a decade when, in 1838, Horace Mann, serving as board secretary, informed the Reverend Packard that the book he had suggested for inclusion in the state's district school libraries "would not be tolerated in Massachusetts." The book had been published by the interdenominational American School Union and was submitted by a respected Congregational minister, but Mann's word had become law.[42]

Exactly as was the case with political instruction, the reformers (Mann chief among them) took upon themselves responsibility for determining what was appropriate and inappropriate for the common schools. They established their version of Protestantism as the only legitimate one for the common schools. Though their critics correctly argued that the approved brand of Protestantism was no more or less than the Unitarianism or liberal Congregationalism the reformers practiced, their arguments were to no avail.[43]

The reformers had taken on a fight they knew they could win. In the words of Timothy Smith, orthodox Calvinism had already become a "dying dogma." Rigid denominationalism was a barrier to progress. The orthodox emphasis on eternal damnation demoralized those who held the future of the republic in their hands. It could no longer be tolerated—at least in the public schools.[44]

3

The Campaign for the Common Schools:
The Enthusiasts, the Indifferent,
and the Opposition

It was easier for the reformers to secure a monopoly on the meaning and practice of Protestant and republican common schooling than it was to attract or compel attendance at their common schools.

The reformers had formulated the solution to all social problems, or so they believed. They had designed the ultimate institution for the socialization of American youth. Their task was now to catalyze public opinion and raise public monies to pay for its operation.

The manufacturers and the common schools

It has been assumed that the reformers were the primary agents in the establishment and selling of the common school movement. This may or may not be true. What is certainly the case, however, is that without the direct and continual assistance of their friends, allies, and supporters from the business world, the reformers would have accomplished very little indeed. Though the most effective of ideologists, they were incapable by themselves of bringing about substantive reforms, either in the schools or in any other social institution.

As Alexander Field has suggested, "Perhaps it is not Mann, after all, who deserves the full-size statue in front of the Massachusetts State House, complete with the inscription, 'Father of the American Public School.' " For Mann would never have become secretary to the board if not first nominated by Edmund Dwight, a wealthy cotton textile manufacturer who persuaded Mann to take the job and supplemented his salary by $500 a year.[1]

Dwight was not the only successful businessman to support the common school crusade. The state boards, in Massachusetts as elsewhere, were chosen from a relatively small group of wealthy merchants, manufacturers, lawyers, and clergy. The lawyers and clergy invariably catered to the manufacturers and merchants, making the occupational diversity on the boards much less significant than might appear.[2]

It is impossible to know who the primary agents of reform were—the businessmen behind the scenes or the reformers on the front lines. What is known, however, is that the two groups worked well together, the reformers supplying the theoretical arguments and propaganda, and the businessmen, the money and political clout.

One of the reasons for Mann's particular success was his connections with the wealthy and powerful in his home state. As his biographer, Jonathan Messerli, has written, from the very start of his first tour of the state, Mann "was attempting to reach the influential people in each community." He was in continual contact not only with the local business elites but with the Lowells, the Appletons, the Lawrences, and the other industrialists and merchants who had amassed fortunes large enough to qualify them as spokesmen for the wealthy and powerful throughout the region.[3]

Though the prosperous and propertied in every walk of life were solicited for aid and support, it was the manufacturers who were most courted by the reformers. It was they, after all, who were most in need of—and best able to profit from—the character-trained and disciplined workforce the common schools intended to provide.

The reformers did not waste their words with the manufacturers. They appealed directly to their self-interest as businessmen whose profit margin depended on worker productivity.

Even Mann, among the most self-righteous and morally committed of the reformers, did not desist from descending to crude
economism in his attempt to persuade the manufacturers to
support his campaign. His entire *Fifth Annual Report* was in fact
"a direct and plausible appeal to industrialists to support public
education."[4]

After sending out questionnaires to several prominent manufacturers, Mann selectively published their conclusions on the
"difference in the productive ability . . . between the educated
and uneducated." As might have been expected, the employers
agreed with Mann that schooled workers were worth more than
unschooled.[5]

Neither Mann nor the manufacturers spent much time emphasizing the effects of schooling on specific work skills or general intelligence. The common schools were not going to be sold
to manufacturers and taxpayers as intellectual or job training
centers. Their contribution to the public welfare was their provision of moral education and character training for the poor.
The real advantages of schooled over unschooled workers were,
as Mann suggested to the manufacturers, the schooled workers'
"docility and quickness in applying themselves to work"; their
"domestic and social habits"; their "personal cleanliness"; their
"dress and their households"; their "deportment and conversa-
tion"; their "economies of housekeeping"; their "standing and
respectability among co-laborers, neighbors, and fellow-citizens
generally"; and their "punctuality and fidelity in the performance of duties."[6]

The manufacturers were unanimous in proclaiming that those
workers with schooling were, as Mann had suggested they
might be, "more orderly and respectful in their deportment,
and more ready to comply with the wholesome and necessary
regulations of an establishment."[7]

J. K. Mills, who was connected with a "house" that had for
the past ten years "constantly employed about three thousand
people . . . in cotton mills, machine shops and calico printing
works," considered common schooling a wise investment. He
reminded his fellow manufacturers of the money they had already spent on their machinery. Only a schooled labor force

could be counted on to protect and multiply these investments while permanently preventing "any unnecessary depreciation."[8]

As Mann summed up his own arguments, now buttressed by the manufacturers' testimony, New England had become the most prosperous region in the union because its schools were the best. It would stay prosperous only if its schools were improved and expanded.[9]

The Midwestern reformers, no less than the Northeastern, directed their attention to the merchant and developing manufacturing classes, attempting to persuade them that common schooling would not only protect property already accumulated but enable them to accumulate still more. Caleb Mills, a private citizen in 1846, later to become Indiana's first Superintendent of Public Instruction, took upon himself the task of enlightening the property holders of the state as to their need for common schools. His "Open Letter" to the Indiana Legislature of 1846 contained a lengthy, densely argued section appropriately entitled, "Diffusion of Knowledge Benefits Property." Mills declared that common schooling would not only discipline the common people to the point where they would not threaten the sanctity of private property, engulf businessmen in a "whirlpool of bad debts," or practice disobedience to their employers, it would also be a direct sign to Eastern and European wealth that the West was civilized enough to safeguard their investments.[10]

It was only in the Southern states that the reformers were forced to do without the support of the more wealthy and powerful. While the Northeastern and Midwestern reformers could direct their attention to leaders in industry, commerce, and banking, Southerners had no similar constituencies to coax, cajole, and frighten into support for the common schools.

The South was for the most part a region of plantation owners with slaves, on the one hand, and small struggling rural farmers, on the other. Although the poor white farmers far outnumbered the plantation owners, their political power and influence was negligible.

The plantation owners of this period were not disinterested

in schooling. They were most concerned with it on two counts: first, that their own children get the best possible schooling and not have to go north to finish it, and, second, that slaves and freed blacks be denied any schooling whatsoever. While some Southern men and women of wealth and property worked, in their own ways, towards expanding the school system to encompass poorer whites, most saw little need for it. Their own children were well schooled—by tutors at home, then in private academies, military schools, or colleges. If the South had any need of improving its institutions of schooling, it was those schools that catered to the children of the wealthy that should be expanded and improved, not the common schools.[11]

The South, by hitching its future to cotton and slavery, ruled out common schooling. The reformers in this region, as dedicated as anywhere else, could find no potential allies. "The northern reformer's economic arguments for educating lower-class children bore no relevance to Negro slaves and poor whites, whom no amount of schooling would have made more useful to the plantation economy or less menacing to the stability of southern society."[12]

The workers, their organizations, and the common schools

Though the reformers and their allies spoke for the working people, the former believed that the workers and their organizations were far less enthusiastic than they ought to be. As Jay Pawa concluded in his exhaustive study, "The Attitude of Labor Organizations in New York State Towards Public Education," those workers who joined pressure groups, political clubs and parties, and trade unions, though not opposed to schooling per se, paid little attention to the common school movement. The subject of common schools was never one to "arouse a great deal of enthusiasm."[13]

For a brief period between 1828 and 1831, in the first flush of Jacksonianism, there were some groups that supported an expanded public school system, but even these groups were never so overcome by the movement that they lost sense of their particular needs as working people. As Sidney Jackson has shown in *America's Struggle for Free Schools*, the working people's program of school reform was never identical to that espoused by the reformers and their businessmen supporters. The working people who called for an expanded and free public school system in the later twenties were still able to look

> the gift horse [public schooling] in the mouth very carefully and [make] specific suggestions and demands for change. They did not like the school atmosphere: discipline was too strict and the growing body too cramped. The curriculum was unsatisfactory: workingmen wanted more than words without meaning and "histories superannuated." They asked "instruction in the laws of our country," and in the art of speaking one's mind about them. Furthermore, it was considered a waste of time when teachers simply placed material before their pupils without calling into action a single faculty of the mind, except the memory. . . . The teachers were not to blame for this, "for few of them know how to think themselves." Nevertheless, there was some room for choice—school committees ought to be more careful in what they offered workingmen's children.[14]

The brief period of critical support for public schooling drew to a rapid close. By the middle thirties the workingmen's groups were totally engrossed by other issues: debtor legislation, court reform, the ten-hour workday, child labor legislation, and the ongoing struggle against the power of the monopolies, corporations, banks, railroads, industrialists, merchant capitalists, and their "bought" men in state and federal government.[15]

The loss of faith in the powers of public schooling did not mean that the workingmen's groups abandoned their faith in education. Unlike the common school reformers, they had never equated education with common schooling. To oppose or be indifferent to the latter had no bearing on their support of the former.

While the reformers had little active interest in educational agencies that were not directly harnessed to the common schools or instrumental in their behalf (like the special lyceums established solely to promote school reform), the workingmen's groups continued to support a variety of educational projects outside the common schools:

—While the reformers sacrificed public libraries in New York through legislation that allowed the districts to divert library money to the common schools, the worker organizations continued on their own to establish and fund reading rooms and libraries.

—While the reformers did their utmost to destroy the private schools and academies which competed with the common schools, the worker groups founded their own mechanics' institutes, lyceums, and lecture series.

—While the reformers disparaged or ignored the possibilities of adult self-education, the workingmen's groups advocated self-culture as a most effective and efficient means of individual and class education. In fact one of the more important arguments made by advocates of the ten-hour day was that the workers needed time off for this kind of self-education.[16]

If the workers and their organizations grew less enthusiastic about the efficacy of common schooling reforms, it was no doubt because they realized that this institution was not, in and of itself, capable of providing the education workers needed, as individuals and as a class. The "monopoly of talent" enjoyed by the more prosperous would not be destroyed by freeing elementary schooling but by leaving the secondary schools, colleges, and universities as they were—absolutely closed to those without the leisure or the funds to attend.

The campaign for school taxes: the reformers vs. the districts

Though the people with wealth and power were the first targets of the reformers, they were politically perceptive enough to realize that if universal common schooling were to become a reality, it would need the support of more than just a handful of wealthy men.

The manufacturers, merchants, professionals, and reformers could not by themselves raise the money needed for expanded common schools. And even if they could, the poor parents whose children had to be schooled would not have accepted the charity. An expanded common school system would cost money, and lots of it. The only source of revenue large enough, secure enough, and not smacking of charity was property taxation.

The campaign for the common schools—through the later 1830s and 1840s—was no more and no less than a campaign for public taxation. The reformers would have preferred any other route towards the realization of their plans, but there was none. Without taxes specifically earmarked for the common schools, there could be no common schools.[17]

Unfortunately for the reformers, because in most states the districts exercised the power of the purse over public schooling, the campaign for school taxes had to be waged in each local district. Fortunately, they could count on support and assistance in just about every district.[18]

Though the statewide reformers, like Mann in Massachusetts and Barnard in Connecticut, too often monopolized the discussion of common school campaigning, it was the local reformers who did a good deal of the work. In every city, town, and village, there were men and women of property, social standing, and unblemished reputation who coordinated the campaigns for school taxation. They were joined by a network of local politicians (mostly Whigs), clergymen, merchants, manufacturers, and professionals. It was the task of the local reformers to keep the issue of public schooling and school taxes before the voter's eye day after day. Towards this end they utilized every available media: they spoke out at district meetings; they bombarded the newspapers with stories about the sorry state of the local schools and the need for reform; they established their own organizations, lyceums, and lecture series to spread the word; and they arranged district and regional conventions that gave the more prominent reformers a platform from which, in the style of the revivalist preacher, they could assail the community for its indifference to the one institution that could save its soul and property.[19]

Whatever the media, whoever the lecturer, writer, or correspondent, the message remained the same. As Mann himself had complained in his *First Report*, the principal obstacle to common school expansion was the "apathy" of the people. The voters and citizens of the local districts—town and country—did not know what was best for them. They continued to ignore the advice of the reformers.[20]

As early as 1820, Daniel Webster had warned that in the modern age of popular suffrage public instruction had become not a luxury so much as "a wise and liberal system of police, by which property, and life, and the peace of society are secured." The reformers through the 1840s would emphasize and reemphasize this argument. Taxpayers should regard school taxes as a form of property insurance, an investment in the social order. One reformer expressed this argument in a resolution offered to a staged convention called to elicit increased support for the common schools:

> Resolved: That the best police for our cities, the lowest insurance of our houses, the firmest security for our banks, the most effective means of preventing pauperism, vice and crime, and the only sure defense of our country, are our common schools; and woe to us, if their means of education be not commensurate with the wants and powers of the people.[21]

Property holders were assailed with arguments that could not be ignored. True, the more prosperous would have to pay higher taxes, but did they not have more to protect from the rapacity of the unschooled? As Caleb Mills warned the "rich land-holders," "merchants," and "manufacturers" of Indiana, they needed the schools as much as the schools needed them. The state—through its establishment and support of common schools—was performing a service for, not taking anything away from, the property holders. School taxes, rather than an infringement on property rights, were the best investment in its security money could buy.[22]

In New England and New York the reformers could concentrate their energies on fighting the battle for school taxes in the local districts. Further west and south however, they had to first secure legislation permitting the districts the right to tax their inhabitants for support of the common schools.[23]

The opponents of school taxes had arguments as long-winded, grandiose, and "American" as the reformers. School taxation, it was declared, was not only illegal, antidemocratic, and un-American; it was also an affront to the most basic right of parents: the right to raise their children as they saw fit. No government could compel support of its common schools; it was up to the individual parents to decide which, if any, of the available schools—common, private, or church—they would support.

Compulsory school taxation was, the opponents continued, more than an attack on American freedoms: it was an attack on the sanctity of the private property system. If American property were truly private, as the Founding Fathers had intended it to be, then no branch of government had the legal authority to confiscate any portion of it through compulsory taxation. Property might be taxed for roads and canals, prisons and police, but only because it could be assumed that all citizens either used or were protected by them. But all citizens did not have children in the common schools. Some had no children at all, others had grown children, still others had children whom they preferred to teach at home or send to private or church schools. To compel these individuals to pay taxes for schools their children would never attend was to rob them of their property.[24]

Horace Mann, perhaps the most theoretically minded of the reformers, devoted almost his entire *Tenth Annual Report* to answering these arguments. The only solid defense of school taxes he could find, however, involved him in an indirect attack on the sanctity of private property. As Mann argued in this Report, those who appeared to have earned and now owned property were merely the "trustees" of the community's wealth. The absolutism of ownership was limited by the cooperation of nature, past generations, and God in allowing accumulation to occur in the first place. The "trustees" had earned not the property itself, but merely the right to oversee it for the community at large. Whether they knew it or not, the property holders of each and every community "owed" the children of that community some share of their wealth. It was their moral, religious, and perhaps even quasi-legal obligation to provide them with the "knowledge and training to good habits" they would need for success and prosperity.[25]

The argument was circuitous, tendentious, and more fitting to a Christian Socialist than a New England Whig. It demonstrates, however, the distance the reformers had to go to answer an opposition argument that rested, perhaps more securely than their own, on the fundamental propositions of the American system.

The debate over the common schools and school taxation did not often take place on this high and lofty rhetorical plain; more often it descended to simple name-calling. The antieducation label was flung at all those who opposed authorizing or raising school taxes. In Pennsylvania, where "permissive" legislation permitting the districts to tax themselves was passed in 1834, the reformers charged that those who petitioned the legislature for repeal or modification were against spending any money at all on schooling the children of the community.[26]

This was clearly not the case. The Friends, as well as the Lutheran, German Reformed, and Mennonite communities—all vigorous opponents of the "permissive" legislation—had on their own established schools, which, though church connected, were open to non-church members and those who could not afford the tuition. These local communities did not oppose universal elementary schooling. They demanded only that they—the local communities—determine what was taught and how it would be paid for. A unified, property-tax-supported common schooling system had become anathema to them only because it meant that the majority would dictate its religion, its language, and its customs to the minority. Surely this smacked more of Old World established religious tyranny than New World democracy.[27]

These communities—some German-speaking, some not—would be placed in an impossible position were the "permissive" legislation passed. They would be forced to either abandon their schools or break the law by refusing to pay their taxes; they could not afford both.

Though in Pennsylvania the common school promoters made much of the fact that many of the petitions opposing the new legislation had been signed in German—or by persons other than the signatories, or with a mark instead of a signature, or illegibly—the fact was that no matter how they signed their names, the common school opponents were neither all German nor all ignorant. They were citizens who considered state interference in local schooling affairs not only unconstitutional but inherently unjust and oppressive.

The campaign for school taxes ended in a stalemate in Pennsylvania. Though the "permissive" legislation of 1834 was never repealed, the grass roots opposition remained so intense that more than half of the districts chose to ignore it, giving up the state aid that would have been theirs had they consented to tax themselves for the common schools.[28]

Compared to their counterparts in the Midwest, the Pennsylvania reformers were fortunate to have emerged from their campaign with a stalemate. In Illinois, the "permissive" legislation passed in 1825 was so unpopular that it was amended to death two years later. Under the amended legislation, the only Illinois citizens who could legally be taxed for the common schools were those who had already agreed to it in writing. In Indiana, the "permissive" legislation passed in 1824 and amended in 1836 was repealed entirely in 1837. Until the early 1850s, no Indiana residents could be required to pay school taxes.[29]

In those Middle Western states without "permissive" legislation and in Pennsylvania, where the permission, though granted, had not been acted on, the common school reformers were temporarily blocked. But even in New England and New York, where the districts had long since been given the right to tax themselves, the campaign for common school taxation had not nearly been won.

In New York State, for example, even though school taxation was the rule in most local districts, the money raised in this manner paid for only 20 percent of teacher salaries. More than half of the total costs still had to come from "rates" paid by the parents. Though state and district laws made provision for granting exemptions to poor and working parents who could not pay their rates, the reformers complained—and loudly—that such a system was far from adequate. There were, they charged, too many poor parents whose pride forbid their asking for rate exemptions and too many penny-pinching districts that refused such exemptions even when requested and deserved.[30]

The reformers wanted to substitute for rate payments local property taxes high enough to compensate for the money now contributed by the parents. Their proposal for "free schools"—free to parents but not to taxpayers—though defeated at the Constitutional Convention in mid-decade, was legislated into existence in 1849. As had happened in Pennsylvania a decade before, the most violent and organized opposition to the state's action occurred after the law had passed.[31]

The opposition to the New York law was so extreme that the State Assembly, on reconvening in 1850, established a special committee to review the legislation. The committee, in issuing its report to the full assembly, expressed its astonishment at the amount and virulence of the opposition to the free school legislation:

> This law has now been in operation some four months only, and yet we are already daily receiving petitions for its amendment, or its total and entirè repeal. Already there have been presented over forty petitions for its amendment, and over two hundred and fifty for its repeal. They come from every corner of the State; from our villages; our secluded districts; from our boards of supervisors; our town meetings; our district meetings; our public officers; public meetings; from the high and the low, the rich and the poor; those who voted for, and those who voted against it; all ages, conditions and classes, are here, and respectfully ask us, either to make essential and important amendments to the law or by its repeal, to place us where we were before. . . . In this manner, and for these purposes, some twenty thousand names, of which over two thousand are for amendments, and over seventeen thousand are for repeal, have been presented to us.[32]

As the committee explained, the free school law was opposed by many of the reformers who had originally supported it. And for good reason. A taxpayer revolt at the local level had made mockery of the law's objectives. Both legislators and reformers had abolished the rates in the expectation that the local districts would raise school taxes to the point where they would compensate for the revenue lost. But the districts had done no such thing. Instead of raising their taxes, they reduced their school year. When the parents had supplemented the tax monies by paying rates for each child, the average school year had been about eight months. Now with the rates abolished, the average school year was only four or five months.[33]

The reformers in New York in 1850, as in Massachusetts and Pennsylvania previously, condemned the district taxpayers for their tight-fisted refusal to raise their property taxes. But here too they missed the central issue. Though the districts opposed to the free school bill were not overjoyed at the thought of paying higher taxes, their opposition was not simply motivated by fiscal self-interest. The free school opponents were not against common schooling per se; neither did they oppose the concept of free schooling for those unable to afford their rates. What seemed to anger them most about the new legislation was the element of state dictation.

Under the old system, the districts maintained, they had taken care of those unable to pay their rates, but they had also been able to refuse exemptions to those who, in their belief, did not deserve them. The new state law removed this right from the local districts. The state legislature—not the district meeting—would decide how to fund the schools and who was to be admitted. There would be no more direct contact between the district and its poor citizens.

The state by interposing itself between the two groups had tied the poor to the backs of the prosperous. Neither group was happy with its new position: the poor because they felt more a burden than ever, the prosperous because they had become more burdened than ever. According to the petitioners from Pompey, New York, the free school law had generated "strifes, division, and animosity in every district." Not only were the prosperous turned against the poor, but division had been created between those whose children had grown old and those whose children were of school age; between those whose children attended private schools and those who did not; between tenants and owners; and between cities with abundant taxable property and rural counties with too little.[34]

The taxpayer revolt was serious enough to force the New York state legislature to resubmit the free school bill to referendum. Again it passed, though with substantially fewer votes than the first time. Still, as had been the case in Pennsylvania, the reformers, though their law was not repealed, emerged with no more than a symbolic victory. In the rural counties, where there existed less taxable property and strong traditions of district autonomy in school matters, the intent of the new legislation was negated. Local taxpayers shortened the school year instead of raising their taxes to cover the revenue lost when the rate bills were abolished.

By 1851 the legislature gave up trying to force the districts to tax themselves. A new school law was passed that substituted a minimal state-levied tax for local property taxes. Because the new state tax was not nearly high enough to cover the cost of schooling, the districts were allowed to supplement it by reinstating the once abolished rates. The reformers' attempt to make the schools free to parents would not be taken up again for another sixteen years.[35]

The inhabitants of the smaller cities and rural counties objected to the new schooling laws because they realized, quite correctly, that more than taxes was at stake. The school district, often no more than an assembly of families small enough to meet together but large enough to support a school, had become an important symbol of an American past rapidly disappearing in the onrush of industrial progress. The shift from local funding to state-mandated taxation had already occurred in the cities. But the cities were beyond reclamation as communities. The fear among the rural populace was that once control of their schools was lost, they too would become more and more like city residents, isolated and estranged from one another.[36]

The state schooling laws were neither the first nor the last nor the most significant assaults on community cohesion and local autonomy. The development of interregional, even international markets had already begun to destroy that economic interdependence that had held the community together. The farmer no longer sold his produce exclusively to the local town. Local artisans no longer produced exclusively for a local trade. The community was becoming as much an anachronism as the district.

Government interference in local affairs was already thought to be too intense. The state regulated commerce, banking, transportation, and now it was attempting to take over the local schools through state legislation mandating taxes and establishing state boards of education and state secretaries and superintendents.

Opposition to reforms mandated by state legislatures and state officials was organized and effective not just in Pennsylvania, New York, and the Midwest but even in Massachusetts, home of the common school campaign, where there was strenuous opposition to the 1837 legislation establishing a state board and paid secretary. It was argued that either the board and its secretary were powerless, in which case they should be abolished as a waste of the people's money, or they had some power, even that of persuasion, in which case they should be abolished as an improper interference with the right of the districts to run their local schools.[37]

The Massachusetts opposition was never powerful enough to depose Mann, though it came within a handful of votes of this objective in 1840. In Connecticut, however, the opposition was able to unseat Mann's friend and fellow reformer, Henry Barnard, who found his position abolished within four years of its establishment.[38]

Further west, the opposition to state supervision of local schooling, clearly a New England import, was more intense. Illinois and Indiana did not have state superintendents or state secretaries or even state boards until 1854. Ohio, which had appointed its first state official in 1837, abolished the position in 1840, only reestablishing it again in 1853.[39]

Who shall teach the children?

The major problem with the common schools was, as described by Horace Mann with the diplomacy of the seasoned politician, "an intense want of competent teachers." Though the reformers in every state found the district's choice of teachers wanting in all respects, their most serious criticism was not of the teachers' lack of learning and intellectual skills but rather their lack of character.[40]

If, as the reformers believed, children learned best by imitating their elders, then it followed that the models for imitation placed before them had to be of the highest quality. The children had to be taught to behave properly, that is, according to the accepted middle-class standards of the day. Farmer's daughters, neighborhood jacks-of-all-trades, rural preachers, and students newly arrived in the cities were not the best models for the young. Only those adults who embodied the desired character traits of self-discipline, moral restraint, diligence, frugality, and temperance belonged in the common schools. Horace Mann, in his *Fourth Annual Report*, made plain the "class" and "characterological" requirements for the common school teacher. He considered only "gentlemen" suitable candidates for reasons he made absolutely clear:

> If, then, the manners of the teacher are to be imitated by his pupils—if he is the glass, at which they "do dress themselves," how strong is the necessity, that he should understand those nameless and innumerable practices, in regard to deportment, dress, conversation, and all personal habits, that constitute the difference between a gentleman and a clown.
> . . . If none but teachers of pure tastes, of good manners, of exemplary morals, had ever gained admission into our schools, neither the school rooms, nor the appurtenances would have been polluted, as some of them now are, with such ribald inscriptions, and with the carvings of such obscene emblems, as would make a heathen blush.[41]

The problem for the reformers was finding an institutional mechanism through which they could intervene in the teacher selection and training process. The solution appeared to be some American variation of the Prussian teacher-training institutions.

Calvin Stowe, commissioned by the Ohio legislature to study the Prussian schools, reported that they were of uniformly high quality because their teachers had been rigidly and rigorously trained in state teacher's seminaries. The Prussians did not allow the local districts to select their teachers nor did they grant to chance or local whim the training those teachers would receive. They had constructed a "system": a regular, standard, prescribed course of study for every prospective teacher.[42]

Here was the answer to the reformers' dilemma. If they could not choose teachers for the individual districts, they could at least take a hand in training those who were chosen. If they could not guarantee that only gentlemen would preside in the common school classrooms, they could at least make sure that those who did had learned their manners and morals.

In his very first report to the Massachusetts state legislature, Horace Mann urged the establishment of normal schools. As he confided to his friend, James Mills, "If I had a few thousand dollars I know I could [by spending it on normal schools] very perceptively hasten the millennium."[43]

Unfortunately for Mann and his fellow reformers, the local communities and state legislatures, who were expected to raise the money for these new schools, were not as convinced of their transcendent importance. The normal schools might elevate the caliber of the teaching staff, but the price was too high. The legislators and districts did not want to pay the money these schools would require, and they distrusted the very concept of state normal schools.

Orestes Brownson, a perpetual critic of Whigs and Prussianizers, articulated the fears and apprehensions of the common school critics: "Who [he asked] are to be the teachers in these normal schools?" The answer was obvious. The government, not the local districts, would choose the teachers. This, Brownson argued, was contrary to the spirit of the democracy.[44]

Mann, fully cognizant of the opposition to the normal schools, used the help of his friend Edmund Dwight, a powerful and wealthy manufacturer, to pry loose state support and funding. Dwight informed the legislature that he would offer $10,000 of his own money for normal schools if it would allocate an equal sum of state money. With this attractive inducement, the normal school bill was passed in 1838. Though the first normal school would open the next year, modestly enough with only twelve students, the opposition remained strong enough to pass through committee a new bill in 1840 recommending the abolition of the normal schools and the return of the $10,000 to Dwight.[45]

Though Mann was able to defeat the 1840 bill and keep the first normal schools alive, neither he nor any of the other reformers entirely overcame the opposition to their Prussianized normal schools. By 1860 there were still no more than twelve in the entire nation.[46]

Though the reformers complained bitterly about the lack of training and poor quality of the common school teachers, they all realized that, in the long run, only better wages would attract better teachers. As long as wages were below what was being offered in the factories and private schools, the common schools would continue to attract unqualified, incompetent individuals.[47]

Part of the problem, the reformers realized, was the changing sexual composition of the teaching staff. By the middle 1830s women had begun to replace men in the common school classrooms, in great part because they could be paid "about 60 percent less on the average."[48]

The reformers did not argue on behalf of equal wages for women. They claimed only that salaries should be at least high enough to attract what Barnard referred to as "young ladies of education and refinement," a phrase with a class connotation as clear as Mann's use of "gentlemen." The wages paid to common school teachers, Barnard pleaded, had to be at least sufficient to afford the young ladies their own lodgings. As he warned the Connecticut state legislature, while "it may not be objectionable to young men, to be thus deprived of a regular and quiet home . . . to young ladies of education and refinement, it is attended with so many inconveniences, that many are driven from this their appropriate field of labor and usefulness rather than encounter them."[49]

Barnard and other reformers blamed the districts for the caliber of the teaching profession. But what they conveniently chose to ignore was the rationale behind the practices they criticized.

Boarding out was, for example, not just a device for saving money, though it was no doubt that. It was also a form of community supervision over the teacher's morals and character. If the teacher were given to a lack of manners, decorum, temperance, frugality, self-discipline, the community would discover it at once. There was no hiding one's character at the dinner table, night after night. The communities similarly kept teacher wages at a minimum not simply because of collective parsimony but because they saw no reason to pay teachers any more. Teaching was not a permanent profession. For the young woman, it was a temporary resting place between adolescence and marriage. For the young man in the city, it was a way to support himself through college or seminary. For those in rural areas, it was a source of livelihood through the winter season when no other work was available. In no case did teachers expect to make this their life's work. And even if they had, it is doubtful that their employers, the local districts, would have substantially increased their salaries.

Teachers in private schools and academies might be people of erudition. The common school "masters" were not, nor were they expected to be. Their primary task was to serve as character models for children to emulate—and to discipline those who preferred to act otherwise. Did such a job deserve higher wages than offered elsewhere? Did the districts really have to raise salaries so that they could attract "gentlemen" and "young ladies of education and refinement"? They obviously did not believe so.[50]

In the case of the normal schools and teachers' salaries, as in that of state-legislated taxes and supervision, the root of the district opposition was not fiscal, as the reformers claimed, but political. Orestes Brownson, among the most vociferous and articulate of the reformer opponents in Massachusetts, confronted the issues directly when he charged that the proposals for state normal schools were a direct, though somewhat disguised attack on district and popular autonomy. In Prussia, "where all the teachers will be the pliant tools of the government and . . . the whole tendency of the education given will be to make the Prussians obedient subjects of Frederick the King," state normal schools, state-legislated taxation, and state supervision might be appropriate.

> A government system of education in Prussia is not inconsistent with the theory of Prussian society, for there all wisdom is supposed to be lodged in the government. But the thing is wholly inadmissible here . . . because, according to our theory, the people are supposed to be wiser than the government. Here, the people do not look to the government for light, for instruction, but the government looks to the people. The people give the law to the government. To entrust, then, the government with the power of determining the education which our children shall receive is entrusting our servant with the power to be our master. This fundamental difference between the two countries, we apprehend, has been overlooked by the board of education and its supporters.[51]

Educational and political principles as well as simple common sense weighed heavily against a state-controlled or state-coordinated schooling system in the United States. Political ties were stronger than educational ones not only for state-appointed administrators and state-educated teachers but also for state boards of education, secretaries, and superintendents, who, because they represented the state and resided far from the district, could not "take the deep interest of parents in each individual school." As Brownson put it, "In the district, we manage the school for our own children, but the board of education [has] no children in the district school. . . . To confide our common schools to the board is like taking the children from their parents, and entrusting them to strangers."[52]

Brownson made it clear that neither he nor any of the other reformer opponents were opposed to schooling per se. On the contrary, the critics of state intervention, he asserted, "bear our unequivocal testimony in favor of universal education and assert the duty of every community to provide the best education in its power for all its children." Reformer name-calling had obscured the true differences between the reformers' and the districts' positions. According to Brownson, "The real question for us to ask is not, Shall our children be educated? but, To what end shall they be educated, and by what means? What is the kind of education needed, and how shall it be furnished?" [53]

4

The Irish and the Common Schools

The reformers had set out on their crusade for common schools in the middle 1830s, a time when the American white population was still relatively homogeneous. They did not pay special attention to the immigrants because there were too few immigrants to merit special concern. Beginning with the early 1840s, all this would change.

The Irish: making a living, building a community

A combination of factors had in the later thirties and forties made life not only uncomfortable but impossible in Ireland. An increase in population, several successive potato crop failures, legislation in England that forbade relief to Irish emigrés, a drop in the price of Irish grain, and new laws that allowed landlords to evict previously unevictable tenants set the stage for what would become one of the largest mass migrations of modern history.

The wave of Irish immigration that began in the late 1830s would not subside until the middle 1850s. During the peak years of the influx alone (1846 to 1853), nearly 1¼ million Irish men, women, and children would disembark in the New World.[1]

Where there had been neither work nor land for the Irish in their own country or elsewhere in the British Isles, there appeared to be plenty of both in the New World. The immigrants would soon discover, however, that the work was of the most menial, degraded, and underpaid variety, and the land, though abundant, cost far more than they could afford.

The Irish found work in the coastal cities where they disembarked. They excavated "ditches for gas and water mains, or were taken in gangs to dig canals or prepare the track of new railroads, or served as engine crews in the omnipresent steamboats. Throughout the [antebellum] period their brawn was laying the foundation for the new material civilization of America."[2]

Across the country the pattern was the same. The Irish filled the unskilled laborer jobs, those with the least security, requiring the least skill, and paying the lowest wages. In Newburyport, Massachusetts, foreigners accounted for almost two-thirds of the common laborers. The majority of these were Irish. In Boston, over four-fifths of the laborers enumerated in the 1850 census had been born in Ireland.[3]

Mrs. Trollope had in the 1820s complained bitterly about the problems of securing servants in this New World where Americans felt it beneath them to serve others. If she had visited the New World after 1850, she would have felt much more at home. The coming of the Irish had solved the "servant problem." The Boston census of 1850 reported no fewer than 3249 "domestic servants." Of these, 2292 had been born in Ireland.[4]

The Irish took the lowest-paying jobs in every industry and every work category. When the invention of the sewing machine enabled employers to increase productivity and lower costs by replacing high priced, skilled tailors with unskilled factory operatives, it was the immigrant Irish to whom they turned. When sugar refining and the manufacture of paper hangings were transformed from workshop to factory production, it was the unskilled Irish who were brought in to replace skilled craftsmen—at a fraction of the original wages.[5]

The Irish not only provided a cheap labor supply for the older, established industries that underwent transformation in this period, they also provided the impetus for the creation of new industries, particularly "in the heavy industries where strong muscles counted most. Scores of new factories, drawing upon the services of hundreds of Irishmen, sprang up in East and South Boston." The number of Irish laborers employed in copper and brass foundries, in new rolling mills, forges, rail factories, and other iron works, increased geometrically as the cheap wages at which the Irish could be hired provided an incentive for capital to invest in these huge manufacturing plants.[6]

The Irish immigrants by necessity moved into the alleyways, converted warehouses, and basements of the larger cities and towns. Earlier in the century, rich and poor had lived in the same neighborhoods, often on the same streets. By the later forties this had begun to change. In Boston the well-to-do abandoned the inner city wards to move to the suburbs or outskirts of the city. The commercial and waterfront districts in Boston, New York, and smaller cities like Newburyport quickly became Irish ghettoes.[7]

While nativists complained of the clannish tendencies of the newcomers, the Irish found their residential concentration to be one of the few reassuring elements in the New World. Whenever the population was large enough, and often when it was not, the Irish tried to pull together their own supportive community in this alien and hostile urban environment. They created parishes, built churches, established fraternal and sororal associations; they started their own newspapers and journals; they organized their own sports and social clubs, picnics, and parades; they founded their own political clubs and patriotic groups, militia companies, and community improvement associations. And, finally, they established their own social institutions: orphan asylums, homes for destitute Catholic children, and parochial and Sunday schools.[8]

Though it was agreed that, excepting the church, parochial schools were the most important community institutions, the costs involved—to the community that would have to build and maintain the schools and to the parents who would have to withdraw their children from wage earning to send them to school—were often prohibitive. Even in New York City, where the Irish had by 1840 succeeded in establishing eight Catholic schools supported entirely by their parishes, and many more that charged tuition, just over 30 percent of the school age population was enrolled. The same situation held true in the other Northeastern cities: community and church had neither the resources nor the teachers required to school the rapidly growing population of Irish Catholic children.[9]

Schools for Irish children

The problems the Irish would confront as they attempted to provide their children with adequate schooling were compounded by the most recent developments in common school history. The Irish had arrived in greatest number after the institution of compulsory property taxation for the support of the common schools. They found themselves in precisely the same situation as the German Protestants a decade earlier. They were faced with the equally unacceptable alternatives of supporting both the common and their own school systems or abandoning the latter because they were too expensive.

The Irish believed that the common schools had been invented for the express purpose of turning their children against them. In these schools, Irish children would be forced to read from a Protestant Bible. Their teachers would be Protestant and their school books would be filled with slurs against the Irish character, history, culture, and religion.[10]

The Irish were correct in their evaluation of the schooling their children would receive. As we have seen, the textbook set the tone and the content of common schooling. And the texts, whether written by Englishmen or Americans, were as viciously anti-Irish and anti-Catholic as the critics charged. According to the widely used *The Village School Geography*, published in 1837, these people were "poor, ignorant, and wicked." They drank too much, worked too little, and got what they deserved: famine, oppression, and poverty. The Catholic church was condemned as not only un-American but subversive of all forms of government, civilization, and morality. According to Ruth

Miller Elson, "several authors even blamed the church for the decline of the Roman Empire." The Pope and his "popish" clergy were described throughout the textbooks as libertine, debauched, corrupt, wicked, immoral, profligate, indolent, slothful, bigoted, parasitical, greedy, illiterate, hypocritical, and pagan.[11]

Because sending their children to the common schools would mean delivering them into a barrage of propaganda, branding them as "Paddies" for life, and forcing them to read the Bible like Protestants, the Irish parents whenever possible kept their young out of common school classrooms. When the parochial schools were too overcrowded or nonexistent and the choice was between common schooling or none at all, some parents chose to enroll their children in the public schools. But they were not happy with the situation. Neither was the church.[12]

The only solution was for the Irish to exert their political influence on city and state officials to have some portion of the tax monies collected for the common schools diverted into their parochial schools. Up until 1825, this had been the standard procedure. The school fund was distributed among the different denominations, including the Catholics, to school their own children as they saw fit. Though this division of funds had been discontinued, the Baptists and Methodists had continued to apply for a portion of the tax money allocated for common schooling.[13]

When Governor William Seward of New York, who believed both in common schooling and in switching the Irish vote from the Democratic column to his own, suggested in 1840 that common schools be established in New York City with teachers of the same faith and language as their students, the Irish Catholics took this as a signal to apply for a portion of the schooling funds.[14]

The Catholic request, though given a hearing, never stood a chance. The Catholics were opposed by a united front of Protestants. Almost overnight, those denominations and communities that had once opposed the common school monopoly on tax support switched sides. Even the Methodists and Baptists, who had asked for the same type of divison of tax money as the

Catholics now requested, argued that tax money should not be used in support of any schools but the "common" ones. The Methodists not only endorsed the "thesis that the control of popular elementary education belonged to the state, but even made the then novel proposal that attendance at these state schools be made compulsory." The Baptists joined in the celebration of the common schools, which, they now admitted, were essentially Protestant and quintessentially American. The parochial schools were accused of being subversive of the civil order and by their very nature profoundly un-American.[15]

By the middle 1840s it had become clear to the Irish Catholics that with this solid front of Protestant denominations lined up against them, they could not expect to receive state assistance for their schools or be relieved of having to support the common ones.

The Irish Catholic community in Philadelphia had attempted a different route to the same end: public schools that their children could attend. By state law, reading in the Protestant Bible, in the Protestant style—without commentary or analysis—was required in all Philadelphia schools. Catholic teachers who had refrained from these obviously Protestant exercises were fired, while Catholic children who did the same were punished for their disobedience. At the very least, the Catholics demanded that some change in this policy be made.

The Catholic petition for change was met with even more hostility in Philadelphia than in New York. When for a brief moment it appeared that the Board of Controllers might accede to some of the demands, nativist mobs led by nativist politicians took matters into their own hands, marching on Catholic wards, burning churches and schools, and rioting with such intensity that only the militia could restore some semblance of public order. Bowing to such pressure, the board backed down completely, preserving the anti-Catholic status quo in the common schools.[16]

The hostility that found expression in destructive mob activity was attributable to more than disagreements over curricula. As we have seen, the independent artisan/craftsmen of the cities and towns were by mid-century fast becoming anachronisms.

Larger production units organized by merchant capitalist retailers were driving the smaller workshops into debt, if not actual extinction. The Irish, unskilled and forced to accept work at
wages far below the skilled craftsmen, came to represent and
embody the new productive system that was destroying the
livelihoods, crafts, traditions, and very self-identities of the
urban artisans. For the first time, workingmen's groups began
to complain of immigrants driving down their wages. The long
term effects of the panic of '37 further aggravated the divisions
and reinforced the hostility between the older established workers and the newly arrived Irish.[17]

That the Irish were forced to pay taxes to schools they would
not allow their children to attend was the least of their problems. In Boston, Protestant laborers had attacked and burned to
the ground a convent school conducted by the Ursuline Sisters.
In New York City, anti-Irish riots were as common on election
days as speeches. In Philadelphia, the common school issue was
the spark that set off the days of rioting.[18]

The reformers' response

The common school reformers were placed in a conundrum by
the arrival of the Irish. It had been difficult enough getting the
local communities to support the common schools through compulsory property taxes. Now with the expansion of the Irish
population to the point where the city schools, if integrated,
would contain as many Irish as "Americans" in their
classrooms, it became even more difficult to attract to the common schools those children whose parents could afford private
ones.

It was not just the well-to-do Americans who were boycotting
the common schools. As we have seen, the opposition of minority groups—German as well as Irish, orthodox Protestant as well
as Catholic—was deep seated and not likely to vanish overnight. Throughout the 1830s the public schools had attempted
to counter this opposition by a variety of means. In New York
City the Public School Society had even recommended in 1837
that two schools in the German wards be staffed with teachers

who understood German. (The classroom instruction would, however, still be offered exclusively in English.) [19]

The common school reformers in every city and state tried to attract the Irish to their schools. They were convinced that the only antidote to the diseases of Irish heritage, Catholicism, and poverty was enforced disciplinary training in the common school classrooms. When the Irish in New York continued to boycott the schools, the Public School Society hired special "visitors" to descend upon Irish wards preaching their benefits. When this strategy failed, the society trustees substituted force for persuasion, recommending to the Common Council that public charity be denied to parents who kept their children out of school." [20]

Though the reformers bemoaned the absence of Irish children from common school classrooms and made all the perfunctory gestures to enroll them, their commitment to common schooling for Irish children was never strong enough for them to advocate the kinds of reforms necessary to do the job. Forced to work as laborers, paid by the day and fired when the job was done—the sewers dug, the tracks laid, the warehouses full—the Irish, like other urban poor, could not afford to send their children to school when their wages often meant the difference between survival and starvation for the entire family. Only child labor laws and subsidies to those families who would lose their children's wages if they were to attend school would have substantially improved the attendance rates of poor Catholic and Protestant children. But, unfortunately, this was the one reform the reformers could not propose. To have done so would have meant the sacrifice of their most enthusiastic supporters, the manufacturers. Besides, even with the will to push for child labor legislation, the reformers lacked the political power to bring it about. [21]

Though all other reforms were, compared to child labor laws, rather negligible, there were still a number of conciliatory gestures that might have changed the attitude of the Catholic parents—though perhaps not the clergy—towards the reformers and their common schools. In Lowell, Massachusetts, an acre of land with a large concentration of Irish Catholics had been made into a separate school district. After consultation with the local bishop and an agreement that the new district's schools would be taught by Catholics and their textbooks purged of anti-Catholic, anti-Irish propaganda, the Irish merged their schools with the public ones. The lesson here was transparent. It was possible, at little cost or sacrifice, to interest Irish parents in public schools. All that was necessary was reforms that would make the common schools a little less common, or to be more precise, a little less "Protestant." [22]

This was the one change necessary to make the schools more palatable to the immigrants, but it was also the one point on which the reformers would never compromise. If, as they believed, the primary purpose of common schooling was to discipline and mold poor children into hard-working, law-abiding, property-respecting workers and citizens, then the mold could not be recast to suit each group fed into the American workplace. The common schools would not be doing their job if they taught children in the ways their parents preferred, especially when those parents were Irish and Catholic as well as poor.

The choice was between changing the schools or abandoning the Irish children, and the reformers chose to maintain the integrity of their schools. Horace Bushnell, a Connecticut Congregationalist with a national reputation and one of the most enthusiastic proponents of the civilizing mission of the common schools, was uncompromising in this regard. He gloried in the fact that the Catholics were being doubly taxed—once for the common schools, again for their own. This was their just penalty for withdrawing their children from the state schools. Bushnell reacted viciously to the argument that the common school fund should be redistributed to the various communities according to their religious preferences. His contention was that such a policy was a direct threat to the sanctity and integrity of the schools, and the state. [23]

From the middle forties on, the Protestant consensus brought about by the arrival of the Catholics became a powerful force in all school political issues. In nine Northern and Midwestern states, specific legislation or constitutional amendments were passed forbidding the expenditure of state moneys on parochial schooling. This restriction on the use of public funds for schooling sealed the fate of not just the Catholics but the Episcopalians, Lutherans, German Reformed, Friends, Mennonites, Methodists, Congregationalists, and Presbyterians—all denominations that at one time or another had attempted to establish their own parochial systems.[24]

The decision to bar state schooling funds for Catholics had not been a difficult one. But it was also not an entirely satisfactory one. In Boston, where by the early 1850s one out of every two births was Irish Catholic, the danger of an unschooled Irish Catholic population was emphasized and reemphasized by school promoters who had, for the past half-century, been arguing that common schooling was the best, perhaps the only, effective and efficient form of property insurance.[25]

In 1848 Mayor Josiah Quincy of Boston, somewhat of a reformer himself, asked the city marshal to ascertain the number of children wandering about, free of institutional supervision. The marshal reported, as could have been predicted, that the great number of "truants" was a problem indeed, one that was making the job of the police much more difficult. Borrowing an old argument of the reformers, he declared that, in the long and short run, it would cost less to school these children than to expand the "Police, Courts, and Prisons."[26]

The Boston School Committee, by the late 1840s composed almost entirely of self-professed supporters of Horace Mann and reform, agreed with the mayor and the marshal on the need to do something about the Irish children. The fact that so many were loose in the streets was taken as direct and positive proof that their parents were not exercising proper control. And, the reformers claimed, when the parents failed to do their job, the state had no choice but to intervene.

In March of 1849 the Boston School Committee proposed to make schooling compulsory for all children. When some legislators protested that such a law "threatened parental rights over the child," the reformers responded that the parents of truants had abdicated their rights by neglecting their responsibilities.

"In 1852, the efforts of Bostonians resulted in . . . a statewide compulsory school law." The schools and their allies, the police, were given new powers to enforce attendance. The new laws were directed at those Irish children who neither worked in factories nor attended school. It was now a crime for children to be free of school or factory. Those who persisted in exercising such illegal freedom were subject to arrest and incarceration in truancy-proof reform schools.[27]

The reform schools of Massachusetts and later of other states in the Northeast were becoming filled with children convicted of this new crime. Though some had been sent away for "larceny" or "stubbornness," quite a number were being incarcerated as truants: "Of children committed to the state reform school at Worcester 367 of 440 boys had been truants from school, a 'crime' exceeded in villainy only by the number who had been addicted to lying, and closely followed by those who used profane language." The percentage who were "foreign" was enormous. The first statistics on "truant and vagrant" children compiled by the Boston marshal in 1849 showed that 963 of the 1066 children charged with these crimes were "of foreign parents." The Boston truant officer William F. Reed reported in 1852 that he had dealt with "36 native and 211 foreign truants . . . during a three-month period. . . . For the year ending June 30, 1853, Reed reported a total of 98 American [sic] and 559 foreign truants."[28]

David Rothman's research shows the same proportions of Irish to "native Americans" in other state reformatories established for truants: "By 1850 only 28% of the residents of New York reformatories were native-born, while over half were Irish. In Philadelphia ⅓ were "American," over 42% Irish. In Cincinnati, over half were Irish or German. . . . Through the country the percentages were the same."[29]

The Irish and other immigrant groups were afforded the special treatment of compulsory school laws and reform schools because, to the minds of the reformers, the defects in Irish homes, neighborhoods, and family life were egregious enough to warrant extraordinary measures.

To Barnas Sears, Horace Mann's successor as secretary to the Massachusetts Board of Education, the conjuncture of urban life and immigrant children was particularly pernicious. Cities, he claimed, "furnish peculiar facilities for the diffusion of corrupt principles and morals." Migrants to the cities found "in their new places of abode, pleasures set before them appealing to every sense, and in gradations adapted to every intellect." So strong was the "current of sensuality," warned a shocked and fearful Sears, "that it too often sweeps almost everything before it. . . . This life of congregated human beings, where money, leisure, shows, and a succession of excitements are the objects of pursuit, is now, with inconceivable power, educating myriads of children." [30]

From colonial times, reformers or their historical counterparts acting in the name of church and/or state had possessed the authority of law, tradition, and common sense to remove children from households that had demonstrated an incapacity to properly care for and raise them. Now, with the coming of the Irish to the urban slums, the reformers extended this right of intervention to its logical (if absurd) extreme. Since the Irish were not only poor but Irish, their material circumstances intertwined with their congenital lack of inner discipline, temperance, and moral fiber to make them *a priori* failures as child-raisers. Therefore, the state was not only justified but required to take responsibility for rearing Irish children away from their parents and transfer it to the state guardians, the school reformers.

In 1853 the Boston School Committee set out the new rules of the game, carefully delineating the changing role of parents and state in child-rearing:

The parent is not the absolute owner of the child. The child is a member of the community, has certain rights, and is bound to perform certain duties, and so far as these relate to the public, Government has the same right of control over the child, that it has over the parent. . . . Those children should be brought within the jurisdiction of the Public Schools, from whom, through their vagrant habits, our property is most in danger, and who, of all others, most need the protecting power of the State. [31]

Horace Mann phrased it a little more succinctly in his diary: "Every child should be educated . . . if not educated by its own father, then the State should appoint a father to it." [32]

By the 1850s Massachusetts was ready to take Mann at his word. An article on immigration in *The Massachusetts Teacher* declared it not only wise but necessary that compulsory schooling laws remove all responsibility for child-rearing from the Irish parents.

> With the old not much can be done; but with their children, the great remedy is *education*. The rising generation must be taught as our children are taught. We say *must be*, because in many cases this can only be accomplished by coercion. In too many instances the parents are unfit guardians of their own children. If left to their direction the young will be brought up in idle, dissolute, vagrant habits, which will make them worse members of society than their parents are; instead of filling our public schools, they will find their way into our prisons, houses of correction, and almshouses. Nothing can operate effectually here but stringent legislation, thoroughly carried out by an efficient police; the children must be gathered up and forced into school, and those who resist or impede this plan, whether parents or *priests*, must be held accountable and punished. [33]

The Irish knew exactly why these new measures had been proposed. It was no longer simply a matter of schooling but rather, in Stanley Schultz's phrase, one of, "Who owns the child?" An Irish newspaper sharply framed the issues:

> The general principle upon which these [compulsory schooling] laws are based is radically unsound, untrue, Atheistical. . . . It is, that the education of children is *not* the work of the Church, or of the Family, but that it is the work of the State. . . . In the matter of education, the State is supreme over the Church and the Family. [A consequence that flows from this principle] leads the state to *adopt* the child, to weaken the ties which bind it to the parent. So laws are made compelling children to attend the state schools, and forbidding the parents, if they be poor, to withdraw their little ones from the school.

The ultimate outcome of such practice was, the newspaper article explained, the destruction of the family and of the Irish people. Schooled children would lose all respect for their parents, their church, their traditions and heritage as Irish. This the Irish would not allow, no matter what the costs.[34]

5

The Legacy of Reform—the Ideology and the Institution

There was never the remotest possibility that the reformers could have succeeded in their ultimate objective of enrolling all the children of the community in their common schools. Even if the funds had been forthcoming and generous enough to build schools as grand as palaces, the poor would not have been able to send their children to them—and not because they did not understand the value of an education.

As Stephen Thernstrom has written regarding the situation of the poor and working parents of Newburyport, no matter how eloquently Horace Mann might extol the benefits of a common schooling, "education for *their* children was simply a luxury the family could not afford."[1]

Universal schooling—for the poor as for the prosperous—would not be attained within the reformers' lifetimes. It was contingent on something the reformers could not produce: the acceptance of child labor regulation by the employers themselves. Without this acceptance—based on the recognition that unregulated child labor was destroying workers before they reached their productive prime—no child labor or compulsory schooling legislation could produce widespread common school enrollment.

Universal common school enrollment was further dependent

on other factors beyond the capacity of the reformers to effect. In the West and in rural areas of the Northeast, there could be no common schooling at all until the population was dense enough to support a school within commuting distance of each household. In the South, universal schooling was unthinkable as long as slavery was maintained.

As we have seen in preceding chapters, while there appeared to be widespread agreement among Americans on the importance of schooling for their children, there was no consensus on the shape that schooling should take. There were differences of opinion over how the schools should be funded; over what form religious instruction should take; and over the qualifications for schoolmasters, the facilities for schoolhouses, the contents and objectives of school books, and the proper language of classroom instruction. In all these areas of dispute, the reformers forced their consensus on local communities not through the power of their arguments so much as through the power of their political coalitions. District by district, state by state, the reformers organized and utilized a coalition of prosperous merchants, manufacturers, bankers, and professionals, in part by presenting common schooling as not simply an agency of popular education but, in the words of one reformer, "the best police for our cities, the lowest insurance of our houses, the firmest security for our banks, the most effective means of preventing pauperism, vice, and crime." [2]

The schools of the nation had always been agencies of socialization as much as of education: they had taught morals and religion, disciplined and trained character as enthusiastically as they had offered instruction in reading and writing. But never before had common schooling been represented so explicitly as the most efficient and effective form of protection against what Mann referred to as "the giant vices which now invade and torment" our society. [3]

The "invaders" and "tormentors" were, in the early years of the crusade, quickly identified as the uprooted and dispossessed, the poor and unemployed, the bankrupt artisans, frustrated journeymen, and failed family farmers condemned to poverty in the city by a lack of capital and marketable skills.

Through the early 1840s this population had been almost uniformly white, Anglo-Saxon, and Protestant, distinguished from the prosperous residents of town and city by their recent arrival and poverty rather than by racial, religious, or ethnic characteristics.

The common schools were designed to control and contain this poor, white, Protestant, male population. But the school model constructed in their behalf was suited to other newcomers to the city: the Irish in the later 1840s, the Eastern and Southern Europeans towards the turn of the century, the blacks who moved northward in the mid-twentieth century. Once the common schools had been defined as institutions of social control, as agencies through which the prosperous and propertied would socialize the poor and working people, it mattered not what color, ethnicity, religion, or geographical area the latter came from. Once political control had been established, the form and content of schooling could be adjusted to the specific characteristics of the lower-class population.

The common schoolers did not succeed in wresting total control from the rural districts and urban neighborhoods. (The next generation of reformers would fight this battle to its conclusion—see Part Two.) Still, by the middle 1850s they had been able to force their conception of a republican, Protestant education on the schools of the Northeast and Middle West. They had also begun selling the country on the principle that what they called moral and political education was as important, perhaps more important, a function of the schools than teaching the rudiments; that teachers should be as close to "gentlemen" and "gentlewomen" as could be afforded; that there should be state standards for schoolhouses and school books; that the state should operate teacher training institutions; and that the only appropriate funding source for the public schools was compulsory property taxation.

The institution of compulsory property taxation for the common schools would never provide the schools with the funds the reformers believed necessary. But where the common schools were not transformed by compulsory taxation their private counterparts were. Because most parents could not afford to pay twice for schooling—first through taxes for the common schools and then through tuition for private ones—the many private schools, church and lay, that had enrolled the children of working people found themselves without a constituency. According to Carl Kaestle, in New York City alone the number of private schools declined from 430 in 1829 to only 138 in 1850, and the percentage of school children enrolled in them from over 60 percent to under 20 percent.[4]

A similar trend occurred in Massachusetts. Here too the private schools for families of moderate incomes, the unincorporated academies, were abandoned by parents unable to pay both tuition and taxes. In the four decades after 1840 the number of such schools declined from 1308 to 350. Only the incorporated, endowed, and expensive academies like Groton and Andover survived the institution of compulsory school taxation. "In Massachusetts between 1840 and 1850 the number of students opting for private education almost halved. . . . For New England as a whole, public enrollment grew by 10 percent; academy [private] attendance *declined* by 6 [percent]."[5]

The common school reformers, though not successful in expanding the enrollment of their institutions as much as they had wanted, were successful enough to drive the private schools, which served moderate income families, into extinction. By the middle 1850s they had realized for their common schools a near monopoly on elementary schooling.

If the reformers' ultimate objectives had been to establish within their lifetimes common schools that would be universally attended by rich and poor alike, they failed. If it was to coax or coerce the Irish Catholics into their common schools, they failed. If it was to diminish to insignificance community control of local schools, they failed. If it was to eliminate poverty, pauperism, criminality, intemperance, workplace indiscipline, political unrest, and social disorder, they failed again.

And yet, though these objectives were not realized, the reformers did succeed in laying the ideological and institutional groundwork upon which later generations of public schools would be erected. Though the crusade had failed in the short run, its long-term effects, especially the shift from family and community to school and state as the guardians of the young and watchdogs at the portal of adult life, must not be underestimated.

II
The High Schools
1895–1915

6

The "Youth" Problem

In the 1830s, the European visitors had been appalled by the behavior of American children—and their parents. The children were undisciplined, ill-mannered, and impudent—and their parents seemed unconcerned.

A half-century later the Europeans might still complain about the children of the New World (as one Frenchman visiting the U.S. in 1892 put it, "a composite photograph of American youth would reveal 'le plus terrible de tous les enfants terribles' "), but they could no longer complain about the adults' lack of concern. The youthful disrespect and unruliness that had once been smiled on as typically American had come to be considered not only unfortunate but positively harmful to the future of the republic.[1]

The invention of "adolescence": G. Stanley Hall

The antebellum reformers, teachers, preachers, and other authorities, had been critical of the behavior of children other than their own, but they had especially focused their attention on the younger children. In their considered opinion it was the earliest years that were most crucial. This was the period in which the child's character would be formed.

The twentieth-century experts were not so certain. What troubled them most was not the youngest children, but their older brothers and sisters. Though they did not deny the importance of providing the younger ones with moral training, they emphasized repeatedly it was the last stage of youth that was the most crucial.

Adolescence as a stage in human development was literally invented during the first decades of the twentieth century. Though, as we shall see, educators and youth workers, lawyers and judges, magazine writers and editors, muckrakers, progressives, and reformers—lay, clerical, and professional—all contributed to the conceptualization, it was the psychologists who gave the new developmental age the patina of scientific explanation it would need to survive.[2]

G. Stanley Hall, a student of William James, president of Clark University, and the first American to invite Sigmund Freud to lecture in this country, introduced the adolescent to the scientific and lay community in 1905 in his massive two-volume work, appropriately entitled: *Adolescence: Its Psychology and Its Relations to Physiology, Anthropology, Sociology, Sex, Crime, Religion, and Education.*[3]

Hall, a self-proclaimed Social Darwinist, theorized that each individual "recapitulated" in his or her development the progress of the human race. Adolescence, in Hall's evolutionary schema, was the individual· stage of development corresponding to the historical period of savagery, vagrancy, and nomadic life. Adolescents, simply put, were young savages, too unrestrained, too filled with the spirit of adventure and the "wanderlust," to adapt easily to the adult roles laid out for them.[4]

The problem was at root a biological one. In each and every individual, according to Hall, as adolescence approached, "sex asserts its mastery in field after field, and works its havoc in the form of secret vice, debauch, disease, and enfeebled heredity."[5]

"In older lands with more conservative traditions," so understood Hall, the society of adults had learned to control, to dam up and rechannel this torrent of adolescent sexuality. But modern American civilization—urbanized and civilized—had not followed the wisdom of the ages. It had abandoned the traditional "regulatives" and increased the temptations to license: "Never has youth been exposed to such dangers of both perversion and arrest as in our own land and day."[6]

Though the risks were enormous, there was, Hall asserted, one way out of this descent into barbarity. It was impossible, and ill-advised, to turn back the clock to simpler times, but it was possible to devise new institutional strategies for coping with the eternal dangers of adolescent sexuality. The "regulatives" must be increased, the temptations decreased, youthful enthusiasm channeled into wholesome activities. As Hall warned the scholarly audience of *Adolescence* and the larger lay audience of the *Ladies' Home Journal*, the war on adolescent sexuality had to be fought on all fronts, including the trousers:

> Trousers should not be too tightly drawn up by suspenders, as boys are prone to do, but should be left loose and lax. They should be made ample, despite fashions often unhygienic. The irritation otherwise caused may be an almost constant stimulus. Undergarments for both sexes should be loose and well cut away, and posture, automatisms, and acts that cause friction should be discouraged. . . . Pockets should be placed well to the side and not too deep, and should not be kept too full while habitually keeping the hands in the pockets should be discouraged.[7]

The "bad boys": who were they?

Hall had shrouded the social problem of adolescence in the pseudoscientific jargons of psychology and biology. In so doing he had elevated the tenor of discussion to the point where other scientists and men of learning felt obliged to add their particular observations and recommendations. There seemed to be almost a national obsession with the subjects of youth, adolescence, and juvenile misbehavior, crime, and delinquency in the decades at the turn of the century. Not only did Hall, John Dewey, and William James, the most important psychologists of the period, lecture the public on their responsibilities in this regard, they were joined by a multitude of lay experts who had their advice and warnings to offer.

In the first decade of the twentieth century, the attention of the nation—or at least its readers—was fastened on the "boy" problem: on juvenile delinquency, crime, courts, and customs. For the popular magazines that, having lowered their prices, could now for the first time claim a mass audience, these themes were irresistible. The *Reader's Guide to Periodical Literature*, which had listed only 13 articles on "boys" and 8 on "juvenile delinquency" for the last decade of the nineteenth century, included over 140 under the heading "boys" for the 1901-1910 period and 75 under "juvenile delinquency" for the 1905-1909 period alone.[8]

Every one of the popular magazines ran its articles on these subjects: *Scribners* published, "Are we spoiling our boys who have the best chances in life?"; *Popular Science*, "Difficult boys"; *The American Mercury*, "Helpless youths and useless men"; *Outlook*, "Getting at the boys," "Being a boy," and "Making good citizens out of bad boys"; *Good Housekeeping*, "Managing a boy"; *Lippincott's*, "Moulding of Men"; *Harper's Bazaar*, "Play suits for little boys" and "Pleas for the small boy"; and *Ladies' Home Journal*, the most influential of all the popular magazines and the first to exceed a million in circulation, "Bad boy of the street," "How and when to be frank with boys," "How I trained my boys to be gentlemen," "How we trained our boy," "Keeping a city boy straight," and "What boys my boy should play with."[9]

As can be seen from the titles, the middle-class public that still made up the bulk of the magazine audience was warned of two separate, but interrelated problems: their own children and those already gone bad.

The reading public knew exactly who the "bad" boys were. Though their own middle-class children would also become corruption-prone as they reached adolescence, it was those who lacked proper family supervision who were most likely to surrender to their baser instincts on reaching the dangerous age. F. H. Briggs, author of the popular guidebook, *Boys as they are made and how to remake them*, warned it was not the natural boys "who come from the home where industry, intelligence and thrift prevail, where books and magazines abound, where the library table forms the center of an interested group, where refinement of thought and life prevail" who were the potential delinquents. It was "the boy over the back fence in your alley" who needed watching.[10]

Those youth "over the back fence" who were now labelled social problems had not risen out of thin air. Most, in fact, had come directly from impoverished farms on both sides of the Atlantic.

The rural exodus that had so disturbed an earlier generation of American reformers accelerated in the decades following the close of the Civil War. Industry had come of age on the farm with the same results as in the city. Smaller productive units were being swallowed whole or forced into bankruptcy by competition with larger, mechanized and capitalized corporate enterprises. The costs of doing business—on the farm as in the city—now included capital to expand production, to purchase new and better machinery, and to store and market the finished products. Those without the capital had to go to the banks or go out of business.[11]

Young men on their own, couples starting out in life, older families with children: all were pulled and pushed into the city—pulled by the hope of finding economic security there, pushed by the impossibility of obtaining it anywhere else.

The census of 1890 revealed the cumulative effect of thousands of individual decisions to leave the farm. During the decade of the 1880s, a period of overall population increase, the farm regions of the Middle West and Northeast lost population: "In Ohio, 755 out of 1316 townships declined in population, in Illinois, 800 out of 1424." Losses were also registered in central Missouri, eastern Iowa, and southern Michigan, all farming areas. In the Northeast the population shift was as dramatic: "Two-fifths of the [counties] in Pennsylvania, a good quarter of New Jersey, nearly five-sixths of New York state . . . three-fifths of Connecticut, three-quarters of Vermont, and nearly two-thirds of New Hampshire and Maine declined in population."[12]

By 1890 it had become clear that the nation, if not yet urban, was headed in that direction. Up to one-third of all Midwesterners, three-fifths of Northeasterners, two-thirds of New Yorkers, and four-fifths of Massachusetts residents now lived in cities. And this happened before the arrival of the "new immigrants" who would even more dramatically effect the demographic shape of the nation.[13]

The Southern and Eastern European peasants who arrived on these shores in the first years of the new century were pushed and pulled by the same forces as the rural Americans. Most had left the Old World because they could see no future without land of their own or the capital to purchase it. They had come to the New World because of the opportunities advertised by relatives already there, by the steamship companies, by agents sent abroad by private industry and state immigration bureaus. Some came to settle, others to accumulate the capital needed for economic independence back home.[14]

They came to work, and they intended to work hard. They were welcomed by businessmen who saw in them a cheap and virtually inexhaustible labor supply. The South, in the throes of one of its periodic rebirths, was particularly anxious to attract these workers to its new cotton mills and its older plantations and tenant farms. Southern businessmen dispatched special agents to European cities, spent money on newspaper ads, meetings, immigration bureaus, and literature in every foreign language to spread the word that the New South offered new opportunity to the immigrants.[15]

The Northern businessmen did not have to extend such efforts. Fortunately for them, the steamships with their cargoes of future workers disembarked near enough to the factories, mills, and workshops of the Northeast to facilitate the rapid recruitment of new workers.

Most immigrants who arrived on these shores in the first years of the new century had few industrial skills to speak of. And even if they possessed these skills, they would not have been likely to find employment that would draw on them. The rapid industrialization of American manufacturing brought with it as rapid a decrease in the percentage of skilled workers required in the newly mechanized workshops and factories, mines and mills. This was not unexpected, but rather one of the reasons why manufacturers reinvested their capital in machinery in the first place. The machinist, tailor, butcher, and steel roller were skilled craftsmen, able to command relatively high wages and control over their working conditions. They were replaced by semiskilled operatives and laborers who could be trained in a day and replaced as rapidly. Not only were these unskilled and semiskilled workers paid less than the skilled, they lacked the bargaining power and the union backing to secure a greater share of the wealth they were producing.[16]

By 1910 the immigrants had become an essential component of the American workforce. Though accounting for only 20 percent of all workers, they held close to 50 percent of the jobs in quarrying, meat-packing, woolen textiles, coal mining, blast furnaces and nearly 70 percent of those in copper mining, suit, coat, and cloak production, and iron mining.[17]

The immigrant and "native" American refugees from rural poverty, would, in the decades surrounding the turn of the century, form the bulk of the new urban population. The "adolescent problem," as we shall see, was at base a problem invented by the older, established urban residents now threatened in any number of ways by these immigrant newcomers.

The urban reformers, educators, and social workers did not blame the immigrants or new urban working class directly; most in fact made it clear that it was not the first generation of urban dwellers but their children who were causing all the trouble. Still, the "adolescent problem" was perceived, diagnosed, and treated as an immigrant problem, one that, if not solved, would rapidly spread to the rest of the population.

The adolescent and the law

Though the psychologists provided the conceptual framework around which the adolescent problem was constructed, it was the reformers who provided the problem with its "solutions."

Jane Addams, who played a vital role in almost every aspect of reform, was one of the most enthusiastic readers and supporters of G. Stanley Hall. From Hull-House, her settlement in the heart of Chicago's immigrant ghetto, she issued a series of recommendations to the magazine-reading public and the politicians, educators, legal experts, and kindred reformers and professionals in other American cities. Adolescents were volatile creatures, capable of the deepest passions, the highest idealism, and the most reckless dissipation. It might not be possible to dampen their ardor or cool their sexually ignited fires, but it was possible to channel their energies into socially meaningful work and personally purifying recreation. In no case should they be left on their own.

Those born into prosperous families were not the problem. It could be assumed that their parents would provide them with the moral guidelines, recreational facilities, and educational supervision they required. But what of the less fortunate, the children of the immigrants and newcomers from rural America to the urban ghettoes? Who would watch over them? Who would protect them from the temptations offered on every street corner? [18]

It was reformers like Jane Addams, working with their professional colleagues, who took up the task of providing these problem children with the supervision they lacked. Because it could be—and was—assumed that the adolescent was constitutionally incapable of self-restraint, these "child-savers," as Anthony Platt refers to them, initiated a campaign to formulate a special legal status for them. [19]

Though New York and Pennsylvania had already recognized the unique nature of juveniles and their potential as social problems, it was the Illinois Juvenile Court Act of 1899, prompted by the Chicago-based "child-savers," that would serve as the model for statutes subsequently enacted in twenty-two states and the District of Columbia. [20]

Under the Illinois statute, any citizen could bring a complaint against any child and his or her parents. The complaint was referred to the juvenile court, where a specially selected judge heard it informally. There was no prosecutor or defense attorney present at these hearings. The rules of evidence and criminal procedure were dispensed with. Juveniles did not have to be accused of a specific crime. Most in fact were brought into court for actions that, had an adult committed them, would not have been considered illegal in any way. "During the earliest years of the Cook County juvenile court, over 50 percent of the delinquency cases arose from charges of 'disorderly behavior,' 'immorality,' 'vagrancy,' 'truancy,' and 'incorrigibility.' " Once found incorrigible, predelinquent, neglected, or dependent, the accused and convicted were declared wards of the state, sent home with a warning, placed under the supervision of a legal guardian, or remanded directly to a state reformatory.[21]

Although, by definition, all adolescents were potential criminals, it was the immigrants and working-class youth who were the targets of these new laws. "It was not by accident that the behavior selected for penalizing by the child-savers—drinking, begging, roaming the streets, frequenting dance-halls and movies, fighting, sexuality, staying out late at night, and incorrigibility—was primarily attributable to the children of lower-class migrant and immigrant families."[22]

When the young did commit actual crimes, they were almost always crimes of property: petty thievery, pilfering, pickpocketing. The children who committed these crimes were not hardened criminals but youngsters who needed the money to have a good time. Most teenagers could not even raise the nickel to buy their way into the theater. A good many of the "pilferings, petty larcenies, and even burglaries" that Jane Addams witnessed in her twenty years at Hull-House were, she believed, the result of this "never ceasing effort on the part of boys to procure theater tickets."[23]

Immigrant or "American" teenagers born in the city of parents new to it were triply victimized: first, they lacked the price of entertainment; second, even their most enterprising attempts to secure it were defined as criminal or delinquent behavior; and third, even when they managed to raise the money to entertain themselves or figured out how to do it for nothing, they were accused of contributing to their own delinquency. Junkers—children who sold junk to junkmen—were *a priori* delinquents whether or not they had stolen the merchandise because, as Addams reported, "with the money obtained they would buy cigarettes and beer or even candy, which could be conspicuously consumed in the alleys." Teenagers who did no more than "gaily walk our streets" were contributing to their own delinquency. No matter how pure their intentions, they were bound to be led into mischief or the temptation that could not be resisted.[24]

Child-saving

The simple truth of the matter was that there was nothing to do, nowhere to play, and no place to work for adolescents born to poor families, immigrant or "American." Though the psychologists proffered and the child-savers accepted theories of biological determinism, the most perceptive among them argued that it was not the biological make-up of this generation of young people but the environment in which they were trapped that undergirded the entire problem.

The common school reformers of a half-century before, charging an earlier generation of rural refugees with parental neglect, claimed that institutional intervention was a necessary response to parental abdication. The reformers who worked in the turn-of-the-century urban settlements could not simply reiterate these charges. They knew from firsthand experience that the immigrant families hadn't only not abandoned their children but that ofttimes they were even stronger than their native American counterparts. The twentieth-century reformers did not, like the common schoolers, blame the families for the indiscipline of their young. Many saw the immigrants instead as the innocent victims of the onrush of industrialization and urbanization—for John Dewey, a revolution as rapid, extensive, and complete as any in history.[25]

The family farm had provided the young with a place to mature under the constant and beneficent supervision of concerned adults, parents, relatives, and friends. But industrialization had, as Dewey viewed it, destroyed this "household and neighborhood" system. What had once been so naturally provided now had to be reconstructed. The child-savers set out to design and establish new institutional substitutes for the traditional "household and neighborhood" agencies of child-rearing and socialization.[26]

The women reformers, though the catalysts of the movement, did not act alone. Their crusade had its publicists; muckrakers; professional consultants (lawyers, doctors, and educators); religious advisers; business advisers; fund-raisers; society patrons; and finally, unpaid and underpaid workers, most often the women themselves. Their movement extended to every social institution that touched the lives of children.[27]

Hull-House in Chicago was the center for campaigns that reached from the juvenile courts to the municipal baths. On the Lower East Side of New York, the settlement house workers were active in each and every citywide progressive movement and organization from the City Vigilance League to the Sanitary Union.[28]

In city after city, reformers themselves assumed the responsibility for seeing that children were properly fed, bathed, clothed, exercised, entertained, schooled, and vacationed. Child workers, they feared, would never survive the perils of the factory long enough to become adults. The reformers took up the call for child labor legislation, and, though ultimately unsuccessful, brought the issue before the public consciousness.

Unhealthy children would not live to become worthy adults: the reformers "coaxed into being community service for the sick." Idleness was but an invitation to moral and physical degeneracy: the reformers established parks, recreation centers, boys' clubs, and opened the schools for after-school and vacation play groups. Dirt was the breeding grounds of disease: the reformers built their own "public baths," and campaigned for municipal ones. Exclusive residence in the urban ghetto broke the youthful spirit: the settlement houses and philanthropic agencies arranged for the children to be sent to the country for a few weeks' rest and rehabilitation each summer.[29]

The reformers, Dewey and Addams foremost among them, by generalizing from their own rural or small-town, Anglo-Saxon, Protestant, middle-class experiences, had romantically reconstructed a preindustrial past in which the young had been gently but efficiently led through childhood and adolescence to their appropriate places in the adult world. Unfortunately the historical record as pieced together was not entirely accurate. The small family farm that the rural American and European immigrants had fled in their journeys to the cities had never been as benignly educative or eternally watchful as the reformers claimed. Such domestic tranquillity required a level of economic security unattainable by the majority of small family farmers.

Even if the household and apprenticeship systems had been as ideal as the reformers believed, their attempt to use them as the model on which to reconstruct a new urban child-rearing and adolescent supervisory system could not succeed. Because the "youth problem" had not been caused by parental or household neglect, it could not be solved by substituting middle-class American surrogates and their institutional substitutes for immigrant and poor parents.[30]

The "youth" problem as a "class" problem

Whether the experts pointed at adolescent biology, the destruction of the "household" and "apprenticeship" system, or the arrival in the city of millions of neglectful and incompetent parents, they always centered their discussion of the "youth" or "adolescent" problems on the poor and immigrant children of the ghettoes. It is impossible to escape the conclusion that at base this problem of urban youth was a problem of poverty. G. Stanley Hall began his study with the empirical demonstration that adolescence was the age of criminality, mostly common thievery. Jane Addams in every one of her articles, speeches, and books confirmed these findings. The youth of the city had been consigned to the ignominy of "social problems" because their lack of money, in an environment based on it, was not only leading them to petty thievery as youngsters but, in the opinion of their social betters, preparing them for more serious and severe acts against property as adults.

For the middle-class settlement house workers, their society patrons, professional colleagues, and businessmen backers, there was no separating the "youth" and "class" problems. Immigrant and poor children—with their bad manners, overripe sexuality, swearing, spitting, and disrespect—were not only aesthetically and morally displeasing, they were also potential recruits for the revolutionary and radical movements building support throughout the country.

The myths of America—of the classless and frictionless society immune to the social dislocations of the Old World—had been sorely tested in the closing decades of the nineteenth century. As early as 1882 an *Atlantic Monthly* writer had warned the public that America's "happy immunity from those social diseases which are the danger and the humiliation of Europe is passing away." By the middle eighties, the editor of the *New York Citizen* could report that "the word 'socialism' . . . a few years ago . . . rarely heard in this country [has become] very common. A spectre of the old world, it is no longer confined to the land of its birth." The editor of *Current* magazine summed up the new mood perceived by the media and its middle-class readership: "The crisis in the affairs of Capital and Labor [has become] the question of the hour."[31]

The question of the hour would remain the dominant question for many decades to come. The American consensus would, in the years surrounding the turn of the century, be shouted down by Populists in the South and West, and by unionists, anarchists, socialists, single-taxers, and utopians throughout the nation.

At the workplace as at the polls, capital was forced (quite literally) to bring in the heavy artillery to maintain the social status quo. It would take a private army of Pinkertons and eight thousand members of the Pennsylvania National Guard to settle the Homestead strike, it would take federal troops to restore corporate order at Pullman, it would take nearly a revolution in political campaigning and seven million dollars (more than twenty times the amount the opposition could raise) to defeat William Jennings Bryan, the Democrat/Populist candidate for president in 1896.[32]

In the developing war between capital and labor, the reformers were self-proclaimed neutrals. Their sympathies for the victims of social change should not be discounted; neither should their ultimate allegiance to the social and productive system that had generated these changes and created these victims in the first place. Though some reformers, including Dewey, identified themselves for a time as Socialists (which they considered the proper name for those interested in promoting social justice, equality, and a society based on cooperation rather than competition), they did not support the radical changes advocated by left-wing unionists, anarchists, and socialists. Such changes were, they believed, not only unnecessary, they were in the long run counterproductive.[33]

For the child-saving reformers as for their colleagues in the larger progressive movement, the route to social amelioration lay in adjusting the people to fit the new productive order, not the reverse. They would "school to order" future generations of American workers and citizens, preparing them for adult life in the new industrial society.

Their task, as they conceived it, was in form identical to that undertaken a half-century before by the common schoolers. In content, however, there were important differences. Though both generations of reformers set out to school to order the young people of their time, their respective conceptions of the end product of this process were different. The common schoolers had been active during the infancy of industrialization and urbanization. The progressives were present as it approached maturity.

In 1860 the United States was still manufacturing less than England, France, or Germany. By the middle nineties, not only was New England per capita outproducing each of these countries, but the manufactured products of the nation as a whole nearly equalled in value that of England, France, and Germany combined. The factory was no longer a vision of the future. It had become the standard for the present. By 1880 the factory system had been adopted in the manufacture of textiles, "boots and shoes, of watches, musical instruments, clothing, agricultural implements, metallic goods generally, fire-arms, carriages and wagons, woolen goods, rubber goods, and even in the slaughtering of hogs." The coming of the factory, the mechanization of the workshop, increased production in all these areas. From 1880 to 1890 alone the mechanization of shoe and boot production doubled output. The increase in steel production was even more phenomenal and in the long run much more significant for the pyramiding effect this basic industry would have on all others. In 1867 less than twenty thousand tons of ingots had been produced. Thirty years later, the output was over seven million tons.[34]

Horace Mann, a half-century before, had argued that with the proper upbringing and internalized disciplinary structure, any young person could make it in the New World. By the turn of the century, this argument, though not yet silenced, was no longer pursued with such self-righteousness by middle-class reformers, especially those who, having lived in the cities and witnessed firsthand the social effects of industrialization, knew full well that perpetual upward mobility for all not suffering from moral or characterological defect was a chimera of the first order. Though some workers would succeed in fighting their way to success and economic independence, the majority would not. The cost of striking out on one's own had simply become too much for even the most dedicated and abstemious worker. Not only had the price of store, shop, business, and farm increased through the post-Civil War decades but the real wages from which the future independent entrepreneurs would have to save their "stakes" were declining. Recurrent depressions, recessions, panics, and crises upset each and every rational savings plan. According to Lewis Corey's calculations, "from 1866 to 1897 there [were] fourteen years of prosperity and seventeen of depression." In each downturn the workers were the losers. Their gains at the other end of the cycle were never sufficient to offset these losses. When successful, strikes helped, but not enough to compensate for the long periods of unemployment that preceded the final settlements.[35]

It was becoming more and more difficult for ambitious young workers to accumulate the capital necessary to raise themselves out of wagework into the mythic promised land of self-employment. Frederick Jackson Turner, the foremost social historian of the period, chronicled the change by shifting the focus of discussion from the coming of industrialization to the passing of the frontier. Jackson claimed that the frontier and the endless opportunities it had created for individual enterprise had, in the nineteenth century, guaranteed upward mobility for the masses and immunity for the society at large from the social turmoil that had unsettled the Old World. Turner was absolutely correct in his assertion that a new page in American history had been turned in the closing decades of the nineteenth century. But the cause of the change was not the closing of the frontier. It was rather the accumulating social changes generated by the triumph of industrialization on the farm and in the city.[36]

For John Dewey and Jane Addams, there was no mystery as to why the newly arrived city residents were so discontented with their social situation that they were beginning to agree with the more subversive spokesmen for radical social change. Twentieth-century wageworkers were frustrated by their present working conditions. The individual worker as such no longer existed. What existed was the production unit: the machinery with its human components. Within the factory or mechanized workshop, the individual workers would produce no finished products. They would have no occasion to demonstrate their singular skills or talents. They would have nothing to be proud of, nothing to look upon as the fruits of their own labor.

The progressives were the first to realize that the emerging industrial order required of its wageworkers a new set of internalized character traits. Earlier in the century the common schoolers had set out to provide the young with the internalized disciplinary structure that would enable them to keep struggling until they had reached their goals as independent, self-made entrepreneurs. Wagework was not considered a permanent station in life but a testing ground, a challenge that, once met, would attest to the individual's worthiness and capacity for self-employment. As the twentieth-century reformers now conceded, such socialization for self-sufficiency had made sense when there were actual possibilities for upward mobility out of wagework. With such possibilities rare, it no longer made sense to socialize workers in this manner. What was now needed was not self-made men and women but team players, individuals ready to sacrifice their personal dreams, hopes, and aspirations for the good of the productive unit.[37]

The public school classroom, if it had not already existed, would have had to come into being to cope with this new situation. As Dewey reminded his extensive readership, the schoolroom was the natural place to begin the task of preparing the new generation for the modern world. The school was, after all, a community in microcosm; after the family, it was the first the children would inhabit. If this children's community were structured properly by the adults who controlled it, it could provide the experiential foundation for future personality development. The idea, quite simply, was to teach the children to play together so that they would grow up to work together; or, as Dewey himself expressed it, "When the school introduces and trains each child of society into membership within such a little community, saturating him with the spirit of service, and providing him with the instruments of effective self-direction, we shall have the deepest and best guaranty of a larger society which is worthy, lovely, and harmonious."[38]

The classroom was the microcosm in which the new society's inhabitants would be trained for the macrocosm of the adult world. The social attitudes of future generations could not be left to chance or tradition. The new behavioral psychologies had demonstrated the ease with which animals could be trained. These scientific methods could and should, it was believed, be transported into the school: "If a rat is put in a maze and finds food only by making a given number of turns in a given sequence, his activity is gradually modified till he habitually takes that course rather than another when he is hungry. . . . Human actions are modified in a like fashion."

There was of course a difference between training rats in a maze and children in a classroom: the rats could be taught to perform their tasks as individuals, but the children had to learn to do their tricks as part of a group.

Setting up conditions which stimulate certain visible and tangible ways of acting is the first step. Making the individual a sharer or partner in the associated activity so that he feels its

success as his success, its failure as his failure, is the completing step. As soon as he is possessed by the emotional attitude
of the group, he will be alert to recognize the special ends at
which it aims and the means employed to secure success. His
beliefs and ideas, in other words, will take a form similar to
those of others in the group.[39]

New activities had to be added to the curriculum, activities
that instilled a sense of group spirit, of solidarity, in the children. An education consisting of "simply learning lessons" fostered competition, not cooperation, leading to antisocial behavior and attitudes. On the other hand, an education that stressed
"active work" instead of "mere learning" would bring children
together. Cooking, gardening, woodworking, and building
with blocks were but some of the activities that would accomplish what was necessary, "the forming of a socialized disposition."[40]

7

The War Against the Wards

The progressive reformers would restructure the classroom and expand the responsibilities of the public schools to fit the changing requirements of the productive order. They were, in a sense, standing on the shoulders of the common school crusaders, adjusting the latter's institutions to the new social situation. Unfortunately, like their forebears, the progressives lacked the power to realize their plans. They were middle-class, Anglo-Saxon, Protestant interlopers in cities filling with poor and immigrant workers. Though they were convinced that they had the answers, they were not consulted; nor was their advice, when offered voluntarily, accepted.[1]

The cities, much to the dismay of the reformers, had become the domain of a new breed of American autocrat: the ward boss and his "machine," politicians who cared little or nothing about productive efficiency, national prosperity, or social morality. The older, established urban gentry and the newly arrived middle class, businessmen and professionals, watched with horror as their democracy went astray. The immigrants, unschooled in democratic principles and practices, continued to vote for the wrong people.

Democracy, the progressives feared, was no longer working in the cities. Perhaps because there was too much of it. The progressives did not propose to abolish democracy, just to curb it enough to secure for their people the positions of power and influence needed to accomplish the task of reform. The solutions to the problems of the city, as they saw it, were to get the right people—the experts, the progressives, the reform-minded men and women of the middle classes—into positions of urban leadership, to replace the elected machine politicians with appointed city managers and commissions, the party men with professionals.[2]

The call to battle

Though the progressive reformers wanted to effect change in every arena of municipal decision-making, from the mayor's office through the police, sanitation, and water works, they focused their attention on the public schools, the most vital of social institutions and, to their eyes, the most corrupt.

The common schoolers had succeeded in mandating state property taxes and state-legislated and state-supervised curricular guidelines. But they had not succeeded in abolishing the decision-making powers of locally elected or appointed school boards. In the rural counties as in the city wards, community representatives still made the important decisions on staffing, text selection, school building, maintenance, and curricula.[3]

The ward system in the cities had no doubt produced its share of crooks and incompetents. But it had also given the urban neighborhoods some say over the schools their children were attending. An informal and unofficial patronage system remained the only assurance the immigrants had that some of their own would be given school jobs: "A ward board, or ward representative, could 'ask around' and talk with people about vacancies and about the particular problems faced in an individual school building. Such a board could also select a few teachers from a recently arrived ethnic group once their numbers became significant. The ward boards governed geographical areas small enough to enable them to give personal attention to problems and to award jobs on personal or ethnic grounds."[4]

The reformers cared little about the democratic niceties of the ward system—or its curiously representative nature. They prided themselves on being pragmatists: what mattered was the final product, nothing else. Were the schools doing their job? If not, why not?

The first question was easily answered: the schools were not doing their job. The urban population was growing more rapidly than the resources allocated for the schools. There were not enough schools, classrooms, or teachers to go around. That this was not the fault of the ward bosses or boards was, for the reformers, beside the point. Led by their muckraker associates, they did not try to understand the problem as much as to publicize its effects. The muckrakers appeared to take especial delight in calling to public attention the horrors of overcrowded urban schools. The judgment they delivered was that whatever was wrong with the schools was the fault of the ward bosses, the ward school boards, and the immigrants themselves who didn't know enough to be rid of them.[5]

Jacob Riis, one of the most persuasive of the muckraker/reformers, spread the blame even further, from the immigrants who knew no better to the responsible middle class who should have. With outrage and indignation Riis claimed that official malfeasance, neglect, and corruption in the wards was aggravated by public apathy. If the responsible people of the cities had given more time to the cause of the poor, then all would have been better off.

Riis and the muckrakers trumpeted the reformers' call to battle: they urged the responsible, reform-minded urban residents to take charge of the public schools in both their own and in the immigrant neighborhoods. As social rescue institutions, the public schools were too important to the welfare of the society to be left in the hands of corruptible immigrant voters.[6]

Business leads the charge

The muckrakers and reformers did not have to fight their holy war without allies. By the time they entered the urban battlefield, the uneasy alliance between the ward bosses and the business community had begun to unravel. Business had tolerated the machines as long as they kept order in the immigrant and working-class wards. Once they stepped beyond the boundaries of cost and decency, they were ripe for extinction.

Municipal corruption had become a drain of profits. Graft, payoffs, gross inefficiency, hopelessly inadequate city services had raised the price of doing business. It had also given the working-class radicals, unionists, single-taxers, anarchists, and Socialists ready ammunition with which to bombard the free enterprise system.

Business was ready to join—more properly, to lead—the war against the wards. If the middle-class reformers provided the infantry for the antimachine crusade, business would provide the heavy artillery and general leadership.[7]

As Samuel Hays has argued so persuasively, it was the "upper-class" businessmen and allied professionals who "initiated and dominated municipal movements." Nowhere does this generalization hold truer than in the case of school reform. Though the groundwork had been laid by the muckrakers and settlement workers, the real work of reform followed directly the founding of businessmen's civic improvement groups dedicated to taking the schools out of politics, i.e., out of the hands of immigrant politicians.[8]

William Issel has demonstrated in his article, "Modernization in Philadelphia School Reform, 1882-1905," that the major agencies of reform in that city, the Civic Club and the Public Education Association, were composed almost exclusively of upper-class businessmen. One hundred percent of the Civic Club and 75 percent of the P.E.A. officers were listed in either the *Blue Book* or the *Social Register*. The Committee of 100, which served the same function in New York City, had an almost identical social composition. According to David Hammack, "Nearly every member of the Committee held a listing in the *Social Register*."[9]

In Horace Mann's day, the manufacturers had been in the forefront of reform. By the turn of the century the financiers and corporate executives were assuming that responsibility. In Pittsburgh, over half of the members of the major reform organization "were bankers and corporation officials or their wives." In New York City forty-nine members of the Committee of 100 were Wall Street lawyers, including thirty-one officers of national corporations, eighteen were bankers. The cofounders of the New York City committee were Nicholas Murry Butler, president of Teachers College and then Columbia University, and Stephen Olin, a leading Wall Street lawyer. Though Butler received most of the headlines and has been given credit (or blame) for the work of reform in New York City, he would not have gotten very far at all without Olin, who provided the reform organization with his own law clerk; with introductions to the important Republican and anti-Tammany politicans in New York City and Albany; with newspaper and magazine contacts; with unlimited funding sources; and with a continual stream of practical advice.[10]

On almost all issues, the reformers, muckrakers, and businessmen were in agreement. It was the fault of neighborhood board members that the schools were overcrowded and understaffed, that adolescent boys were not staying in school long enough to learn "how to work," that the youth problem was becoming more serious day by day. The immigrants and their school boards were held directly accountable for juvenile delinquency, illiteracy, and aimlessness. The schools were failing, and the problem was one of poor management. The solution was to fire the old managers and replace them with new ones.[11]

In every city, the coalitions followed the same strategy. They knew full well that their odds of attracting ethnic, Jewish, and Catholic working-class voters for their white, Anglo-Saxon, Protestant, Social Register school board candidates were not very great. Only if they were successful in convincing the state legislatures to replace election by ward with citywide voting would they stand a chance. In elections conducted at large rather than in the neighborhoods, their near monopoly of newspaper support, professional, legal, organizational, and financial resources would compensate for their obvious political liabilities.[12]

By going over the heads of city politicians and residents to

the state legislatures already gerrymandered to minimize the ur-
ban/immigrant influence, the reform coalitions had explicitly
raised the issue of home rule. The businessmen, lawyers, college presidents, "aristocrats," and "pink tea ladies" had allied
themselves with the anti-city, anti-immigrant, anti-machine
state politicians. Their opponents were those who—on principle
or for self-interest—believed in home rule; neighborhood, religious, and "landsmen" groups; teacher-and-principal organizations; city politicians, both pro- and anti-machine; a majority of the city's elected representatives in the state legislature;
and a majority of the City Board of Education recently appointed by anti-Tammany Mayor William Strong.

The principals and teachers, the most organized and vociferous opponents of reform, were no doubt stirred to action by self-
interest and the machines to which many owed their jobs. But
they also had no use for a centralized system that would increase supervision of their work by outsiders who were not either neighborhood residents, parents, or educators.

Though a disparate group, the reform opponents were united
under the banners of home rule and popular control of local institutions. They opposed centralization on political and educational grounds. Not only was it antidemocratic and un-
American, it was also bound to adversely affect the schools'
functioning. Ward boards and ward trustees, representing as
they did the varied ethnic, religious, and occupational groups
in the community, enjoyed the confidence of parents and
teachers. Centrally elected boards and their professional staffs
could not. The "pink tea ladies" and Wall Street "aristocrats"
did not attend the same churches as the neighborhood people,
or speak the same language, or even send their children to public school. How then were they going to look after the neighborhood's classrooms? [13]

The reformers responded to such arguments with ridicule.
They characterized their opponents as no less than "the forces
of evil," "a horde of bandits and barbarians," joined by "scores
of incompetent teachers." Questions of democracy, home rule,
and popular control were beside the point. As Stephen Olin put
it, the neighborhoods did not control the police, nor did they

assess their own taxes or select their own health inspectors. Why then should they be allowed to run their own schools? [14]

The reformers, professionals, and big businessmen claimed for themselves alone the objectivity and vision needed to look after the interests of the city as a whole. They knew what was best not only for the local communities but for the larger society of which the neighborhoods were but the smallest particle. Replacing the informal, almost personal leadership of local ward trustees and boards with a more formal bureaucratic structure would make the schools more efficient as instruments of Americanization, socialization, and disciplinary training. [15]

Reform coalitions proffered this administrative model (centralized school board, superintendent, and professional staff) as desirable for rural as well as city schools. Schooling had become far too important a social institution to be left in the hands of parents and neighborhood residents, rural or urban. Parallel to the urban reformers, the rural coalitions submitted to the state legislatures their "reform" bills aimed at replacing locally elected district school boards with consolidated county ones. [16]

The coalitions did not succeed at first in many states. But they tried again and again, and were eventually successful. Rural consolidation bills were submitted to state legislatures until they were passed. Though the reformers would, in years to come, continue to complain about the small, inefficient, isolated rural districts, many of those that had existed in the nineteenth century did not survive the twentieth: "Between 1897 and 1905, some twenty states authorized the consolidation of schools. . . . while certain other states, operating under some form of the county-unit system, slowly began the work of school consolidation." [17]

The reform of the city schools, though a more difficult task, was accomplished more rapidly. By the second decade of the twentieth century, almost every major city system had been centralized. [18]

The New York City public school reorganization bill, defeated in the state legislature in 1895, was resubmitted and, in the form of a compromise bill, passed and signed into law in 1896. [19]

Like New York, "St. Louis went through a familiar cycle of exposure of corruption and inefficiency by muckrakers, a call for a better 'class of men' in office by elite civic groups, and a successful appeal to the state legislature to change the structure of control of the city's schools." Under the charter passed by the Missouri legislature in 1897, the ward system of election was replaced by election-at-large. The percentage of "big businessmen and professionals" on the board was increased from under 15 percent to over 80 percent.[20]

The war against the wards took longer to win in Philadelphia than it had in New York City or St. Louis. The home rule and neighborhood coalitions in the former city were powerful enough to defeat the first five reform bills submitted to the Harrisburg legislature. Not until 1905, with the help of local and nationally known muckrakers and with President Eliot of Harvard leading the reform campaign, did a Philadelphia school reorganization bill pass the Harrisburg legislature. Ward boards with under 12 percent of their numbers listed in the *Blue Book* or *Social Register* were replaced by a centrally elected board with 76 percent of its members so distinguished.[21]

Chicago was the last major city to have its schools reformed. The teachers' union in that city, led by Margaret Haley, built an antireform coalition that was successful in defeating the reform bills submitted to the legislature at Springfield in 1899, 1901, 1903, and 1905. Reform would not come to Chicago until the First World War.[22]

Chicago was the exception. By the second decade of the new century the reform coalitions had accomplished their task in every other major American city. The ward system of school board election and representation had been state-legislated out of existence in New York, St. Louis, Philadelphia, Baltimore, Buffalo, Pittsburgh, San Francisco, Boston, Cleveland, Detroit, Los Angeles, and Milwaukee. By 1916 it was estimated that "more than three-fifths of the members of city [school] committees were merchants, manufacturers, bankers, brokers, real estate men, and doctors and lawyers."[23]

The reform coalitions, though they had replaced the ward boards with centrally elected ones composed of their own people, would discover soon enough that their victory was a hollow one. They could make the important decisions, but these decisions, if they were going to be successfully implemented, had to be sold at the local level to the community that would have to deliver its tax dollars, to the parents with school-age children, and to the teachers who would have to teach them.

The business community, though in the twentieth century capable of exerting a much more direct effect on public school policy than ever before, could still not do as it pleased. The myth of democracy had to be maintained, the illusion protected that the schools were, and would remain, institutions by, for, and of the people. As we shall see in coming chapters, the more business tried to adjust the schools to meet its own requirements, the more difficulty it would have convincing local communities, parents, teachers, and students that such "reforms" were in their interests also.

8

Reforming the High Schools

The reformed boards, their superintendents, and their professional staffs had their work cut out for them. As we have seen, the city and some rural school systems had never been able to catch up with the expanding school-age population. Overcrowding was particularly a problem in the urban areas of the Northeast and the Midwest. In New York City alone, "at the turn of the century 1,100 willing children were refused admission to any school for lack of space." The situation was as bad in other city school systems.[1]

The overcrowding was no doubt contributory to the high rate of failure and growing percentage of overage students in the city schools—over 40 percent of the total in the Boston, Chicago, Detroit, Philadelphia, Pittsburgh, New York, and Minneapolis systems, according to Colin Greer.[2]

One might have expected that the major thrust of reform at the turn of the century would be these urban schools. But this was not the case. As the nineteenth century gave way to the twentieth, the major concern of the public school reformers was not the overcrowded elementary schools, but the relatively underattended high schools.

Though the elementary schools were not doing their job as well as might be hoped, they were at least keeping upwards of

70 percent of the school-age population off the streets and under proper supervision through their most tender years. The same could not be said of the secondary schools. As late as 1890, more than 90 percent of the fourteen-to-seventeen-year-olds (those potentially dangerous adolescents) were free of any institutional supervision. Here was a potential "social problem" much more dangerous than overcrowding and failure in the elementary grades.[3]

"Youth" problems, "class" problems, and some early attempts to solve them

The progressive reformers and their colleagues had succeeded through the closing decades of the nineteenth century in drawing attention to the "youth" and "class" problems. The problems, as they themselves had pointed out, were interconnected. Problem adolescents were not going to become model wageworkers; they were much more likely to become problem workers.

The solution proposed to the youth and class problems was an institutional one. If only a greater proportion of the adolescent population could be induced to enter and remain in high school, a solution could be reached. Increasing the enrollments in secondary schools would not only remove potentially troublesome teenagers from the streets, it would provide them with the preparation and training they required as future manual and industrial wageworkers.

There was one thing wrong with this approach. In theory the high schools might have been the perfect institutional solution to the social problems generated with the maturation of the new industrial order. In practice they were not. As youth redemption centers and industrial training grounds, they were sadly inefficient, even worse, counterproductive. The reformers and muckrakers were not the only nor the most powerful of those who would criticize and attempt to transform the high schools in the new century. In this case, as in that of the common school crusade, it is difficult to determine what the driving force behind the movement was—the reformers out front or the business interests, more often in the background.

Michael Katz, who studied the founding of high schools in Massachusetts in the middle nineteenth century, found that most of them were established in urban and manufacturing areas by men of business, usually associated with commerce. High school, as they well knew, would provide their own children with free secondary schooling and their businesses with a literate, more productive workforce.[4]

The early high school promoters were more concerned with expansion than with reform. The traditional classical curriculum with a little bookkeeping thrown in suited them fine: it would provide their clerks with the skills they needed and their children with an entrée into higher-status professional positions.[5]

It was not until later in the century, from the middle 1880s on, that business critics of secondary schooling shifted their focus from the quantitative to the qualitative. The high schools, they began to argue, were not only not reaching enough students, especially males; they were improperly schooling those they did reach—filling their heads with all sorts of inappropriate expectations which, unmet, might drive them into the clutches of the socialists, anarchists, utopians, single-taxers, and unionists. As one critic assessed the situation, "Too much education of a certain sort, such as Greek, Latin, French, German, and especially book-keeping, to a person of humble antecedents, is utterly demoralizing in nine cases out of ten. . . . After a good deal of observation . . . I have arrived at the conclusion that our system of education . . . when it goes beyond . . . a grammar school, is vicious in the extreme—productive of more evil than good."[6]

Many businessmen did more than just complain. They established their own high schools and pressured the public ones to reform. The reforms they had in mind were in the direction of trade and manual training. They would replace the traditional high school program of outmoded, irrelevant, and dull "booklearning" with practical courses that taught "real" skills: sewing, cooking, and drawing for the girls, and carpentry, metal and machine work for the boys. Boys and girls, when manually trained in school, would become better workers not only because their manual skills had been sharpened but because their schooling had given them a sense of the dignity of their own labor.[7]

Manual training was promoted in much the same terms as common schooling had been a half-century earlier: its value lay as much in the moral training it offered as in the manual. Those most in need of such moral uplift—blacks, juvenile delinquents, and the wayward children of the immigrants—were identified as the natural constituency for the manual training schools.[8]

If the reforms had taken root when first proposed, in the 1870s, 1880s, and 1890s, there would have been less cause for businessmen and reformers to complain about the high schools in the new century. But they did not take root; there were too many people opposed to them.

Educators opposed them out of a mixture of self-interest (they did not want to lose their jobs to manual trainers) and concern for their students (they still believed that a proper education had to be a "classical" one). [9]

Organized labor opposed them as an obvious attempt to circumvent apprenticeship rules and create a larger, cheapened labor supply.[10]

And the students for whom the schools were intended opposed them by simply staying away. Though the manual trainers had argued that such schools, because they were not "literary," would attract those students in need of moral uplift, the schools did nothing of the sort. Manual training, no matter how enthusiastically promoted as social and moral panacea, did not attract large numbers of young people to the high schools. By the 1889–1890 school year no more than 7 percent of the fourteen-to-seventeen-year-olds of the nation were attending any school—public or private, manual training or "literary."[11]

High schools and white collars

The manual training and trade schools had been designed for the children of the working class. It was taken for granted that the middle class would want a more traditional, academic education for its offspring. Unfortunately for the reform-minded, the workers too wanted that kind of education for their children.

The major problem with the manual, trade, and vocationally oriented high school programs was that they had not been established to prepare young people for the type of work they wanted. It was difficult enough for poor families to support their children through high school. Those who made the sacrifice of the income their children could have been earning had they foregone high school were not going to settle for anything less than the traditional education they believed, not improperly, might provide their young with a way out of manual wage and factory work into a white-collar job.

Though advancing industrialization reduced the possibilities for self-employment—as independent craftsmen, shop owners, or small family farmers—it stimulated the development of what appeared to be another category of employment superior to manual work in almost every regard. The growth in the non-agricultural workforce in the late nineteenth and early twentieth centuries was greatest in that area the census classified as "clerical occupations." Between 1880 and 1910, this category increased its percentage of the total workforce from 0.9 percent to 4.6 percent. Clerical work was the largest though not the only white-collar field expanding year by year. There were by 1910 another 1.3 million jobs for salesmen, saleswomen, and clerks in stores. All told, where only 3 percent of the workforce in 1880 was employed in clerical or sales positions, by 1910 the percentage had risen to 8 percent and was steadily climbing.[12]

In terms of "status" (not to mention security from layoffs and future prospects), these white-collar positions were considered more desirable than manual labor, skilled or unskilled. They also paid substantially higher wages. According to Harry Braverman, author of *Labor and Monopoly Capital*:

> In the United States, in 1900, clerical employees of steam railroads and in manufacturing establishments had average annual earnings of $1,011; in the same year, the average annual earnings of workers in these industries was $435 for manufacturing and $548 for steam railroads. And there are other

indications that the average pay of the clerical classification was about double the production and transportation workers' average; in 1899, for example, the average pay of all full-time postal employees was $955.[13]

The choice of white-collar over manual work was made even easier by the fact that opportunities in the former fields were expanding while those in the latter were in a state of terminal decline. Manual work had come to be associated almost exclusively with work within the factory. The small, independent craftsmen, artisans, and manufacturers with their secure if not wildly profitable workshops had been all but eliminated by competition from large-scale corporate concerns. For the young person who dreamed of wealth or merely a secure future, white-collar work appeared to be the only possibility.[14]

As the children of working-class "American" families continued to bypass the factory whenever possible, the immigrants who could not afford this option assumed an ever larger role in the industrial workforce. By the turn of the century they had begun to outnumber "native Americans" in many industries and individual factories.[15]

The manufacturers were not opposed to the immigrants dominating the "bottom ranks"—the unskilled and menial laborer positions. There were in fact good reasons for maintaining on the factory floor a "judicious mix" of workers from a variety of immigrant groups. What the manufacturers feared was the developing situation where the absence of "American" workers was granting the immigrants a *de facto* monopoly over the supervisory and skilled positions as well.[16]

Still, other than complain about the young "Americans" and their dandyish, lax ways—the industrialists did nothing to improve the conditions in their factories that were responsible for keeping the native-born away. They neither raised wages, eliminated the numerous health hazards and accident traps, nor provided their workers with the job security and possibilities for self-advancement they sought. They instead blamed the high school, a convenient scapegoat, for the reluctance of the young "Americans" to enter the factory.

There could be no doubt that the high school was playing a

central role in broadening the horizons of that minority of working class students who could afford to attend it. It was more than coincidental that the growth of high school enrollment followed directly the upward curve of white-collar employment in the decades surrounding the turn of the century. In the last decade of the nineteenth century, enrollments more than doubled. In the first decade of the twentieth, they nearly doubled again. [17]

Before 1890 the high school had been a luxury for town as well as student. Neither the employers nor the society-at-large appeared to care very much if its workers, businessmen, or professionals had graduated from or even attended high school. About the only type of job that a high school education helped secure was schoolteaching (for women) and clerking or bookkeeping (for men). As these areas of employment expanded in the late 1800s, the value of the high school diploma increased commensurately. Teenagers who had earlier looked to high school as vocationally irrelevant at best were now beginning to enroll in significant numbers. The earlier reluctance of taxpayers to increase their support of public schooling by building and funding high schools on top of common ones was rapidly eroding. Towns and cities once indifferent or positively hostile were, in the name of civic pride and prosperity, establishing their own public high schools. [18]

The change in the high school population was more than quantitative; the backgrounds of the students were changing as well. As Charles Skinner, New York State Superintendent of Schools, warned the educators assembled at the 1897 National Education Association convention, "Whether agreeable or not, we must recognize the fact that it is the children of the plain people, in city and country, who are crowding our schoolrooms today, and these will always be in the majority. The children of the masses and not of the classes will rule us." [19]

The high schools: a new weapon in the battle for exports and against the unions

As we have seen, American manufacturing came of age in the closing decades of the nineteenth century. But the rapid and apparently irreversible increase in production did not set the minds of the manufacturers at ease. There was a catch in the logic of expansion, a cause for anxiety in the pyramiding of production. Where was the market for all these goods? The nation's capacity for consumption could not increase as rapidly as its production. (Unless of course there were some change in the distribution of wealth—for the business interests, a "cure" far worse than the "illness.")

There were, fortunately, new markets to conquer, new frontiers that beckoned. American industry, following the successful example of American agriculture, began to look abroad for markets in which to sell the increasing quantities of finished goods. By 1902 Frank Vanderlip, a vice president of the National City Bank of New York, was writing

> jubilantly of the American "Commercial Invasion" of Europe. "American locomotives, running on American rails, now whistle past the Pyramids and across the long Siberian steppes. . . . Three years ago there was but one American locomotive in the United Kingdom; today there is not a road of importance there on which trains are not being pulled by American engines. . . . America has sent coals to Newcastle, cotton to Manchester, cutlery to Sheffield, potatoes to Ireland, champagnes to France, watches to Switzerland, and 'Rhine wine' to Germany!" [20]

Vanderlip gloated, but his pride, his apparently unbounded optimism, was more than compensated for by the equally pervasive anxiety that haunted the business community. The tariff system had protected American manufacturing through most of its nineteenth-century infancy. But now, with industrialization having grown to full maturity, the Americans could no longer hide behind walls of protection. Their future prosperity was dependent on their securing and maintaining export markets overseas.

Industry come of age had to expand its markets—or be suffocated by overproduction. When those markets could not be peaceably opened, there was military might to pave the way. As William Appleman Williams has so rigorously argued, it is no accident of history that the modern age of American imperialism followed almost directly on the economic and social crises of the middle 1890s. The logic was clear. Lack of markets led to overproduction. Overproduction led to depression. Depression led to social chaos and the prospect of endemic class conflict. The solutions, then, to business prosperity and social and class harmony were new and expanded markets, no matter how secured.[21]

There was a direct link, in the minds of the industrialists, between the problem of the export market and that of the high schools. Nineteenth-century businessmen might have been able to rely on the "laws" of supply and demand to provide them with a workforce, reasonably disciplined, at reasonable prices. The twentieth-century corporate industrialists would not rely on such unpredictable "laws" for the recruitment and training of their workforce. Organized into a number of national organizations, including the National Civic Federation for the corporate giants and the National Association of Manufacturers (NAM) for the smaller and more moderate sized firms, business entered the arena of high school reform.

In the nineteenth century, local commercial interests had been in the forefront of high school reform. Now, in the twentieth century, the corporate leaders of industry and finance, whose business interests were national and international, interjected themselves into what one nationally known educator referred to as the "deluge of discussion [that] has overspread the entire world of secondary education."[22]

In 1905 the NAM established its own Committee on Industrial Education. In 1906 it joined and almost immediately became the most active participant and funding source for the National Society for the Promotion of Industrial Education (NSPIE), an organization formed explicitly "to bring to public attention the importance of industrial education" and "to promote the establishment of institutions for industrial training."[23]

The NAM entered the high school campaign with two enemies in view—the Germans, now emerging as chief competitors in the export markets, and the unions, now blamed for the problems the American manufacturers were having competing with the Germans.

While the corporate giants represented in the National Civic Federation had come to terms with the unions, the smaller manufacturers of the NAM continued to regard them as irreconcilable obstacles to progress and prosperity. The unions, having seized control of the last remnants of the apprenticeship system were, the employers charged, manipulating it to keep the supply of workers down and wages up. If industrial training and certification for the skilled and supervisory positions could be removed from the factory to the public high schools, then the unions would be unable to exercise any control on the size of the industrial workforce. The resultant gain in industrial efficiency (and decrease in wages) would, the manufacturers predicted, enable them to compete successfully in the increasingly important and ever-expanding export markets.[24]

Spokesmen for the business community could not help but announce to the world their new discovery, their secret weapon against the Germans and every other world competitor. Frank Vanderlip of the National City Bank presented the good news to the 1905 convention of the National Education Association. The miracle of German industry, he had discovered, was no miracle at all, but rather the end result of adjusting their secondary schooling system to the manufacturers' requirements. "I am firmly convinced that the explanation [for Germany's economic success] can be encompassed in a single word—the schoolmaster. He is the great corner-stone of Germany's remarkable commercial and industrial success. From the economic point of view, the school system of Germany stands unparalleled."[25]

The NAM's Committee on Industrial Education, in its 1905 report, claimed to have made the same discovery and drawn from it inescapable conclusions: "The German technical and trade schools are at once the admiration and fear of all countries. In the world's race for commercial supremacy we must copy and improve upon the German method of education. Germany relies chiefly upon her [high school] trained workers for her commercial success and prosperity. She puts no limit on the money to be expended in trade and technical education."[26]

Industrial schooling: for whom?

The 1905 NAM committee report did more than simply outline the rationale for industrial schooling in the public schools. It made it abundantly clear who it wanted to be placed in these programs and trained for these jobs: "We should not depend on Europe for our skill; we must educate our own boys." Throughout the report, it was asserted directly and unequivocably that it was "our boys," "American youth," "American boys" who were needed in the factories.[27]

The manufacturers were not interested in spending their own or the American taxpayers' money on training immigrants for the unskilled, menial laborer jobs they were already performing quite adequately. Such schooling would not only, as they considered it, be a waste of time, it might also give these laborers the idea that they were worth more in wages. The industrial schooling plans were not intended for immigrant factory workers but rather for those "American boys" who were not now but ought to be filling the supervisory and skilled positions on the factory floor. As Frederick Clark, treasurer of the Talbot Mills in Massachusetts, told a symposium audience at an NSPIE convention, "I think the aim of the trade school should be to produce skilled workmen with a thorough theoretical [sic] and as much practical knowledge as possible, men fitted to fill the positions of Foremen, Overseers, Superintendents, etc."[28]

Eldon Keith, a Massachusetts shoe manufacturer, took the same position: "What we are looking for more especially, is the promotion of schools for the training of foremen and superintendents."[29]

Henry Hess of the Hess-Bright Manufacturing Company of Philadelphia agreed: "The aim of the trade school should be to fit its students as mechanics . . . and give beyond this a groundwork which would be of benefit in enabling those who want to rise to take leading positions."[30]

Even the labor representative at the symposium, John Tobin, general president of the Boot and Shoe Workers Union, saw no other reason for trade schools than the training of future foremen.[31]

The unions, controlled by and for native American workers (with some exceptions), joined the industrial schooling campaign and the business-dominated NSPIE because they saw the new schools as directly advantageous for their constituency and its children. Industrial schooling would provide "American" students with training and direct entrée into the better factory jobs. And it would provide their parents with an incentive to keep their children in school until they were ready to assume their rightful places in the skilled and supervisory positions on the factory floor.[32]

Industrial schooling programs were not intended for everybody. The sons and daughters of the middle class were certainly not expected to enroll in them. Nor were the children of the immigrants who, more often than not, had to drop out of school long before they reached the secondary level.[33]

The new schools were designed exclusively for "American" boys and girls. Since working-class "American" girls had to work for a living, they too deserved to be specially trained and prepared for the more respectable trades. Industrial schooling programs would channel the "American" girls away from the "unskilled occupations" where they would have had to work alongside men " 'of shiftless and irresponsible character' in an environment . . . conducive to reckless moral behavior" to skilled occupations like dressmaking, which "offered a moderate income in an acceptable work environment."

The *raison d'etre* for industrial schooling was the same for both sexes. Industrial training programs in the public schools would direct "American" boys into the supervisory factory positions and "American" girls into the "more wholesome trades." The necessary but low-paying, unskilled jobs in the "sweat shops" and on the factory floor would be left to the immigrants. They alone would be sacrificed to the work that led nowhere but to ruined health and reputations.[34]

9

New Studies for New Students

The traditional high school education, by unfitting its graduates "for work with their hands," encouraging them instead to look beyond the factory for their future employment, had become more of a problem than a solution. Still, despite its faults, it remained the only viable institutional solution to the "youth" and "worker" problems. To eject working-class youth from the institutions best situated to ease them through the perils of adolescence into the responsibilities of adulthood would serve no good purpose.[1]

The task confronting the business community and the critics of the high schools was a complex one: they wanted to bring as many "plain people" as possible into the high schools and keep them there through their teens, but in such a way that their expectations for life after graduation would not be inappropriately raised.

Industrial schooling appeared to be the solution. Not only would such programs direct students towards realistic and realizable futures, but they would also attract many working class students who, the experts claimed, had been frightened away by the traditional secondary school curriculum.

The masses, it was said, were not entering or remaining in the high schools because the high school curriculum had not been adjusted to their special needs. The muckrakers took great delight in calling attention to what they considered the failure of the high schools to move out of the dark ages. The secondary schools' exclusive emphasis on "culture," it was argued, might have been appropriate to an earlier era, but was most definitely not appropriate to the modern age. "Our medieval high schools: shall we educate children for the 12th or the 20th century?" asked a *Saturday Evening Post* article somewhat ingenuously in 1912, the conclusion having already been reached that the schools were at least eight centuries behind the times.[2]

Industrial schooling for the "plain people"

The critics of the public high schools, especially those from the business world, accepted without question the inability of the "masses" to proceed at the same academic rate as the "classes." The working-class children were failing because they could not keep up with their middle-class counterparts and, in fact, were totally incapable of learning the same kinds of things. The NAM Committee on Industrial Education, in the section of its 1912 report headed, "Three Kinds of Children—Three Kinds of Schools," scientifically categorized children according to their class backgrounds and "innate" abilities:

> Differing as children do from one another, they may, nevertheless, be divided educationally into three great classes:
> 1. The abstract-minded and imaginative children, who learn readily from the printed page. Most of the children whose ancestors were in the professions and the higher occupations, so-called, are of this class, as well as many from the humbler callings.
> 2. The concrete, or hand-minded children. Those who can only with extreme difficulty, and then imperfectly, learn from the abstractions of the printed page. These children constitute at least half of all the children of the nation, being that half who leave our schools by the end of the sixth grade . . .
> 3. The great intermediate class . . .[3]

The NAM had no quarrel with the traditional classical curriculum for the "abstract-minded" children "whose ancestors

were in the professions and the higher occupations." These
children belonged in classrooms where the classical subjects
were taught, where the acquisition of intellectual skills was
stressed, where the mental "faculties"—memory, judgment,
taste, fancy, imagination, and reason—were exercised and developed.

What the NAM wanted was more practical schooling for the
50 percent of the nation's children who, without financial resources to continue their schooling, were dropping out before
high school. It would have been nice if these "hand-minded,"
working-class children had been capable of profiting from the
traditional secondary school curriculum. But, the NAM committee assured its public, they were not.[4]

Earlier in the century, such undemocratic assumptions might
have been countered by the educators themselves. Up until the
middle years of the 1900s, curricular debates at NEA conventions had discussed the one curriculum proper for all students,
not different curricula for different students. When, for example, President Keyes of the Throop Polytechnic Institute of
Pasadena lectured the 1895 convention on "the modifications of
secondary school courses most demanded by the conditions of
today," he made clear that manual training courses should become part of *every* student's education. He explicitly rejected
the notion that nonacademic courses should be offered to only
some high school students. Manual training subjects, if educa-
tionally valid, belonged in the curriculum of all of them, regardless of academic talent, family background, or future vocational
plans.[5]

It was only towards the middle of the first decade of the new
century that the educators themselves took up the call for new
curricula "differentiated" for the new students. In 1903 the first
proposal was made at an NEA convention for separate manual
training high schools for working-class, nonacademic youngsters. In 1907 the president of the Manual Training Department
of the NEA introduced his speech by commenting that "no
single topic has engaged the attention of educational conventions more frequently, during the past two years, than has this
topic of industrial education. Certainly there is no question

which has been so insistently urged as being of immediate and vital concern to the country at large." By 1909 the convention was overwhelmed by educators anxious to add their voices to the chorus of affirmation. Not only was the keynote speech at the general session devoted to "The Need, Scope, and Character of Industrial Education," but no fewer than five papers were offered on the subject at the Department of Superintendence meetings; another four at the Round Table of Superintendents of Smaller Cities; two more at the National Council of Education assembly; two of four at the Department of Secondary Education; and the Presidential Address of the Department of Science Instruction treated it as well.[6]

The NAM and the NSPIE, as well as dozens of smaller local businessmen's groups, had done their work—and done it well. The NAM Committee on Industrial Education had published its first report in 1905; the NSPIE had only been founded in 1906. And yet, by 1909, industrial schooling was not only receiving a hearing from the educators at their national conventions, it was virtually monopolizing all discussion.

Still, it must be borne in mind that these NEA educators, consumed by excitement for the new proposals, were not representative of the administrators and teaching staff in the schools. The conventions were overloaded with upper echelon administrators, county, city, and state superintendents, graduate school professors and college presidents. It was the educational establishment, not the educational community, that had so quickly assented to the businessmen's proposals.[7]

Differentiation:
the new democracy in secondary schooling

The educational establishment had always listened attentively to the leaders of the business community. After all, as the business community claimed (and the educators by and large agreed), what was good for business was good for the larger society, employees and employers alike.

During the common school era, there had been apparent harmony between the interests of students and the requirements of the larger social order as defined by its business leaders. The disciplinary training offered in the common school classrooms would provide the employer with hard-working, dependable wageworkers. Likewise, it would provide the individual worker with the skills and habits needed for wagework for the time being and self-employment later.

By the turn of the century the educators could no longer assume the existence of this community of interest between employers and employees. The path from wageworker to self-employment had been barricaded. The educators had to choose: would they train their students to be independent, self-directed individuals or dependent wageworkers? The workers themselves might opt for the first alternative; their future employers would most certainly choose the latter.

The educators did not often phrase their dilemma in these terms. They talked instead of "idealism" and "realism," of anachronistic dreams and modern realities. The schools might once have been the proud bearers of the democratic tradition. Communities and educators might once have been able to take pride in the one-room schoolhouse where, so the story went, rich and poor learned their letters together. But the new industrial world of the twentieth century could no longer afford to cater to such dreams. The workplace was not and could not be a democracy. As Ellwood Cubberley, Dean of the School of Education at Stanford and one of the most powerful individuals in the educational establishment, wrote in 1909, it was high time that the schools "give up the exceedingly democratic idea that all are equal, and that our society is devoid of classes. . . . Increasing specialization . . . has divided the people into dozens of more or less clearly defined classes, and the increasing centralization of trade and industry has concentrated business in the hands of a relatively small number." The days when moral character and internalized discipline alone were a guarantee of economic success were long gone. "No longer can a man save up a thousand dollars and start a business for himself with much chance of success. The employee tends to remain an employee; the wage earner tends to remain a wage earner."[8]

It was the big guns in the educational community—the deans

and presidents of the graduate education schools, the teachers of future superintendents and principals, the convention keynoters and textbook writers, the state and city superintendents—who carried the message to the rest of the community.

Cubberley at Stanford was not the only university spokesman for realism in the public schools. Dean James Earl Russell of Teacher's College in New York City was no less virulent in his denunciation of the idealists. He too warned the education community to take stock of the world around it and adjust its practices to changing social realities. Unmet expectations were a danger to the individual and to the society. The school that did not dampen the youngster's dreams of future economic independence, of professional or white-collar positions, was not doing its duty to that youngster and his society. As Russell warned the 1908 NEA symposium on "The Place of Industries in Public Education":

> How can a nation endure that deliberately seeks to rouse ambitions and aspirations in the oncoming generations which in the nature of events cannot possibly be fulfilled? If the chief object of government be to promote civil order and social stability, how can we justify our practice in schooling the masses in precisely the same manner as we do those who are to be our leaders? Is human nature so constituted that those who fail will readily acquiesce in the success of their rivals. . . . Is it any wonder that we are beset with labor troubles?[9]

Russell's advice would have been strangely jarring to the earlier generation of common school crusaders who had assumed as part of their ultimate responsibility the duty of raising the spirits and aspirations of the young to more noble pursuits than life as subordinate wageworkers. Russell was recommending the exact opposite. The new task of the public school teacher, as he presented it, was not to urge students onward to economic independence but to lower such expectations and adjust those who would fail to the probability of failure.

Russell had entitled his speech "Democracy and Education: Equal Opportunity for All" without a trace of irony. It was his

position that only "differentiated" schooling—different curricula for different classes of students—was democratic schooling. High schools that offered only an academic education were
not meeting the needs of those who would "do the rougher
work of life." Because students faced different futures, they
deserved to receive different educations depending on those futures. Russell praised as ultimately most democratic the "negro
schools of the South, the county agricultural schools of Wisconsin, and the trade schools of some of our eastern cities." These
schools had properly differentiated "the school courses and
school work" of their pupils in accordance with their "definitely
known . . . future vocations."[10]

This, then, was the new educational democracy. The school
was to assume the reality and inheritability of social class. Democracy meant offering every student the opportunity for an
education equally adjusted to what school officials assumed
would be his or her future vocation.

David Snedden, a graduate professor at Stanford and then at
Teacher's College, later to become commissioner of education in
Massachusetts, urged schoolmen to pay attention to the "conditions under which the economic status of the family affect the
educational careers of children under the age of fourteen."
Snedden accepted as given the existence of an urban proletariat
with no choice but to deliver its children to work as soon as
possible. A democratic education for these children would have
to be differentiated even earlier than the high school they
would probably never attend. Snedden suggested that the public schools follow the European practice of "extensive differentiation at [age] twelve or earlier."[11]

Differentiated schooling became the new watchword of educational leaders, the sign that they too had come of age, jet-
tisoning their earlier idealism, ready and willing to adjust their
schooling practices to the requirements of the new social order.
J. Stanley Brown, a high school principal from Illinois and
frequent speaker before the national conventions, congratulated
his 1910 audience on the distance they had traveled since the
days of Horace Mann and the common schools:

> In the early days of secondary education when schools were somewhat small and poorly equipped and when funds were more difficult to obtain than at present, we had the same set of studies provided for all, regardless of sex, previous condition, or future employment, and we considered that we were rendering the best service to all, and it is now reported that there are some remote regions east of the Alleghenies even now where such an opinion is making a struggle to survive.[12]

The remote regions might not have accepted the wisdom of differentiation, but the audience of educational leaders to whom Brown spoke certainly did. Every session of the 1910 NEA Department of Superintendence meeting was devoted to the topic. Papers were offered on the ways in which children differed in mental alertness, moral responsibility, mental attitude, physical condition, environment, and vocational aims.[13]

The educators found in the concept of differentiation and the notion that some students were incapable of academic work the perfect alibi for past and future failures—and at a time when they were being called to account for those failures. This was the era of the professional school survey and muckraker journalism, both of which were documenting astounding failure rates in the public schools, especially the high schools.

Before 1905 the educators had responded to their critics by avoidance or the simple denial that statistics on attrition, dropouts, and overage students were accurate. The minority who took to heart the evidence that the schools were not doing as well as they might looked to the classrooms for the reason. One particularly courageous commentator, a principal from Illinois, suggested at an NEA convention that the teachers might be responsible for the high rates of failure, especially in the first year of high school. Only when the teachers began to take their work more seriously, more professionally, would the rate of failure begin to decline. Teaching, he believed, had to become a true profession and considered as such by the society-at-large, by taxpayers, by teacher-training institutions and, of course, by the teachers themselves.[14]

This line of reasoning was unique and never again replicated—at least before an NEA convention. The educational establishment had, by the middle 1900s, accepted the reality and inevitability but not the responsibility for high failure rates.

The new students:
what they wanted, what they got

That the plain people were not doing as well as they might could not be doubted. But the fault was hardly their own. The minimal pedagogical progress (prompted by Dewey and his followers) that had been achieved in the elementary grades had progressed no further. Within the secondary school classrooms, the style, content, and form of instruction remained as it had always been. Teachers presented students with a mass of trivia, facts, and figures to be memorized. There was no attempt at interesting the students in the subject matter or giving them a clue as to why it should be learned in the first place. Students who could not adapt to the routine found it difficult to remain in school long enough to graduate.

The chief reason for the high rate of attrition was neither boredom nor academic incapacity. Most of those who dropped out before graduation or never went in the first place did so out of economic necessity. They left school for work, either because their parents needed their income to help support younger siblings or because they needed the income and the independence it would bring.

As had been predicted, "the children of the plain people" had begun crowding the schoolrooms. The middle-class finishing school had become a mass institution. That the characteristics of the high school population had changed could be seen in the drop in the percentage of students whose family income enabled them to consider going on to college. In 1890 some 14.4 percent of the public high school enrollment was in this position. By 1905 that percentage had fallen to 9.6 percent; by 1909, to 5.6 percent.[15]

In retrospect, what is most remarkable about this first generation of plain people to enter the high schools *en masse* is not their failure or drop out rate but rather the enthusiasm with which they entered the schools and selected for themselves precisely those courses the experts had decreed beyond their interest and capacity. They were not going to settle for anything less in the way of a secondary education than the traditional academic program that their middle-class predecessors had enjoyed.[16]

In the 1889–1890 school term, 35 percent of the then predominantly middle-class public high school population had enrolled in Latin classes. By 1905, after the first wave of "plain people" had entered the high schools, the proportion of students taking Latin had increased to just over 50 percent. The increase in the percentage of students enrolled in other academic courses was as impressive. Within the same fifteen-year period, the percentage of students taking algebra increased from 45 percent to 58 percent; geometry, from 21 percent to 28 percent; and German, 11 percent to 20 percent.[17]

Obviously, no matter what the experts said, the children of the plain people wanted the same type of education that had been traditionally provided the children of the middle class. The more the educators—with the applause of the business community—moved to adjust the curriculum to their "requirements," the more they elected the traditional academic courses. High school to them meant Latin and algebra, not metalworking and sewing.

The educational establishment might have taken pleasure from this vote of confidence given the academic curriculum. Certainly the Latin and algebra teachers could not but have been pleased by the increasing enrollments in their courses. But among those represented at the NEA conventions there was no joy in these developments. Though some educators might have believed that a classical, academic education would serve working-class children by strengthening their minds, they knew also that such schooling had the unfortunate effect of raising expectations unrealistically. This they could not allow.[18]

The educational establishment, by the middle 1900s already committed to differentiation, now had to take upon itself the task of diverting the new students, no matter what their choices, from the traditional academic courses into others more "suited" to their capacities and future vocational needs.

The children of the plain people were greeted with new electives and then new courses of study specially designed in their behalf. In school after school the course and curricula offerings grew at almost the same pace as the enrollment.

Patricia Graham, in her study of the schools of Marquette, Michigan, found a direct correlation between the increase in school population and the increased diversity in course offerings. "In much of its early period the high school had served the children of the middle- and upper-middle classes" almost exclusively. On entering high school, these children were offered a choice, not among electives, but among four strictly structured curricula: "Classical (requiring both Greek and Latin), Latin-Scientific (Latin, but French or German instead of Greek), Scientific (either French or German but no ancient language), and English (no foreign language and only a 3-year course)." Only as the masses began to enter the high school towards the turn of the century did the Marquette educators— with the prodding of local businessmen—take up the argument that a "more appropriate curriculum was necessary." The high school curriculum was expanded to include such vocational subjects as

> bookkeeping, commercial arithmetic, stenography and type-writing, business correspondence, and commercial law. In manual training students could study mechanical drawing, woodwork, ironwork, pattern making, and reflecting the dominant industry of the region, advanced ironwork. . . . In domestic science . . . cooking, sewing and design work, dressmaking, household economy, and in keeping with the early twentieth-century fetish of scientism, laundry science.[19]

The curricular revolution in Muncie, Indiana, reported by Robert and Helen Lynd in *Middletown*, was as thorough as in Marquette, Michigan. As the plain people entered the high school, so did dozens of new subjects enter the curricula. In 1889, entering Middletown students "had to choose, as Middletown high school students had done for thirty years, between two four-year courses, the Latin and the English courses, the sole difference between them being whether one did or did not take 'the language.' The number of separate year courses open to them totaled but twenty." By the early 1920s, instead of two curricular choices there were twelve (general, college preparatory, music, art, shorthand, bookkeeping, applied electricity, mechanical drafting, printing, machine shop, manual arts, and home economics), and instead of twenty subjects to choose from, there were now over one hundred.[20]

This opening up of curricula was not confined to the city and town schools. In the countryside also, the schools were beginning to offer vocational courses. The rural high schools of Johnson County, Indiana, introduced agriculture as a course of study at precisely the same time as the city schools were adding their own vocational subjects.[21]

The reformers, educators, and enlightened businessmen who supported these new, socially efficient schooling programs believed they were acting in the best interests of their "plainer" students. Classical or foreign languages for future factory hands, English literature or algebra and trigonometry for future clerks, bookkeepers, and secretaries, would only waste the time, energy, and money of students, teachers, and community alike. Better that these students be directed to a more useful course of study. As John Dewey himself put it, "The simple facts of the case are that in the majority of human beings the distinctively intellectual interest is not dominant. They have the so-called practical impulse and disposition." It was neither fair nor logical to ask these nonintellectual students to take traditional subjects that had been designed with "mental training" as their objective. Why even attempt to exercise or train minds that were substandard, especially when the bodies that housed these minds were not substandard and could be schooled to provide greater productivity in adult life?[22]

A socially efficient schooling system would select the minds best suited for mental training and the bodies best suited for manual training. The problem was convincing those who were to be denied the traditional high school education that this was for their own good. If the high schools were to differentiate between students capable of academic work and those who were felt not to be, some process of distinguishing the gold from the dust had to be established and legitimized as more than social class, ethnic, or racial discrimination.

Later in the century, the scientists would provide the schools with standardized testing: an antiseptic, brutally efficient technique for weeding out the "best" minds from the "substandard." In the prewar period, however, the selection process was more haphazard, though the experts were already attempting to find workable solutions to this sticky problem.[23]

It would have been preferable had the students differentiated themselves. But, as judged by the course enrollments in Latin and algebra, the schools would have to do the differentiation for them.

The carrot and the stick were used to direct the working-class students away from the academic courses into the new vocational curricula. Students were promised that the industrial training, commercial, and domestic science courses would lead to more useful lives with more secure wages and warned that the academic subjects would lead nowhere but to frustration and unemployment. Subjects like Latin and algebra—once prized for their disciplinary training, for their intellectual merits—were degraded to the status of "college preparatory" and recommended only for those who could afford postsecondary schooling.[24]

Even the elementary school teachers were enlisted in the task of differentiating their students. As Charles W. Eliot, president of Harvard University, suggested, since it was already too late to differentiate students once they had arrived at the high school, the elementary school teachers should be given the assignment: they "ought to sort the pupils and sort them by their evident or probable destinies."[25]

The fully developed schooling system would begin to differentiate students according to "probable destiny" as early as the elementary school. Immigrant children and blacks who, it was assumed, would have to drop out before ever reaching high school were offered the least academic training. "American" children whose probable destiny was supervisory or higher level blue-collar work were given some academic work in the elementary schools, then directed into manual, nonacademic high school programs. Only those middle- and upper-class children whose probable destiny was white-collar work or further schooling in college were allowed to remain through high school in the traditionally rigorous, classical, and "gentlemanly" academic courses.

As long as the schooling system, through the agency of the lower-grade teachers and counselors, was sorting students according to their probable destinies, the fiction was maintained that academic capacity as measured by success in school was the ultimate determinant of that final destiny, that those who lasted longest in school and performed best were the most capable. As we have seen throughout this study, however, it was not academic ability or motivation that differentiated drop outs from graduates—in either elementary or high school. It was economic need. Immigrant children dropped out before even graduating from elementary school not because they were inherently poor students but because they had to go to work. Blacks dropped out for the same reason. Throughout this period, it was only those students from middle- and upper-class white families who could afford to postpone work until their later teens. These were the students who were considered college material because these were the students who could afford to go to college.

Social efficiency in secondary schooling

Ultimately, the fully developed schooling system—and the fully developed ideological equation between schooling and economic worth—would provide legitimation for workplace discrimination between "Americans" and immigrants in the North as well as whites and blacks in the South.

In this era, prior to World War I, though the black migration northward had already begun, "most Negroes [were] concentrated in a very small area of the United States. Of the 9,927,763 Negroes in the entire nation at that time, 90 percent were living in the South."

Through the 1870s and 1880s, black and poor white children had suffered together from the South's disregard for their education. There were virtually no compulsory schooling laws for either race nor was there any great effort to raise local or state taxes to adequately support what few public schools there were. Alabama, not unrepresentative of the Southern states, was by the turn of the century still "spending about $.50 per school age child for educational purposes in contrast with the national average of $2.84." [26]

It was only during the twenty-year period surrounding the turn of the century that the South joined the rest of the nation in its concern for public schooling. Enrollment in the public schools began to grow much faster than the funds earmarked for public education. The South's solution to the funding problem was predictable. Up until the 1890s, funds had been distributed by state law almost equally between the black and the white school systems. But now, as the schools increased their enrollment and importance, this equality was no longer acceptable. State after state changed its laws to allow local superintendents considerable leeway in distributing school funds as they saw fit. In those areas where blacks predominated, funds previously allocated for black students were shifted to the whites: "In Lowndes County . . . in 1912 for every dollar spent on education for a black child, $33.40 was spent for a white child." [27]

Throughout the South, state and local officials joined in the high school movement by building new public high schools for whites only. Blacks were left on their own or to the paternalism of white missionaries and their Northern industrialist capital.

Those industrialist/philanthropists who were at all concerned about secondary schooling for blacks never intended that this schooling should be equal to that available for whites. As William H. Baldwin, J. P. Morgan's Southern manager and one of the most persuasive proponents of black schooling, argued before the Second Conference for Education in the South (1899), though schooling opportunities for Southern blacks should be expanded, the type of schooling offered them should be directly related to the type of work they would be called on to perform after graduation.

> In the negro is the opportunity of the South. Time has proven that he is best fitted to perform the heavy labor in the Southern states. . . . The South needs him; but the South needs him educated to be a suitable citizen. He will willingly fill the more menial positions, and do the heavy work, at less wages, than the American white man or any foreign race which has yet come to our shores. This will permit the Southern white laborer to perform the more expert labor, and to leave the fields, the mines, and the simpler trades for the negro.[28]

Under no circumstances was schooling for blacks to be allowed to create competition between them and the poorer whites. In fact there were those who argued that until the skills of the whites were sufficiently raised, no "industrial schooling" of blacks should be permitted. As the president of the Georgia Institute of Technology argued, industrial schooling, if established in the South, should be for whites only, not for blacks:

> When the colored race all become skilled bricklayers, somebody will have to carry the mortar. When they all become plumbers, who are going to be the helpers, the men who carry the tools? When they become scientific farmers, who are going to be laborers? Are Southerners, we Southern whites? No. We have settled that question long ago, but unless we have trade and industrial schools [for whites exclusively], our boys will have to carry the mortar for somebody, even if they have to emigrate to do it.[29]

In the North industrial schooling was established to assure "Americans" a headstart towards the supervisory positions in the factory. In the South industrial schooling was, in similar fashion, designed to prepare whites for the factory work, leaving, as Baldwin had put it, "the fields, the mines, and the simpler trades for the negro."

Blacks and immigrants were caught in an impossible situation: they were excluded from the high schools, by law or by the economic necessity of having to work as teenagers, and then told that because they had not attended these high schools they were not worthy of the better jobs available for working-class youth.

As differentiated schooling won acceptance as the socially efficient way of running a school system, distinction was made not only between the middle- and upper-class children bound for college, the working-class children newly enrolled in high school, and the immigrants and blacks who would drop out of grade school, but also between boys destined for work and girls whose place, the experts decreed, was in the home.

Before differentiation had become acceptable, girls had competed in the classroom and, more often than not, performed better than the boys; so much better, in fact, that one of the more common complaints voiced about the nineteenth-century high schools was that the boys were less likely to succeed than the girls.[30]

Now, with the entrance of the plain people into secondary schooling, it was solemnly declared that too much academic learning might be not only useless but positively dangerous for girls, especially those from working-class families: "Superintendent J. H. Francis of Los Angeles was reported to have declared at the NEA meeting in 1914 that the study of algebra had caused many a girl to lose her soul." The principal of the Washington Irving High School for Girls in New York City referred to Latin for his students as no more than a "horrible nightmare."[31]

It was now decreed by the established authorities that the entire course of secondary study for girls had to be reconsidered in the light of the new social efficiency criteria: "It was desirable in the education of women, thought Superintendent H. J. Wightman of Altoona, Pennsylvania, to weigh Latin against cooking, solid geometry against dressmaking, and algebra against household duties." The new standards by which the courses were to be evaluated were succinctly described by an editorial in *Education:* "Where does trigonometry apply in a good woman's life? Will it contribute anything towards peace, happiness, and contentment in the home? Will it bake any bread, sew on any buttons or rock any cradles?"[32]

Only for the middle-class girls was instruction in the traditional academic and cultural subjects judged at all socially efficient. They after all would in their future vocations as wives and mothers have to serve as cultural guardians of middle-class households. For working-class women such course work was not only worthless but a serious diversion from more relevant schooling.[33]

We saw in an earlier chapter how industrial schooling courses for girls had been aimed at channeling those American girls who would have to work before (and probably during and after) marriage into more respectable trades. Domestic science programs, the female equivalent of industrial schooling, were promoted for the same reasons: not only would they prepare the young for what one NEA speaker declared "the vocation of every woman . . . marriage," but they would also provide them with entrée into the better jobs available for working-class women.[34]

As Mrs. W. N. Hutt informed the 1910 NEA convention, "The graduate in home economics may teach cooking, sewing, bacteriology, chemistry, and any of its various branches. She may have supervision of the food and sanitation of institutions such as hospitals, asylums, mercantile establishments, cotton mills, and homes of correction."[35]

The social efficiency experts were not content with simply differentiating curricula according to the students' "probable destinies." Even those subjects like history, still required of all students, were brought under the magnifying lens of social efficiency. No longer could a teacher claim that his or her subject was worthwhile because it broadened minds or trained the intellect. The question was how did that particular subject contribute to the social welfare of the nation.[36]

It was difficult, if not impossible, for those who still believed in the value of academic subjects as "mental trainers" to answer the efficiency experts, who now demanded "socially valid reasons" why these subjects should be taught. David Snedden, one of the most articulate and powerful proponents of socially efficient schooling, applied this standard alone to the traditional curriculum and found most, if not all of it, wanting. "In 1913," Edward Krug reports, "[Snedden] found algebra to be in a particularly hopeless state. . . . The only socially valid reason for algebra, in his opinion, applied to 'small numbers' who would use it as a professional tool. . . . A year later, he included Latin with algebra as a subject for which no socially valid purposes could be identified." In 1917 Snedden turned his sights on history, declaring that it too "could no longer 'be regarded as an end in itself.' " The teaching and content of this subject, like all the others, had to be sharply reformed if it was to remain part of the high school curriculum. Snedden even suggested that history as a subject might be so grossly inefficient it would eventually have to be replaced by some other kind of social studies.[37]

By the time the Lynds began their study of Middletown in the early 1920s, Snedden's threat had been realized. Though some history was still being taught, the emphasis was now placed on a more socially efficient social studies program, one designed explicitly to deal with the social pressures that had arisen during and immediately after the Great War.

Social efficiency rendered academic subjects no more than empty shells to be filled by the efficiency experts. In the middle 1920s the social studies courses, for example, were directed towards the still struggling but surviving Russian Revolution and the stifled but not defeated revolutionary movements that threatened the stability of Western Europe and the United States. The fact that the schools were being used for propaganda purposes was nothing new. The common school texts had certainly not been impartial in their presentation of the American way of life. The difference was more one of emphasis. As Dean Russell of Teachers College put it in a 1925 report, "Good Citizenship as an aim in life is nothing new. . . . But good citizenship as a dominant aim of the American public school is something new. . . . For the first time in history, as I see it, a social democracy is attempting to shape the opinions and bias the judgment of oncoming generations."[38]

Courses such as history could be adjusted in form and content to meet the requirements of the efficiency experts. Courses that did not lend themselves to such modification would not survive the new century.

Latin was the first casualty. The initial step in its decline and fall was its removal from the list of requirements to the waste-land of "college preparatory" subjects. According to the Lynds, the study of Latin, in the 1890s required for four years of more than half the Middletown students, was by the middle 1920s required of no one. Nationwide, its removal from required sta-tus, combined with the propaganda barrage directed against it, succeeded in turning away the large numbers of plain people who had once chosen to enroll. Latin enrollments, which had increased from 35 percent to over 50 percent of total students from 1890 to 1905, began to decline after 1905. By 1915 only 37 percent of all students were taking Latin; by 1922, only 27.5 per-cent.[39]

Algebra was headed towards the same fate. Again the figures on enrollment describe its history. With the entrance of the plain people into the high schools, the percentage of students taking algebra increased from 45 percent in 1890 to 58 percent in 1905. Only during the decade after 1905 (not coincidentally the decade of the NAM committee, the NSPIE, and the differentia-tion campaign) did the enrollments in algebra, as in Latin, begin to decline. By 1922 no more than 40 percent of high school students were taking the subject.[40]

The secondary school reform movement, led by the business-men and their organizations and subsequently supported by the educational establishment, succeeded in devising a new standard of evaluation and then having it applied to the high school curriculum. No longer would subjects be evaluated according to the degree to which they trained, disciplined, and exercised the minds of the students. The high school had en-tered the new industrial age: social efficiency had become the major factor in curricular decisions.

10

Reaction, Resistance, and the Final Compromise

The first wave of excitement about differentiated, socially efficient schooling crested before much opposition was raised. The public and professionals, when not adulatory, were indifferent. Even the unions, which might as a matter of course have opposed schooling programs designed to undercut their dwindling role in worker training and certification, appeared to support the reforms. It was only as the reform proposals moved closer to implementation that this union support—and public and professional indifference—gave way to a more active posture of outright opposition.

The union response

The American Federation of Labor, not willing to be left behind as the movement for industrial and vocational public schooling gathered momentum, established its own committee on industrial education in 1908. Though suspicious of business's enthusiasm for the new schooling programs, the committee nonetheless asserted in its first report that the reforms deserved the support of labor as long as they were "administered by the same authority and agency which administers our public school systems." [1]

It was not until the close of the first decade of reform that the A. F. of L. began reconsidering its support of industrial and vocational schooling. The Committee on Education, in its 1915 report to the convention, expressed its "apprehension that this proposed industrial education may ultimately give way to an attempt on the part of large commercial interests [to limit] the opportunities of the workers' children for a general education," and in so doing make those children into "more submissive and less independent" workers.

The unions were beginning to recognize that industrial schooling was not adding new courses to the standard curricula as much as substituting vocational for academic ones. Boys were enrolled in metal shop instead of in Latin; girls were learning sewing but not geometry. The 1915 A. F. of L. Committee on Education report, adopted by the full convention, put industrialists and educators alike on notice that in the future industrial education programs would only win union endorsement when "equal attention [was] given to the general educational studies and requirements of the school children. Your committee believes the latter [i.e., general education courses] of greater importance to the future welfare of the workers than the former instructions [in vocational subjects]."[2]

The "plain people's" response

The A. F. of L.'s reluctance to support without reservation the new curricular reforms was matched by the reluctance of the working people the union claimed to represent. Both parents and children knew what they wanted—and that was to escape the workplaces the new programs were designed to prepare them for. The reformers were attempting the impossible—to lure young workers back into the industrial workplaces without making any substantial changes in the work environment and social conditions that had driven them away in the first place.

As W. B. Prescott of the International Typographical Union warned the industrial schoolers assembled at the 1907 NSPIE convention:

I do not think the establishment of trade or any other sort of schools will induce American boys, of what our manufacturers deem the desirable class, to go into factories and mills. Those who will do so will go unwillingly and as a last resort, as long as the present regime attains. It is not alone inability to work with their hands that keeps the desirable ones out. It is the failure of society at large and especially a class of employers— to recognize the dignity of labor. . . . The mechanic is being lowered in social esteem as a result of iniquitous shop rules, and boys with spirit and red blood in their veins will not submit to such tyrannies. So, Messieurs Employers, if you want the flower of American youth to follow industrial pursuits you will have to treat them less like prisoners of necessity and more like men. . . . Until you do, it is my belief you will look in vain for American boys to enter your factories as willing workers.[3]

The children of the plain people, who had begun entering the high schools in large part because they believed a high school education might offer them entrance into the white-collar world, were not going to be detoured through industrial schools back into the factories.

Working-class students and adults were not blind to the changes being made in the secondary school curricula. Many agreed implicitly with the A. F. of L. committee that if a choice had to be made between general and vocational education, the former was ultimately of more value because of what the students might learn and because of what they might become. General education trained the mind, strengthened the character, and prepared youth for citizenship; it also provided them with the intellectual training and certification deemed necessary for entrance into the preferred white-collar jobs.[4]

The schooling reformers could not accept the public's hesitancy to endorse their new curricula. They continued to complain about the slowness of the people in responding to their programs, as if the problem were not the programs themselves but the students' and parents' inability to understand them. Public apathy, even hostility, was regarded as a public relations problem.[5]

The U.S. Bureau of Education, taking its lead from the NSPIE, devoted an entire chapter of its 1916 Bulletin on Vocational Secondary Education to the organization of a vocational schooling public relations campaign. The chapter, appropriately entitled "Some Ways in Which Vocational Education May Be Introduced," warned vocational and industrial schooling enthusiasts of the groundwork necessary before such programs could be introduced into public school systems. "A continuous campaign of publicity" would be crucial in bringing "about a local demand" for an investigation and report on the feasibility of new schooling models; new and reprinted documents of possible programs would have to be published and distributed and the support of local newspapers solicited and secured. Speaking engagements would have to be arranged with "lantern slides and moving pictures [to] serve as effective means for impressing those present" (fortunately the NAM had already developed the appropriate material for such presentations); exhibitions held, advisory committees formed, and the direct support of influential community leaders, "boards of trade, labor organizations, civic and educational associations" enlisted.[6]

Unfortunately for the high school reformers and their propagandists, the sad fact was that not even the best organized public relations campaigns could possibly elicit public acceptance for the new industrial and vocational schools. The gap between student and parent expectations for a high school education and what the vocational advocates were prepared to offer was too wide to be papered over by publicity.

J. Stanley Brown, long an advocate of industrial training, took the floor of the 1915 NEA convention to warn the vocational proponents to prepare themselves for a long-term struggle for secondary school reform: "Probably the largest factor in determining what is to be the place and function of the high school in our American education is seen in the struggle between the individual parent and the boy or girl on the one hand, and the manufacturer, the business man, and the industrialist on the other hand." The sides and issues had, according to Brown, already been drawn—and tightly. The parents and their supporters from "social, ethical, and religious organizations" sought for the student "the right to develop his own life in the way which seemed best to his parent and himself and that his duties as a citizen demand." They were committed to a high school education that recognized "the obligation of the community and the state for a higher and better development of the individual." The "manufacturers, the commercialists, or the industrialists" on the other hand were concerned not at all with "human character, right living, and good citizenship" or with schooling the individual to be "the best citizen, the most honest and careful man." They were committed only "to [making] every individual employee subordinate to the production of his particular institution."[7]

Brown wondered aloud how such a conflict could be harmoniously resolved. As the first flush of excitement for the new reforms began to fade, other educators—at the national, state, and local levels—came to share the same concern.

The educators' response

In the beginning, the supporters of the new schooling had been quick to quiet the fears of the traditionalists by stressing that the new subjects would satisfy the criteria established for the old. The manual training, industrial, and vocational subjects, it was claimed, were worthy of inclusion in the secondary curricula because of their inherent disciplinary value. As President Keyes of the Throop Polytechnic Institute of Pasadena informed the 1895 NEA convention, the aim of manual training courses was not specialized vocational training but

> the development of conscious, skillful energy and the subordination of every other power of body and mind to the action of the will. Its chief product is never the accurate drawing, the beautiful sketch, the well-made garment, the well-cooked dinner, the exactly fitted joint, the perfectly adjusted machine, the intricate and ornamental iron-work, the thing of beauty which seems to speak to us from wood or clay; but it is the self-controlled, self-centered young man or woman.[8]

Such deference to traditional educational values and objectives did not last long. Within a year of the founding of the

NSPIE, the climate had already shifted enough to permit the New York State Commissioner of Education to boldly pronounce that the new vocational schools in his state were going to "be sharply distinguished from any schools that are now known in America. . . . They will have a distinct individuality and a definite object of their own. They are neither, primarily, to quicken mentality nor to develop culture. . . . The 'culturists' are not to appropriate these new schools."[9]

The culturists, needless to say, were not reassured. As it became clear that the industrial and vocational schooling advocates were not only uninterested in "quickening mentality" and "developing culture" but were actively opposed to such schooling objectives, the rank-and-file teachers and local administrators abandoned their earlier stance of benign neutrality for active opposition.

Teachers and administrators opposed the new schools out of self-interest—they did not intend to be replaced by vocational trainers—but also because they continued to believe in the value of a traditional, academic education for all, regardless of future occupation. They might have supported vocational subjects if added on to a more traditional program, but they would not support them as substitutes for the "real" courses.

The teachers had begun taking themselves more seriously, setting up their own national organizations, their own unions, their own process for establishing credentials within the profession. Perhaps as importantly, they had began to internalize the schooling ideology developed and disseminated by the common school crusaders a half-century before. The public school "professionals" now considered themselves the moral guardians of the democratic order. They would determine the character of those who would be the nation's leaders—and followers. Public schooling was the last bulwark of stability in a society perpetually on the brink of chaos. The teacher's duty to the republic was paramount; they could not allow themselves to be replaced by job trainers.[10]

The vocational schoolers had given up trying to win these traditionalists to their side. As Commissioner Draper of New York stated quite plainly, the "culturists" were the enemy. At all costs, the new vocational schools had to be placed beyond their reach. They were not to be allowed any contact with the vocational students; they were not to be allowed any control whatsoever over curricula, funding, organization, supervision, or staffing of the new schools.[11]

The vocational and industrial schools, if they were to succeed, had to be cut loose from the rest of the public school system. This was the principal recommendation of every state commission and every NAM and NSPIE proposal advocating industrial schooling. Without such institutional autonomy, it was feared, the vocational and industrial schools would be reduced to nothing more than manual training annexes to academic institutions.[12]

Vocational schooling, though to be made separate from academic schooling, was not going to be allowed absolute autonomy. Just as the academic high schools were answerable to local school boards, so too would the vocational schools be accountable to local business leaders.

Strong ties between the schools and business might have been desirable in the case of the academic high schools, but they were absolutely essential in the case of the vocational schools. As David Snedden, Massachusetts commissioner of education, reported to the NEA Department of Superintendence meeting in 1914:

> The vocational school must be in a position to go constantly to the world of economic activity, in order to derive clear knowledge of the purposes which should control it. It should be governed by or possess an advisory committee containing men who are intimately identified in the occupation for which it learns, both as employers and employees. The vocational school should divest itself as completely as possible of the academic atmosphere, and should reproduce as fully as possible the atmosphere of economic endeavor in the field for which it trains.[13]

The teachers and local administrators could, of course, be counted on to resist such attempts to divest their schools of academic atmosphere and remove them from public control. The local school boards sided with the teachers and administrators.

They had been elected or appointed to look after the welfare of all children regardless of class background or "probable destiny." They were not now going to yield this responsibility to businessmen advisory councils.

In Massachusetts, where a commission established by Governor Douglas, owner of one of the largest shoe manufacturing businesses in the state, recommended that the industrial schools be organized independently of local school boards, grassroots opposition was sufficient to sidetrack the project indefinitely. Despite "intensive propagandizing" and the offer of additional state aid if the local school boards and communities agreed to establish new and separate industrial schools, "few cities in Massachusetts actually instituted them under the Commission's guidelines." [14]

Though rebuffed in Massachusetts, the separate schooling proposals were not consigned to the oblivion of politically inexpedient reforms but were submitted in one form or another in other Northeastern and Midwestern cities. [15]

The major proponents of the separate schooling plans on the local as on the national level were the businessmen, organized into "nonpartisan" political clubs and civic improvement associations. In Chicago the plan for a separate system of vocational schools was commissioned by the Commercial Club and supported by the Illinois Manufacturers' Association, the Industrial Club, the Hamilton Club, the City Club, the Association of Commerce, and the Civic Federation, all, in the words of George Counts, representing "the great employing interests of city and state." [16]

The business groups and their paid and unpaid propagandists based their arguments for a dual schooling system on the need for industrial efficiency. They claimed that without vocational and industrial schools American industry would inevitably fall further and further behind in the battle for exports. Their opponents did not directly disagree. They argued instead that a dual system, though it might enhance industrial efficiency, was so patently undemocratic that it would erode the social fabric that supported private enterprise.

The Cooley Bill, named after the former superintendent of

schools who had been hired to draft it, was opposed by the teachers, unions, local city politicians, and neighborhood groups. It was submitted to and defeated by the Illinois state legislature in 1913, 1915, and 1917.[17]

Secondary schooling: for industrial efficiency or for democracy?

The debate for and against separately administered industrial schooling programs was joined not only in the state legislatures but at the annual NEA conventions, where only a few years before the speakers had been unanimous in their praise for the new reform models. At the 1914 meeting of the Department of Superintendence of the NEA, W. C. Bagley of the University of Illinois confronted the issues of efficiency versus democracy in a widely reported debate with David Snedden. Bagley reminded his NEA convention audience—and Snedden—that a dual schooling system with separate vocational schools would be a socially stratified schooling system. In the inevitable choice that would have to be made between social and industrial efficiency and schooling democracy, Bagley made clear where his—and where he believed the public's—sentiments lay: "A stratified society and a permanent proletariat are undoubtedly the prime conditions of a certain type of national efficiency. But wherever our people have been intelligently informed regarding what this type of efficiency costs, they have been fairly unanimous in declaring that the price is too high." [18]

The Snedden–Bagley debate was reprinted and commented on in the educational journals, the consensus being that Bagley's arguments had won the day. As the *School Review* reported, rather tongue in cheek, Snedden's "advocacy of a separate system of administration for vocational and industrial education . . . did not receive warm approbation from the rank-and-file of superintendents in the field." [19]

It certainly did not win the support of the man considered by many the founder of the curricular reform movement, John Dewey, who was outraged by the undemocratic uses to which his progressive pedagogy had been bent. To his mind, the proposals for separate industrial schooling were no less than "the greatest evil now threatening the interests of democracy in education." The vocational schools, once removed from public control, would, Dewey predicted, be taken over from top to bottom by the business community, which would convert them into job training centers supported by tax money. A bifurcated public schooling system would not only be an insult to the American people but a direct danger to the future of American democracy.[20]

Dewey and Bagley recognized immediately the fatal contradiction between schooling for democracy and schooling for industrial efficiency. Germany (as the business organizations never ceased to point out) might have been able to efficiently separate those bound for the factory from those headed to the front office, offering each group differentiated schooling adjusted to its probable workplace destiny. But Germany was not, nor did it pretend to be, a democratic, classless society.

American society could not harness its schooling system to the requirements of its industrialists as efficiently as Germany did. American schools had other purposes to serve. They had to maintain the illusion of democracy in a society where the increasing agglomeration of wealth in the hands of the few was rendering negligible the political power of the many; they had to maintain the appearance of the classless society in a new industrial order established on the separation of labor from capital; they had to maintain the pretense of unlimited upward mobility in a society where such movement was becoming much more the exception than the rule. In short, they had to preserve and present the myths of America to each new generation of Americans.

Differentiated, separated secondary schooling might increase industrial efficiency, but only at the cost of social harmony. Working-class students segregated in their early teens from their more prosperous contemporaries would not easily be convinced that they lived in a land of unlimited opportunity. If a choice had to be made between restructuring the public schools for the defense and service of the traditional American myths or fashioning them to meet the requirements of American business, the majority of rank-and-file teachers and administrators, the unions, and a sizable proportion of the nationally known educational leaders were ready to choose the former. W. C. Bagley spoke for all of them when he declared, "We mean to keep open the door of opportunity at every level of the educational ladder. It is a costly process, but so are most other things that are precious and worthwhile."[21]

Neither Bagley's determination, Dewey's defense of democracy, nor the organized strength of the teachers and unions would succeed in keeping that door open. But they would at least make sure that it was not completely closed.

The industrial and vocational schoolers never achieved the reforms they advocated in the decade of enthusiasm following the NAM's 1905 report from its Committee on Industrial Education. This does not mean they gave up trying. Led by the NSPIE, the vocational promoters, having come to recognize— though somewhat belatedly—that community and teacher acceptance was beyond their reach, shifted their lobbying focus from the local and professional level to the federal. If the local and state boards of education were not going to grant the money and allow the vocational schools the autonomy they required, perhaps the federal government could provide the proper funds—and pressure. After years of lobbying, the vocational schoolers were rewarded with the Smith-Hughes Act of 1917, a piece of legislation with so many purposes to serve it could barely accomplish any of them.[22]

Even with the allocations of federal financial support from the Smith-Hughes Act, the states and local communities continued to resist the new schooling reforms: "In 1912–13, after industrial education had been generally accepted but before federal funding was in effect, 6.9 percent of high school students were enrolled in industrial and trade courses; in 1924 when utilization of federal aid was near its peak, 6.7 percent of high school students were in such courses."[23]

The final compromise:
the comprehensive high school

The secondary schooling system would emerge full grown in the twentieth century as somewhat of a compromise between the ideas of the vocationalists and the traditionalists. Differentiated schooling had become a necessity, but so too had the continuation of some form of common schooling experience beyond the elementary grades.

The high schools were becoming so firmly harnessed to the social order that they reflected all the contradictions of that order. They were called upon to do the impossible: to uphold the myths of the "classless" community while at the same time preparing young people for their future lives in a society based on class divisions.[24]

The schools were infused with the contradictions of their society not only within the walls but in their governance procedures as well. The reformers' attempts to remove control from the community could never entirely succeed. No matter who made the rules, no matter who decided the ultimate questions of curricula and scholastic requirements, the schools could not function without the at least tacit support of parents, teachers, and students. This support was, unfortunately, not always easy to secure. The parents and high school students still believed that the schools should remain educational and cultural agencies as well as pathways to upward mobility for those who did their work well. The teachers saw themselves as educators, the real guardians of the American way of life. Neither teachers nor parents and students were likely to abandon their more traditional vision to that of the school reformers. Transferring all control from the local community to centralized boards that looked to the state legislatures and later to the federal government for funds and leadership did not resolve the conflict, it only institutionalized it.

The "comprehensive" high school, where academic and vocational subjects were taught and administered under the same roof, would become the standard model for secondary schooling in the twentieth century because it provided the substance of differentiation without the appearance. Comprehensive high schools differentiated students into curricular "tracks," but then undid the damage to democratic pretensions by bringing them back together again into a microcosmic, quintessentially American, democratic community to eat lunch, take recess, learn their "civics," attend assembly, and cheer their athletic teams to victory.

Unfortunately, because it had to be all things to all people, the comprehensive high school failed in both its objectives. It could not be democratic as long as it continued to segregate students by social class into vocational or academic tracks. And its efficiency was impaired, as had been predicted, by housing the vocational offerings within what were administered and celebrated as academic high schools. Because the vocational programs within the comprehensive high schools were obviously second-class in terms of funding, teaching, and, perhaps most importantly, the social class of the students enrolled, they could never attract in sufficient number, nor could they school effectively, those students for whom they had been designed in the first place.[25]

The comprehensive high school, in the long run, failed because it was so well-integrated into the American social order that it was strangulated by the contradictions that permeated that order. As we shall soon see in Part 3, the laying on of an additional layer of mass schooling after World War II was in part a response to the failure of the reformed high schools to serve the economic (manpower) requirements of the new industrial order while upholding the democratic myths of an older America.

As a social panacea, the secondary school system was eclipsed after a mere fifty years. It survives today, but only as a staging area for youth on their way to work or higher education.

III
Higher Education
1945–1970

11

Between the World Wars:
To School or To Work?

An American schooling system was being built—piece by piece. By the second decade of the twentieth century, a second story had been added to the common school foundation constructed in the decades before the Civil War. An institutional path to adult life—from near infancy through adolescence—had been carefully laid out for young Americans to follow.

High school: for whom?

In 1890 it made little economic sense to attend high school. There were more direct paths to fame and fortune. In the forty years after 1890 this changed. The establishment and growth of the national corporations led to technological improvements in the factory and the "scientific management" of the labor force. This, in turn, affected the composition of the working class. The final result—from the perspective of the public school system—was an increase in the economic value of the high school diploma. The degree became more valuable as an admission ticket into white-collar employment, and white-collar employment was replacing self-employment as the surest path to economic security.[1]

The independent artisan/craftsmen had been absorbed into

the factory system in the first half of the nineteenth century. Small retailers and manufacturers were meeting the same fate in the first half of the twentieth century. They too found it difficult, if not impossible, to compete against the larger corporate units that were efficiently and profitably invading their local markets. As the Lynds reported from Middletown in the middle twenties:

> A swarm of chain stores is pressing hard upon the small independent retailer, who had things far more his own way in the nineties; during an apparently characteristic ten months from April, 1924, through January, 1925, three Middletown clothing stores and one shoe store were taken over by selling agencies having at least one store in another city, and four new chains entered the city with one or more branches.[2]

The small, independent farmers were as affected by the triumph of the corporation as their self-employed counterparts in town and city. The American family farm had never been as well off in fact as in fiction. Even in 1890, only one-half of all farms had been mortgage-free. By 1930, this percentage had dropped to one-fourth.[3]

One of the advantages of self-employment had been the opportunity for one generation to hand down its business to the next. Children followed their parents' path from infancy to adulthood, picking up the family skills, business, and property along the way. The coming of the corporation interred this process. As the corporation swallowed up the smaller independents or made life that much more difficult for those that survived, many families found they had nothing to turn over to their children except debts to wholesalers and mortgages to banks.

More adults were now worrying about their children's futures. Parents no longer assumed—or wished—that the next generation would follow the path of the previous ones. As the Lynds discovered in Middletown:

> Many parents . . . not satisfied with the vocations chance has dealt them . . . want to do something more for their children, but, particularly among the working class, they are frequently at a loss as to how to go about it. Such ideas as working class parents have for their children's future are largely negative: "I

hope they won't have to work as hard as their father"; or, "*He*
don't want the girls to go into no factory if he can help it."[4]

For those parents without a business, property, or specialized
skills to hand on to their children, further education seemed—if
not the answer to the mysteries of the job market—the best substitute for one. A high school education would at least give
them a better chance to land a "respectable" job. Young women
might find work as teachers in the common schools, as bookkeepers, secretaries, stenographers, file clerks, telephone opera-
tors, receptionists, and typists in the offices, and as saleswomen or cashiers in the department and retail stores. For male
high school graduates, the opportunities for employment in office or retail store were even more promising: the white-collar
jobs opening for them offered better wages and greater possibilities for advancement.[5]

As the diploma became more valuable in terms of the work it
helped secure, more students sought it. The increase in high
school enrollment that had begun in the last decade of the nineteenth century continued through the first decades of the twentieth.

While prosperity increased high school attendance, depression did not decrease it. For the depression decade of the 1930s,
unemployment rates, 20 percent for adults, were twice that for
young men and women. If, in better times, they had been lured
towards attaining their diplomas by the promise of a better job,
during the depression they were pushed into high school by
lack of employment.

The percentage of teenagers attending high school increased
through each decade of the twentieth century. In 1920, 32 percent of fourteen-to-seventeen-year-olds were in high school; by
1930, the percentage had increased to 51 percent; by 1940 it was
73 percent.[6]

Only the coming of World War II reversed the trend. Young
men and women who were of less value than their elders as
workers in peacetime became indispensable in wartime. For the
war's duration, their place was no longer in high school but on
the front lines for the boys and the assembly lines for the girls.

College: for whom?

The high schools were not the only layer of the academic system to grow in enrollment during the first decades of the twentieth century. Enrollments in higher education expanded as spectacularly, and for many of the same reasons.

As the corporate giants grew in size and profitability, absorbing or eliminating the smaller concerns that tried to compete, the need was created for a new layer of upper- and middle-level white-collar occupations. The captains of industry now looked for advice to a squadron of what Stuart Ewen refers to as "Captains of Consciousness": public relations specialists to keep the public appreciative of the goods and services the corporations had to offer, advertisers to excite a public need for those goods and services, labor relations specialists to smooth out labor problems, personnel managers to "manage" the personnel.[7]

The number of these new specialists, experts, managers, directors, and executives increased almost yearly. As Thomas Cochran describes it,

> The problem of the right amount of management for the production involved was never solved, but the trend was distinctly upward. A study of manufacturing industry puts the increase in administrative employees between 1899 and 1929 at 330 percent, while production employees increased less than 90 percent.[8]

In Middletown, the Lynds reported that in the course of one generation "the 'general manager' of the glass factory . . . [had] been succeeded by a 'production manager,' a 'sales manager,' an 'advertising manager,' a 'personnel manager,' and an 'office manager.'"[9]

The newly expanding world of the business corporation was somewhat confusing to those outside that world, without capital or skills. The path to the lower levels of white-collar employment in office, school, and retail store appeared to lead straight through the high school. But how did one reach the middle and upper levels of corporate management?

Parents uncertain about their children's future were able to assuage their anxiety somewhat by pushing their children as far as possible in school. For those with money, the members of what the Lynds called the "business class," higher education was taken for granted. Thirty-seven of forty Middletown business-class families expected their children to go to college.

The working-class Middletown families had much the same dreams. But their answers to the question of future schooling had to be phrased "in terms of 'hope to' or 'want to' [or] 'if we can afford it.' " In many households, a college education for the children meant the postponement or sacrifice of other dreams for the parents. Families would give up their plans for a house of their own; mothers would return to work to support older children in college. As one working-class father told the Lynds, "I don't know how we're going to get the children through college, but we're *going* to. A boy without an education today just ain't *anywhere!*" [10]

College had become important to working-class families for many of the same reasons as high school. Just as the high school diploma appeared to be the ticket to the lower-level white-collar jobs, a college degree was perceived as the admission ticket to the upper levels of the corporate bureaucracy. The small town grocer or neighborhood druggist might have hired a young man simply because he knew his parents and liked his ways. The larger corporations wanted something more. While hiring policies were not coldly procedural, it was apparent that college boys were getting the better jobs and climbing the bureaucratic ladder with greater speed. Andrew Carnegie might prefer the veteran workman to the college grad wet behind the ears; his personnel managers did not.

The college diploma was even more valuable, often indispensable, for aspiring professionals. Where once there had been many routes to professional work, now only one remained: higher education.

The college education—for the corporate executive, for the professional, for the higher-level white-collar worker—was valuable in part because it was expensive enough to be a badge of social standing. The college diploma did not necessarily prove that one had learned much; what it did demonstrate was that one had had enough money to delay entrance into the work world.

During the first half of the twentieth century, college, though not as blue-blooded as it had once been, was still restricted primarily to those who could afford it. Neither student nor parents could expect help from federal government, state, local, or college funding sources. The costs of college had to be borne by the families themselves, and these costs were not insignificant. In the school year 1929-1930, when per capita income was roughly one-third what it would become in 1974-1975, the costs per family of college attendance were 9 percent higher. [11]

In Middletown, the Lynds found that working-class families were saving for their children's college education. Small businessmen and farmers were doing the same—and for obvious reasons. In the heyday of frontier capitalism, hard work, self-discipline, and all those other character traits associated with a common school education might have been considered sufficient ingredients for economic success. By the 1920s the suspicion had grown that one needed "contacts" and "credentials" as well. College was the route to the better jobs in the professional and corporate workplace because it provided both. [12]

In some ways a college education was a sort of finishing school for the future professional and corporate leadership. There were, at the time, no stringent admission requirements. If you had the money, you would be admitted. At college, whether one of the more prestigious schools of the East or one of the larger state universities of the Midwest, the children of the rich and prosperous met others of their class and those newly invited into the "elite," made contacts that would in the future prove valuable, refined their manners, and soaked up enough culture to distinguish themselves from the rabble. [13]

One could expect a similar curriculum regardless of the institution one attended. From Michigan to Massachusetts, in the public and private colleges and universities, the liberal arts remained at the core. Liberal arts courses were considered indispensable and irreplaceable in the manufacture of the nation's social, cultural and political leaders. They were not only the repository of the culture of the West but the best intellectual training for young minds destined for leadership. Even in the land grant universities of the Midwest intended to serve the farming communities directly, the liberal arts were an important part of the curriculum. Many students attended these schools not to study agricultural science but to acquire a liberal arts education with which they could escape the farm entirely for professional or corporate offices.[14]

College or university training provided future generations of business and government leaders with a rudimentary but common culture. Wherever they enrolled, they most probably had suffered the same regimen of disciplinary exercises and imbibed from the same well of patriotic, cultural, and moral precepts.

When, in the middle 1950s, C. Wright Mills set out to investigate the postwar "power elite," he discovered that one of the invisible threads that bound them together was their college background. As a group, the leading business executives were nine times more likely than the rest of the population in their age group to have graduated from college in the 1920s.

This is not to imply that their business success was a result of their college education. On the contrary, it was their parents' previous success that allowed them to attend college in the first place. According to Mills, almost all these corporate executives had been "born with a big advantage: they managed to have fathers on at least upper-middle-class levels of occupation and income; they [were] Protestant, white, and American born. These factors of origin led directly to their second big advantage." Their family wealth enabled them to get the college education that sealed their initial class privilege with a veneer of upperclass culture and sharpened intellectual skills.[15]

Those born without comparable advantages—of wealth, class background, nativity, and, of course, race and sex—rarely made it into college in the 1920s and 1930s. Though the percentage of all youth attending college rose through the decades, by the coming of World War II not even 15 percent of the college-age group was actually enrolled in any institution of higher education. College was less restricted an institution than it had once been but still remained very much an "elite" one.[16]

As we have already seen, one cause for the increase in high school enrollments in the first four decades of the century was the decrease in employment opportunities for young teenagers. Although immigrant youths were employed in the mills and factories well into the new century, the overall rate of employment was declining steadily. The Lynds reported that in the 1920s the entire working population of Middletown started working anywhere from two to five years later than they had in 1890. Nationwide, the percentage of fourteen-to-nineteen-year-old males who were working dropped from 62 percent in 1900 to 40 percent in 1930. This drop in employment was correlated with an increase in the percentage of fourteen-to-seventeen-year-olds in high school, from 11 percent in 1900 to over 50 percent in 1930.[17]

The relationship between employment and enrollment held for college-age youth as well. One reason that college enrollment did not, in this period, increase as much as high school was that employment opportunities for college-age youth did not significantly decline. The drop in employment for twenty-to-twenty-four-year-old males was less than 2 percent in the first three decades of the century.[18]

In fact, through these first decades of the new century young men seemed to be faring better on the job market than ever before. As plants and factories were modernized, new machinery was brought in to replace the skilled minds and hands of the master craftsmen and skilled mechanics. Work in these modernized plants was becoming in large part machine tending. Under these circumstances, employers were turning to younger men to replace the older skilled workers. The younger men gave less trouble, followed orders, and had no traditions of worker independence to throw back at foremen pushing them to pay more attention to their machines.[19]

The coming of automation meant more than a gradual reevaluation of labor, a downgrading of the older and skilled, a preference for the unskilled but young and strong. "Modernization" ultimately meant a higher rate of unemployment and anxiety—for workers of all ages. Though working people had never had the security of steady employment enjoyed by their bosses, the incidence of shutdowns, layoffs, work slowdowns, and slumps seemed to affect them more in the twenties than at any time in recent memory. A full decade before the coming of full-scale depression, the crisis of overproduction was already reaching into the lives and homes of America's working families. The newly modernized, automated factories were producing more goods than could be sold. The newly modernized chain department stores were stocking more goods than could be sold. The new middle managers, cost accountants and production managers made life that much less secure. Under their management, as the workers of Middletown reported to the Lynds, layoffs had become "much more automatic" than when the plants were smaller and the owner personally knew all his workers.[20]

Through the "prosperous" twenties, unemployment continued to play with the dreams of working people in Middletown and elsewhere. The workers interviewed by the Lynds in 1924 were all concerned about the unemployment problem. The official unemployment rate had doubled from 2.4 percent in 1923 to 5.0 percent in 1924. Only from the vantage point of the thirties would the twenties be considered a decade of prosperity and full employment.[21]

12

One Depression Cured, Another Prevented: Planning for War and Postwar

The depression burst upon the nation in the summer of 1929 and did not subside for a decade. Unemployment was computed officially at 8.7 percent in 1930, 15.9 percent in 1931, and 23.6 percent in 1932. It did not dip below 20 percent until 1936, and it would not go below 5 percent until 1942.[1]

As the figures demonstrate, the appearance of FDR in the White House, whatever it did for the nation's "spirit," did not solve the problem of unemployment. FDR's first attempt at a cure for the country's economic ills was the same as Hoover's— balancing the budget—and similarly unsuccessful. Balancing the budget by reducing spending was the exact opposite of what J. M. Keynes, the English economist, had prescribed for the depressed economy. Keynes argued that in a depression public spending had to be increased, not decreased, to put people back to work. The nature of their jobs was not as important as the salaries they earned. It was their paychecks that would start the economy going again as they used them to buy goods and services, pumping money into the depressed economy. As Keynes himself put it:

> If the Treasury were to fill old bottles with banknotes, bury them at suitable depths in disused coal-mines which are then

> filled up to the surface with town rubbish, and leave it to
> private enterprise on well-tried principles of *laissez-faire* to dig
> the notes up again . . . there need be no more unemployment
> and, with the help of the repercussions, the real income of the
> community, and its capital wealth also, would probably be-
> come a good deal greater than it actually is.[2]

What Keynesian logic could not accomplish, the German and
Japanese threat to the "free world" and its "free economy"
could. "In the Second World War the equivalent of the . . .
buried bottles full of money were the tanks, the bombers, and
the aircraft carriers." They did the job, as Keynes had predicted. In the course of the war, the nation spent itself out of
the depression. The spending began before Pearl Harbor and
continued to accelerate through 1942. "In 1942 alone the proportion of economic activity devoted to war production grew from
15 to 33 percent, and by the end of the following year federal
spending for goods and services exceeded the total product of
the economy in 1933. The federal budget, about $9 billion in
1939, rose to $100 billion in 1945."[3]

Fighting the war the American way

To properly mobilize the economy to meet the demands of wartime, FDR called in a consulting team of corporate specialists.
Henry Stimson, though a lifelong Republican, left his corporate
law firm at the president's invitation to become secretary of
war. Stimson stayed at the War Department for the duration.
Other experts from the world of big business and finance com-
muted regularly between the private and the public sectors. For
Stimson, as for the president and his dollar-a-year men, ad-
visors, and cabinet officers, the wartime economy would
operate on the same hallowed "profit" principles as the peacetime. As Stimson put it, "If you are going to . . . go to war . . .
in a capitalist country, you have to let business make money out
of the process or business won't work."

No effort that would facilitate production was spared. And
since there could be no production at all without the promise of
profits, no effort was spared to guarantee these profits. The war

economy was a planned economy, planned by and for the larger corporations. They were given governmental help in keeping wages at a reasonable level. They were guaranteed large profits on war contracts "negotiated on the basis of cost plus a fixed fee." They were granted federal subsidies and low cost loans to tool up for war production. The tax laws were changed to guarantee them faster "write offs for expansion and retooling." And come time for reconversion to peacetime production, they were promised that their newly expanded plants, "financed by government funds, would be available at bargain-basement prices for postwar use."[4]

While the largest corporations were doing better than ever, the smaller manufacturers were struggling to survive. Those without war contracts of their own, and this was by far the great majority, were forced to subcontract to the industrial giants under less than optimum conditions. When war production was reduced in the winter of 1943, they lost even these subcontracts. They were still not allowed to produce consumer goods.

The smaller concerns looked anxiously to reconversion, when they would be able once again to produce for a "free market" without government interference. The larger corporations were quite pleased with the new planned economy. The corporate community firmly entrenched in Washington during the war had discovered that the rhetoric about free enterprise notwithstanding, cooperation between business and government was good for business. The corporate leaders had brought the economy under control during the war and profited from it. They did not plan to loosen their controls come peacetime.[5]

The planners, within and alongside the federal government, were agreed that any return to prewar economic conditions would be a return to depression. It was now accepted knowledge that the depression of the thirties had been caused in part, surely intensified, by the restrictive trade policies of nations that had, between the wars, closed their doors to American goods. There could be no return to these policies in postwar. In order to sustain business production and prosperity, to forestall depression, the U.S. government would use the strength it had gained from wartime victory to knock down all barriers to the free and unfettered flow of American goods and investment capital.[6]

But could the immediate increase in exports ever be large enough to put the twelve million soldiers and twenty million civilians in war plants back to work? The United States had survived one decade of unemployment, but not without serious threats to the social status quo. From left and right, the free enterprise system that led to the debacle of overproduction was severely criticized in the thirties and rightly so. Business, with the help of government, weathered the crisis with its private property and profits intact. But could it survive another dose of unemployment, especially when those without jobs would be returning veterans?

The G.I. Bill

By the summer of 1943 the Washington correspondent for the *New Republic* was already looking ahead to the war's end, but with fear and trembling rather than the customary jubilation: "When demobilization day comes we are going to suffer another Pearl Harbor, a Pearl Harbor perfectly foreseeable—now—a Pearl Harbor of peace, not of war." The peacetime Pearl Harbor would be even more devastating than the wartime because the attackers would come from inside, rather than outside, the American system. The soldiers were coming home.[7]

One did not have to be a very astute student of history to realize that returning veterans without jobs could become a revolutionary mass just waiting to explode. A past commander of the American legion reminded the House Committee on World War Veterans Legislation "that after the last war, except for England, this is the only country where the men who wore uniforms did not overthrow the government on either side of that conflict." Although his history was not quite correct, the general thrust of the comments was well taken.[8]

From a different political perspective, the liberal journal *Harper's Magazine* voiced the same warning as the war came to a close:

The veterans are not going to accept unemployment with the
bewildered docility which was characteristic of most of the
jobless in the last depression. . . . What action will result
from that attitude? . . . Nobody knows, of course. But we
have some hints, and they are hints which should make any
American start worrying. One of them is the report of a historian who watched fascism rise in Italy and Germany after the
last war.[9]

The best solution to the problem would have been guaranteed
employment. The Selective Service Act of 1940 attempted to
provide the first draftees with such a guarantee, requiring employers to rehire at the same pay, in the same position, workers
who had gone off to war. The postwar planners would have
been only too happy to guarantee work to all veterans. But they
knew better. There were simply not enough jobs to go around,
nor could enough be created to put all the demobilized soldiers
back to work.

In the early summer of 1942, Frederick Delano, head of the
National Resources Planning Board, a chief planning agency of
the government, asked permission of his nephew, the president, to "appoint 'a small planning committee' to analyze problems of 'the demobilization of men in the armed forces and industry.' " The president would not publicly sanction the
creation of such a committee because he believed postwar planning at that early date might divert "people's attention from the
winning of the war." He suggested, however, that Delano begin unofficial, unpublicized work on the problems.[10]

Within a year, the Delano committee delivered its recommendations to the president. The committee was convinced that the
"postwar economy would be depressed," with mass unemployment the inevitable consequence. To forestall such unemployment, the committee first considered delaying the discharge of
any soldiers until there were civilian jobs available for them.
This plan, though it would have solved the unemployment
problem, was scrapped. The servicemen and their families
would never have accepted it. And as the committee reluctantly
conceded, there might never be enough jobs for all the veterans.

The final recommendations were based on the principle that

the best way to keep veterans off unemployment lines was to send them to school. It was specifically recommended

> that all veterans be given the opportunity to embark on one year's education or training with substantial federal aid. . . . Not only did education benefit the country in traditional ways, the authors of the . . . report thought, but veterans' education would also help alleviate unemployment after the war. If unemployment rose, a system of federal scholarships would help cushion the impact.

FDR did not go public with his own concern over the veterans' future until the summer of 1943. At the conclusion of his July 28 fireside chat, he assured his audience:

> While concentrating on military victory, we are not neglecting the planning of things to come. . . . Among many other things we are, today, planning for the return to civilian life of our gallant men and women in the armed services. They must not be demobilized into an environment of inflation and unemployment, to a place on the bread line or on a corner selling apples. We must, this time, have plans ready—instead of waiting to do a hasty, insufficient and ill-considered job at the last moment.[11]

By the winter of 1943 the relevant congressional committees were already discussing postwar veterans' legislation. With the American Legion pushing hard—and in the same direction as the presidential planning commission—Congress made its decision. The G.I. Bill of Rights became law without a dissenting vote. Unlike earlier veterans' legislation, this bill, though its nickname might indicate otherwise, was primarily directed towards solving the problems of the postwar economy and only secondarily towards those of the returning veterans. There were no provisions for the traditional "cash bonuses" here, no heavy emphasis on pensions or medical benefits for the wounded and handicapped. The central features of this bill—and subsequent amendments—were the provisions for federal aid to veterans' education.

Neither the postwar planners who had initiated the discussion, the congressmen who sponsored the bill, the commit-

teemen who reported it out, the Legionnaires who lobbied for
it, the congressmen and senators who approved it, nor the president who signed it into law were overly concerned about veterans' education per se. As Keith Olson has written in his full-
length study, *The G.I. Bill, the Veterans, and the Colleges:*

> The origins and motives for enactment of the G.I. Bill re-
> vealed a widespread awareness of the past and an attempt to
> ward off a recurrence of undesirable conditions and events.
> . . . The persons responsible for the legislation clearly indi-
> cated by their statements and testimonies that the primary
> problem lay with the economy, not the veteran. Almost every-
> one realized that war spending had ended the depression.
> . . . Politicians and other leaders had little faith that the econ-
> omy could sustain full employment as it moved from war to
> peace, yet they were convinced that the United States could
> not safely allow extensive veteran unemployment. If the man
> in uniform would go from the battle line to the breadline, the
> common theme ran, he probably would demand radical eco-
> nomic and political changes.
>
> At its root, the Servicemen's Readjustment Act of 1944 was
> more an antidepression measure than an expression of grati-
> tude to veterans.[12]

The only sponsors of the bill concerned with its educational
impact were those from the higher education community itself.
From the very beginning, the American Council on Education,
a nonprofit organization of educational associations, colleges,
and universities, had cooperated with the federal planning
committees. The A.C.E. committee on the "Relationship of
Higher Education to the Federal Government" agreed almost
completely with the government and congressional committees.
Only when it came to granting "all veterans four years of
schooling" did the educators disagree. They believed it more
sensible to guarantee them only one subsidized year. For the
next three years, benefits would be limited to a much smaller
and "select group."[13]

The higher educators did not emphasize their differences
with the governmental planning committees—nor the legislation as ultimately enacted. The colleges had not yet recovered

entirely from the drastic drop in enrollments during the war years. As postwar approached, tuition-paying students would be necessary if higher education were to stage its own recovery.

Though most schools had suffered during the war, the smaller colleges and universities had been hurt much more than the larger ones. The large, prestigious universities had been able to sustain reasonable enrollments by offering draft-deferrable hard science and engineering courses and by housing, feeding, and schooling the mass of student soldiers and sailors whose training brought them to the college campuses with full federal funding to pay their way.

The larger universities benefited from federal support not only for student soldiers but for faculty who had joined the war effort. World War II, unlike previous wars, was fought as much by new weapons as old: new weapons that had to be researched and, in some instances, designed and developed by the nation's scientists, the majority of whom were affiliated with the larger universities. The cooperation of university and federal government was beneficial to both parties. The government obtained the weapons it needed, while the larger universities expanded their research facilities and received a new source of income to maintain them.[14]

It was only after the G.I. Bill had been signed into law—and victory and peace had come within view—that the higher educators who had doubts about the legislation began to openly express them. James B. Conant, president of Harvard University, let it be known in his 1945 Annual Report that, in his view, the act was " 'distressing' because it failed 'to distinguish between those who can profit most by advanced education and those who cannot.' His ideal G.I. Bill would have financed the education 'of a carefully selected number of returned veterans.' " In an early version of the "opening the floodgates" scenario, Conant warned that the bill would tempt schools in need of students and their tuition to admit veterans that didn't belong in college: "Because of the G.I. Bill 'we may find the least capable among the war generation . . . flooding the facilities for advanced education.' "

Robert Hutchins of the University of Chicago had much the

same fears. In the December 1944 issue of *Collier's Magazine*, he warned of "The Threat to American Education" posed by the veterans' legislation:

> Colleges and universities will find themselves converted into educational hobo jungles. And veterans, unable to get work and equally unable to resist putting pressure on the colleges and universities, will find themselves educational hobos. . . . education is not a device for coping with mass unemployment. [15]

It is of course not entirely coincidental that the presidents of two of the nation's most prestigious and prosperous institutions, in strong financial shape in part because of wartime research contracts, were the ones to speak out most vehemently against the veterans' legislation. Still, when the time came, neither university closed its "floodgates." Both welcomed the returning veterans—and their federal funds.

The nation's colleges and universities did more than just receive the veterans. They actively prepared for their arrival. Since it was the veterans themselves who would choose where to enroll, the amount of federal funds each institution received depended entirely on the number of veterans it could attract. Given this situation, it was the "better" universities that attracted the bulk of the students—and the accompanying federal funds.

> Veterans flocked to the Ivy League schools, the state universities, and the better liberal arts colleges and technical schools. They enrolled only as a last resort in junior colleges, teachers colleges, and less-known, small liberal art schools. . . . "Why go to Podunk College," *Time* magazine asked, "when the Government will send you to Yale?"

Although Yale and its like had a giant headstart, almost every other institution of higher education joined the battle for the veterans and the dollars that would follow them onto the campus. Most schools had by mid-1943 established veterans' planning councils. By V. J. Day, almost all had modified their admission procedures "to admit by examination veterans who had not graduated from high school." Women's schools began to admit men. School calendars were adjusted; refresher courses were designed; special counseling centers were set up; advanced credit for military "learning experiences" was offered. The schools did everything in their power to help the veteran adjust to the school, and the school to the veteran. Everything, that is, that didn't cost too much.

Though budgets continued to grow, they did not keep pace with enrollments. The colleges and universities coped with the new problem of overused facilities and faculties by increasing class sizes and the proportion of graduate students and lower-level faculty who did the teaching. At the University of Wisconsin, "Classes doubled and tripled their prewar size and public address systems in class became common. The number of faculty at all ranks also set new records, but the most significant increase came at the lowest levels." Between 1939–40 and 1947–48, the number of associate and full professors at Wisconsin increased by 41 percent. But the number of graduate assistants and instructors increased by almost 110 percent.

Nothing however seemed to discourage the returning veterans. Housed in prefabricated slums, their classrooms in Quonset huts or barracks, the veterans continued to enroll:

> Veterans broke very conceivable enrollment record. . . . By the fall of 1947, at the peak of veteran enrollment, the number of males registered and the percentage of persons eighteen to twenty years old enrolled in colleges had more than doubled the prewar records; total college enrollment, greater by over a million, had climbed by seventy-five percent. For three years the majority of all male students were veterans and one semester veterans came within a fraction of a percentage point of being the majority of all students.[16]

Some of these students would, of course, have gone on to college even without the federal funds. But there were many who would never have had the chance.

When Joe College of the newspaper cartoons began to look more like G.I. Joe of the trenches than Dink Stover of Yale, it was clear that a significant shift had occurred in the college and university student population. No one had planned this "democ-cratization." In fact, the original committees had at first pro-posed granting veteran's benefits only to students whose schooling had been interrupted by war. But this legislation was never a real possibility. Given the pressures of wartime, the lobbying of the Legion, and—above all else—the specter of an army of unemployed veterans marching on government and corporate headquarters, it was almost preordained that benefits would be extended to as many veterans as possible for as long as possible.

The legislation as passed offered aid to all who sought it. Contrary to the experts' predictions, large numbers did seek it—more than 2.3 million veterans in all. Of these, the most conser-vative estimates concluded that almost a half million would not have been able to attend college without the federal scholar-ships. These were the veterans who came from the least wealthy and least formally educated families, who had never dreamed of entering a profession, who were most likely married, and who "had been out of school longer, served longer, been overseas longer."

Surprisingly enough, for the higher education experts at least, these veterans who were not traditional "college material" man-aged to do as well as those who would have attended college, benefits or not. Every test, evaluation, and survey showed the same results: "The veterans who would not have gone to college without the G.I. Bill 'earned slightly better grades relative to ability than did those who probably would have attended in any case.'" When all veterans were measured against nonvet-erans, the differences in performance were even more striking.

During the early autumn of 1947, Benjamin Fine [of the *New York Times*] toured campuses throughout the East and Middle West and found college presidents and professors impressed by the "maturity and eagerness and better than average grades" of veterans. "The G.I.'s," Fine wrote, "are hogging the honor rolls and the Dean's lists." *Newsweek* pointed out that not one of Columbia University's 7,826 veterans "was in serious scholastic difficulty at the last marking period." Dur-ing the spring semester of 1947 only thirty-five of the 6,010 veterans at the University of Minnesota suffered academic dismissal, about one-half of one percent compared to the normal civilian rate of over ten percent. At Hobart College four civilians flunked out for each veteran.

The returning veterans were doing this well even though they had avoided the softer academic programs prescribed for them. The higher education experts, Hutchins among them, had predicted that the "nontraditional" students on G.I. benefits would enroll in the vocational rather than the more rigorous and intellectually demanding liberal arts courses. They were wrong. At the University of Wisconsin, the percentage of veterans enrolled in a liberal arts curriculum was 38.1 percent compared to 25.5 percent for nonveterans. The percentage of veterans in the School of Commerce was 13.9 percent compared with 44.0 percent for the nonveterans.[17]

The veterans knew precisely what a college education should entail—and they settled for, and received, nothing less. They were fortunate that they didn't have to. Because the G.I. Bill was not intended as an "educational" measure, but as antidepression, unemployment relief, it was not used to reform higher education from above. No power of the purse was wielded in connection with the funds. No control was imposed on the students or the institutions that received their tuition money. The higher education system did what it pleased with the income generated by its new veteran/students. And the students themselves, with one exception, determined which institutions would receive the money. Only in the case of the unaccredited Negro colleges of the South were benefits denied because of this lack of accreditation. But in this instance also, the federal assistance simply maintained the status quo without intervening in the normal functioning of the academic system. The Negro colleges had always been discriminated against. The G.I. Bills perpetuated the practice.[18]

The World War II veterans were the first generation of nontraditional college students, i.e., those from families who could not afford to pay their way. In future decades, many more students, veterans and nonveterans, would follow them into college, but with one crucial distinction.

The veterans, as we have seen, were invited into institutions to sit and learn in classrooms already populated by those whose class background and family income assured them a seat, regardless of state assistance. In the middle 1960s, though millions of nontraditional students would be offered assistance to continue their schooling after high school, very few would be given such latitude in choosing their institutions and curricula.

If the G.I. funds democratized the student population without transforming the institutional structure of higher education, the state assistance that would begin to flow freely again in the middle 1960s would have the opposite effect: it would transform the institutional structure but without democratizing the student population.

The G.I. Bill planning process, perhaps more than the legislation itself, established a dangerous precedent. As President Hutchins of Chicago complained, the state planners were using the colleges and universities to solve social problems that had nothing to do with them. "Education is not a device for coping with mass unemployment," he argued. But no one listened. The state planners were not primarily, or even secondarily, concerned with the future of the higher education institutions. They were worried about the stability of American society in postwar—and the irreversible effects of immediate and massive veterans' unemployment. If the colleges and universities could be utilized to alleviate the problem, federal funds would be diverted in their direction. The lesson was clear: the colleges and universities were an important national resource, not simply as educational institutions but as all-purpose problem solvers.

13

In the "National Interest": The Private Universities in Postwar

The war came to a close more rapidly than had been predicted. From beginning to end, the alliance of state, corporation, and university fought it the American way. Government provided the funds, industry the planes, the university the bomb.

Contrary to those dire warnings, no second Pearl Harbor befell the nation in the months following V.J. Day. The depression never returned. The American consumer—tempted, taunted, and teased by the promise of automatic toasters, electric coffeemakers, compact dishwashers, ice cube-ejecting refrigerators, static-free radios, and brand new all-American homes to contain these items—embarked on a buying spree that knew few limits. By the time their wartime savings had been spent, business and government were well on their way towards fashioning more permanent (though no less foolproof) safeguards against the threat of recurrent depression.[1]

Fortunately for the corporations and the economic and political systems whose security was tied to their prosperity, the peace was much shorter than the war that preceded it—or the war that succeeded it. Cold War followed World War, and the economy that had been mobilized to fight the Germans could be redirected towards another set of enemies without ever having to be demobilized.

From World War to Cold War:
the state and the corporation

The American people were told that the nation was going to war so soon again not because government wanted it that way but because it had no choice. The Cold War, like the Second World War, was presented as a moralistic, defensive war of "containment." Still, in spite of the rhetoric, the Cold War was waged not to defend the American way as much as to extend it. Communism had to be rolled back so that American goods and capital could be rolled into every corner of the world.[2]

The United States alone among nations emerged from the war in better economic shape than it had entered. The question for state and corporate planners in 1945 was not how to return to prewar normalcy but how best to use American dollars and military strength to pry open the door to raw materials, investment possibilities, and new and expanded markets.[3]

The Cold War provided the justification and rationale on which renewed state support for the corporations could be sustained. The federal government opened foreign doors for American business with military pressure and "financial aid" packages. It also supported the industrial giants by buying their goods directly in the name of national security.[4]

As industry and government discovered during the war, military spending is the perfect public works project. No sooner is one generation of weapons off the assembly line than another must replace it. As *U.S. News and World Report* editorialized in the midst of the Cold War: "Government planners figure they have found the magic formula for almost endless good times. . . . *Cold War* is the catalyst. Cold War is an automatic pump primer. . . . Cold War demands, if fully exploited, are almost limitless."

Just as World War II military spending brought the country out of depression in the early forties, Cold War defense spending would keep it depression-proof in the fifties.[5]

From Cold War to Korea to Cold War to Vietnam, the defense budget was redirected to different weapons for different enemies but would never significantly decline as a percentage of the Gross National Product. From the Cold War, 1946 to 1950, through the Korean War, 1951 to 1953, military spending jumped from 5.1 percent of the GNP to 12.3 percent of the GNP. Throughout the fifties, it would continue at a rate of 10 percent of the GNP.[6]

Though the state, even in its most "laissez-faire" incarnations, had supported the profit-making activities of big business and the capitalist system that made them possible, "the New Deal and World War II forced business and government to work more closely together." In the postwar period the relationship became nearly incestuous. Eisenhower's secretary of defense, Charles Wilson, former president of General Motors, perhaps put it a little too bluntly for the public when he told the Senate Armed Forces Committee that he, for one, always assumed that "what was good for our country was good for General Motors, and vice versa."[7]

There was no conspiracy here. The state did not bother to hide its interest in maintaining business prosperity. In fact, it continued to argue, with increased emphasis, that the only way to protect and preserve the American way was to protect and preserve the corporate way.[8]

In the battle of ideology, American goods stood stronger than American words. The American way was the better way because it included a chicken in every pot, a car in every garage, and a new refrigerator for every kitchen. Though schoolchildren were duly warned of Khrushchev's threat to bury us, business and government were convinced that, given the proper assistance, the American corporation could by itself win the Cold War, burying the International Communist Conspiracy beneath tons and tons of modern capitalist commodities.[9]

For business to really prosper, much state assistance was needed. The government was already pledged to purchase at noncompetitive prices a significant part of industrial output in the form of military goods and hardware. But American industry, dominated by the giant corporate monopolies, needed support not only in selling its goods but in producing them.

Production and distribution costs are a primary element in the business of profit making. The lower these costs, the greater the profits. In the postwar period, the federal government expanded into areas such as highway building, satellite launching, and waste disposal, in part because improvements in these areas assisted the corporations in cutting their basic costs.

Better highways cut production and distribution costs by cutting the price of transporting raw materials to the plants, finished products to the stores, workers to work, and buyers to markets. Satellites cut the cost of overseas communications for multinational corporations transacting business around the world. Federal support for local sewage treatment centers used tax money to dispose of corporate wastes. Through the mediation of the state, the corporations got what they needed without any one of them having to pay for it exclusively or disproportionately. [10]

State assistance to business was not a new phenomenon in American life. The state had provided the nineteenth-century railroads with enough free land to pave their way west with considerable profit. The differences between these nineteenth-century "incentives" and the twentieth-century assistance were in scale and dimension. More money was offered the postwar corporations—and in more ways.

The R&D explosion

Relative to the discussion in this book, the most striking departure from prewar practice was the increasing level of state support for scientific research and development. Such support had not been proffered earlier in the century in part because it had not been sought. American industry was far behind its European counterparts in appreciating the dollar value of scientific research. [11]

It was only during and immediately after World War II that the American corporations began to discover the long-term profitability of R&D investments, especially when paid for by the state. President Truman was warned repeatedly that federal support of basic research and development initiated during the war had to be continued. It was crucial not only to the Cold War struggle against the communists but in the export war against all competitors.

The science editor of the *New York Times* summed up the new situation in testimony before a Senate subcommittee. No matter what the policies of the past, the postwar state had to step into the middle of the scientific enterprise—with funding, coordination, and long-term planning:

> We have followed in scientific and industrial research what the economists call the laissez-faire policy which is now outmoded in economics but which still prevails in research.
>
> Now, I strongly disapprove of anything like the imposition of a state philosophy or ideology upon every shade of human thinking of the kind you have in Russia.
>
> On the other hand, I have nothing but admiration for the organization of science such as constituted in Russia. There you find that science is propagated on all fronts. [12]

Postwar planners—from the scientific community, from industry and government—continued making the same point, though never with the suggestion that we should follow the Russian example. Still, acknowledged or not, the United States in postwar abandoned its earlier laissez-faire attitude towards research and development, opting instead for the Russian or German model.

Federal expenditures in the area of R&D "grew at an annual rate of 24.9 percent" between 1940 and 1964. While in 1940 less than 1 percent of all U.S. budget outlays had been spent for R&D, by 1965 the proportion had jumped to 12.6 percent. In the 1950s alone the percentage of the Gross National Product devoted to research and development increased from 1.1 percent to 2.78 percent. [13]

Most of the R&D money came from the federal government and went to industry for "development." A good deal, however, went to the universities in support of "fundamental research." Higher education, which in 1938 had received about $6.2 million for R&D, by 1947 was receiving $150.0 million, by 1952, $220.0 million, by 1963, 760.0 million. [14]

Private industry benefited directly and indirectly from this increased funding for university R&D. Not only was the profit margin on military production enlarged by the federal subsidy for research and development, but the spin-offs from such research provided nonmilitary production with new materials, new products, and new technologies at almost no cost. In the immediate postwar period, "many specific developments financed largely by defense appropriations . . . proved to be of great benefit to industry in general, for example, the jet aircraft and the electronic computer." According to J. R. Killian, distinguished American scientist and chairman of the Corporation of MIT, the "close relationship" between industry and university in the postwar period "made it possible for new ideas, new discoveries, and new data to flow more easily from university laboratory to application. . . . Research and development in scientific and engineering institutions [have] made major contributions to the origin and growth of the computer industry. The chemical, electrical, and nuclear industries have derived much from research carried out in both university and nonuniversity laboratories."[45]

Federally funded research laboratories, on and off campus, were especially helpful in American industry's never-ending battle for new products to sell a public not yet weary of the old. Teflon and Tang were but two examples of new, space-age products developed in federally funded laboratories.[16]

The universities were doing double duty for private industry. They were carrying out basic and applied research while simultaneously training the personnel private industry would one day employ in its own laboratories. The arms and new product races had generated an enormous need for engineers, scientists, and researchers in all fields, at all levels of specialization. Between 1954 and 1965, the annual rate of increase in R&D personnel averaged over 7 percent, compared with a 1.5 percent increase in the labor force as a whole. By 1965 over one-half million researchers were employed throughout the country, 70 percent of them by the corporations.[17]

Though the shock of the Russian success with Sputnik in October 1957 is often credited with much of the increase in federal funding for research and the schooling of researchers, the rate of growth in this area was no greater after than before "this devastating blow to the prestige of the United States as the leader in the scientific and technical world." What Sputnik did was provide corporate scientists, educators, and politicians with a new context in which to argue for federal aid to education. The Cold War had generated the arms race; the arms race precipitated the "scientists" or "knowledge race."

In the weeks and months after Sputnik, federal legislators spared no rhetorical flourishes in expounding the dire need for funding to close the "scientists' gap." Educators who in the past had viewed federal intervention with alarm found it much more difficult to voice their reservations when the question was phrased in terms of "national security."[18]

Though it was difficult to reach a consensus on issues related to education in a Congress divided along religious and sectional lines between those who supported and those who feared the ultimate social implications of federal aid, money could be spent to develop suggested science and math curricula and to entice local public schools to adopt them. Money could also be spent to close the "scientists' gap" at the point of production: the graduate schools.[19]

In the past, funds had not been allocated for the training of student scientists per se. The prestigious and prosperous universities received the bulk of their federal funding for specific research projects. Graduate students were trained by working on these projects as unpaid apprentice/assistants. Only after 1958, when the U.S. and the U.S.S.R. were engaged in a full-fledged "knowledge" race, did the federal government begin to supply scholarship, fellowship, traineeship, and loan money to aid these students through their graduate training. By the mid-sixties it was estimated that up to four-fifths of all graduate students in the natural sciences were receiving some form of federal assistance.[20]

Of research and education

As we have seen, the universities that accepted federal research funds during World War II were not concerned with the educational impact of such funding. They had been asked and had accepted a new assignment "in the national interest." Between World War and Cold War, there was no opportunity for institutional reflection on the long-range thrust of such a commitment. The universities simply supplied the government with what it wanted—and was willing to pay for. The Cold War, Mc-Carthyite "Red Scare" atmosphere of the middle 1950s muted potential critics and provided supporters of the new university role with an ideological screen to deflect criticism. In the name of value-free rationality, of "academic freedom," university faculty could not be questioned nor could scrutiny be given the funding or the projects for which it was granted.[21]

If function is dictated by funding, then the leading universities were becoming more and more research centers and less and less educational institutions. For the 1959–1960 academic year, Cal Tech, MIT, and Princeton received over 75 percent of their total budget from federal R&D funds; the University of California at San Diego and the University of Chicago, more than 50 percent; Harvard, the University of Michigan, Cornell, and Stanford, more than 24 percent.[22]

It is theoretically possible that the universities receiving the bulk of the federal funds could have undertaken their research tasks without drawing energy and funds away from their traditional educational role. But this was not the case. As the institutional funds devoted to "organized research" increased between 1930 and 1958 from 3.5 percent to 16 percent of the "total current expenditures," the money allocated for "resident instruction" decreased from 44 percent to 32.5 percent.

A good deal of the federal funding allocated for university research never even reached the campuses. By 1960 as much money was being spent in off-campus affiliated research centers as on campus. These off-campus centers were not only "not connected with graduate training" but, according to Fritz Machlup, competed "with it by draining the teaching faculties of some of their personnel."[23]

Even when we consider that research conducted on campus, it is not clear that it had any positive impact on the education of students, graduate or undergraduate. In 1961 Alice Rivlin tried to directly answer, for the Brookings Institute, the question we are asking: "To what extent is research support aid to higher education?" Although she concluded that "in many ways, the university as a whole benefits from . . . federal research support" when such support went towards research conducted on campus, she also concluded that

> heavy involvement of regular faculty members with federal research is not without costs, both to the university and to the students. Even where the government undertakes to compensate the university for the full indirect costs associated with individual research projects, some administrative and other costs of a large volume of government research still may not be fully compensated. Moreover, although the government may pay a portion of a faculty member's salary in order to compensate the university for the time he takes away from teaching to devote to government research, the portion may be unrealistically small. Some of the faculty members with government research projects spend most of their time on research and the administrative and fund-raising activities associated with sponsored research to the neglect of their students, especially their undergraduate students.[24]

If the impact on education was at best uncertain in those few universities that received huge amounts of federal money, what of the vast majority of colleges and universities that received nothing at all? Clark Kerr, writing about the "federal grant university" in 1966, reported that only six universities were receiving 57 percent of all federal R&D money, while twenty were receiving 79 percent of the total—and this was an improvement from earlier periods when the money had been even less widely distributed.[25]

The have-not institutions suffered greatly from their comparative lack of federal money and the scientists it supported. As Rivlin concluded: "They [the majority of schools without research funding] find it more difficult and expensive to maintain a good faculty and a stimulating atmosphere than if the federal research money were being spent entirely outside the academic marketplace—or not at all."[26]

The universities and faculty members who welcomed the research grants—from the Defense Department and the Atomic Energy Commission throughout the fifties, from these sources and the national health and space agencies throughout the sixties and seventies—adjusted their traditional mission as educators to meet the requirements of the postwar productive order. The new funds—and the new university role they engendered— increased the independence of the professors in such a way that the university as an educational agency was weakened. As Harold Hodgkinson concluded in *Institutions in Transition*, a Carnegie Commission Report, one of the more significant changes in higher education in the postwar period was the "rather striking increase in the numbers of faculty who do not teach." The "institutional reward structure for faculty" was transformed by the inflow of federal money. Faculty were no longer rewarded with status or material benefits because of their educational role. According to Alain Touraine, "Recent developments, in fact, have led university people to define themselves increasingly in terms of their scientific role; neither teaching nor administrative problems are major preoccupations."[27]

As Clark Kerr, himself a former president of a "federal grant university" summed up the postwar institutional changes, "some faculty members [have tended] to shift their identification and loyalty from the university to the agency in Washington. Their concern with the general welfare of the university is eroded. . . . The university . . . becomes to an extent a 'hotel.' The [federal funding] agency becomes the new alma mater."[28]

New funds and functions

In the postwar period, the universities and their faculties welcomed funding from any and all sources. Those who paid the piper called the tune. From the 1950s on, besides the space, defense, atomic energy—and since the middle sixties, health— agencies, only the foundations and some of the larger corporations could afford the price.[29]

The foundations could not in the 1950s hope to exercise the influence they had once held. Though the sums available for dispersal had increased, they had not risen as rapidly as the basic costs of operation of the colleges and universities. If, to borrow an example from Curti and Nash's *Philanthropy in the*

Shaping of American Higher Education, "the Carnegie Corporation's annual appropriations [in its early days] were a 15th of
the yearly income of higher education institutions, by 1940 the
fraction had decreased to a 140th."[30]

Still, the foundations had money to spend and specific purposes for which to spend it. A primary purpose (though perhaps less important after the war than earlier in the century)
was to withdraw from public view the corporate Mr. Hyde,
screening him with the foundation Dr. Jekyl. Henry Ford and
John D. Rockefeller, not the most benevolent of men, established the Ford and Rockefeller foundations: family and corporate names were rescued from opprobrium, their fortunes
from too large a tax bite.

Earlier in the century the industrial giants had endowed
schools of business at the leading universities. In the postwar
period their foundation descendents created schools of industrial management and international institutes for the same reasons: because the corporations required but could not afford to
train such specialists on their own.

As the corporations reached out to markets, labor, and raw
materials in every corner of the world, the need grew for international marketing experts, foreign language and culture specialists and "foreign relations" advisers for corporate, CIA, and
State Department offices. Foundation money was spent to establish Russian Institutes at Columbia and Harvard, a School of
International Studies at Columbia, an Institute of International
Studies at Berkeley.

Money spent in the universities was justified by the foundations that spent it—and the universities that accepted it—in the
name of "national security." The international institutes, it was
claimed, would be instrumental in the Cold War struggle
against communism. That they would also be important sources
of foreign specialists for the larger corporations with multinational interests was not advertised.[31]

In all these expenditures, the foundations saw an absolute
congruity between corporate needs and the national interest.
Expertly trained foreign specialists and industrial managers
would in the long run protect and preserve the American

way—by preserving and extending the corporate capitalist system. The federal government officially recognized this corporate contribution to the national welfare by establishing tax laws that, in essence, allowed the corporations to spend as much federal money as they did their own. Of every dollar of corporate money donated to higher education, fifty-two cents would have gone to the government in taxes if not spent "philanthropically."[32]

Up until the 1950s, most corporate money spent for higher education had been funneled through the nonprofit foundations. Only after a favorable court decision in 1951 did the corporations begin to make substantial contributions on their own.

The corporation money went almost exclusively to the private colleges and universities. Irving Olds, former chairman of the board of United States Steel and one of the more important champions of corporate aid, solicited contributions by emphasizing the symbolic and direct ties between the private universities and the private enterprise system: "Capitalism and free enterprise owe their survival in no small degree to the existence of our private independent universities. . . . If the day ever comes when our tax-supported competitors can offer the youth of America a better education than we can—and at a lower price—we are through."

The private universities were rendering the corporations a valuable service by training future executives and specialists, and by providing faculty expertise for corporate problem-solving research. As Olds and other corporate sponsors warned their colleagues, such services could only be guaranteed as long as the private universities remained solvent without federal financial assistance—and the inevitable control it would entail.[33]

Though a good deal of corporate money went towards supporting the private universities, and no strings were attached, more than half was spent for specially designed "social research" projects. According to Haydn Smith, vice-president of research for the Council for Financial Aid to Education, which oversaw much corporate giving, overall corporate support of higher education increased through the fifties and sixties because research grants had proven to be good investments. "For many industries the productivity of funds allocated to research has been much higher for university-sponsored programs than for 'in-house' efforts."[34]

Foundation and corporate funds for "social research" were not of the magnitude of federal funds for scientific research. Yet, in the long run, they exerted the same type of influence. If the federal funding agencies had become the alma mater of university scientists and engineers, the foundations and corporations came to play the same role for the social scientists, and with the same results. The larger universities and their faculty were diverted from their traditional educational role into a new one: the buying, selling, and management of specialized knowledge of value to the corporations.

Theoretically, grants to support social research might have enhanced the educational role of the university and its faculty. But, as was the case with the impact of the federal R&D money, the opposite occurred. Grant recipients "found [themselves], willingly or not, completely relieved of teaching responsibility, at least as it concerned undergraduates."

As Curti and Nash concluded, describing the impact of foundation funding in almost the same terms Clark Kerr had used to describe the effect of federal research funding: "The millions of dollars of foundation philanthropy have encouraged a gradual redefinition of the role of the professor within the framework of American higher education. . . . Colleges and especially universities have tended to become places where talented scholars hang their hats while pursuing the answers to problems of advanced research rather than institutions primarily concerned with instruction."[35]

The postwar corporate order was more reliant on new products, markets, technologies, materials, and specially trained executives and specialists than ever before. The federal government took on itself the financial burden of providing the corporations with the research and the trained personnel required to maintain a "reasonable" profit margin. The university's role was as middle-management or subcontractor. It oversaw the dispersal of the funds and provided the researchers and corporate personnel trainers with the staff and facilities they needed.

Unfortunately the funds flowing through the universities did not leave them untouched. The federal funding agencies, foundations, and corporations bought a piece of the university and used it for their own ends, which were not necessarily educational.

Higher education, which had up until the Second World War been subjected to some criticism for its "irrelevance," its unconcern with the society around it, would no longer have to answer such charges. As Daniel Bell so proudly reported, by the middle seventies, the university had become "the primary institution of the post-industrial society. In the past twenty years, the university—and by 'the university' I have in mind the elite group—has taken on a vast number of enlarged functions: in basic research, as a service institution, and in the expansion of general education."[36]

Unfortunately, as we have already seen and as we shall see again, none of these enlarged functions had much to contribute to the educational role of the private universities and colleges.

14

A "Rising Tide" of Students: The Public Sector

Like other patriotic institutions, higher education enlisted for service in World War II and re-enlisted for the Cold War. The universities and colleges enthusiastically provided the military and private industry with trained personnel and scientific R&D and the society-at-large with the best unemployment insurance federal money could buy.

The G.I.'s, over two million of them, were welcomed into the institutions of higher education, where, as we have seen, they prospered. The schools that accepted them did as well: the money the veterans brought with them enabled the institutions to survive and remain relatively solvent through what could have been a difficult period.

Though the G.I. Bill had the effect of bailing out the nation's colleges and universities, it was originally designed not to aid education as much as to deter unemployment. In this it was most effective. Between 1945 and 1948, with G.I. enrollments close to one million, the unemployment rate stayed below 4 percent. Only in 1949, with veteran enrollment on the decline, did the rate climb back above 5 percent where it remained until the outbreak of another war.[1]

Though the postwar buying spree and the diversion of veterans from unemployment lines to college campuses had forestalled a postwar depression, the specter of massive unemployment was not entirely exorcised. The Employment Act of 1946 codified what would become a chief task of the federal government throughout the postwar period: the maintenance of unemployment levels at a rate high enough to provide employers with a reserve army to draw from but not high enough to recreate depression conditions and the possibility of social explosion.[2]

Fewer "good" jobs and more job hunters

Holding unemployment down to a reasonable level through the fifties and sixties was no simple task. The corporations—through automation at home and relocation overseas—displaced workers; the federal government was expected to get them back to work or at least defuse the social discontent and potential economic catastrophe they represented.

The unions took little responsibility for the shrinkage in the number of workers. They asked management instead for a simple *quid pro quo:* higher wages and better fringe benefits for those workers who kept their jobs. The corporations obtained from the unions the agreement not to interfere with cost-cutting, labor-saving improvements. Those union members with jobs got wage increases high enough to at least keep pace with inflation. The consuming public paid the bill in higher prices and a generalized inflationary spiral.[3]

While, from 1950 to 1970, the absolute number of "blue-collar" jobs increased slightly, the percentage of such jobs in the total workforce stayed about the same or declined. The Bureau of Labor Statistics figures, as reported by Harry Braverman, showed an actual decline in employment in the "manufacturing, construction, and other 'goods producing' industries" from 40.9 percent of the total nonagricultural workforce in 1950 to 33 percent in 1970.[4]

All things being equal, this moderate decline in blue-collar employment would not have been serious. But, unfortunately for those out of work, the decline in blue-collar employment occurred at the same time as the demand for these jobs was expanded by the addition of millions of rural workers to the working-age population.

Between 1940 and 1970 over twenty million had to leave the land, most displaced by the mechanization of the farms they had worked. Many of the white migrants moved close by to expanding cities and towns with jobs for them. The Southern black migrants, over 4 million of them, could not move to the adjacent Southern cities. Centuries of racism would have made life there difficult, employment impossible. The majority of black migrants moved into the Northern cities where they believed work would be available.[5]

As we have seen throughout this study, the newcomers to the cities have always been consigned to the bottom levels of the workplace hierarchy. The differences between the bottom in the nineteenth and twentieth centuries were, however, enormous. The old and new immigrants, the Irish and Italians, though relegated to the lowest, dirtiest, worst-paying jobs, could still find work—if only on a day-to-day basis. The blacks had a much more difficult time. They were not only victimized by discrimination and prejudice to a greater degree than any of the previous migrant groups. It was also their historical misfortune to have been forced into urban areas at a time when employment was declining in those job categories that had traditionally been filled by the newly arrived city residents.

The rural migrants, both black and white, were not the only ones to enter the urban marketplace in the postwar decades. Women, recruited for work during the war, in postwar preferred—or were compelled by economic necessity—to maintain their places. Many were not willing to return to their dependent unpaid status as workers in the home when they could achieve some degree of independence as paid workers outside it. Through the fifties and sixties, many women went back to work because they wanted to; many more, however, had no choice. With the relative decline of blue-collar employment, working-class women often found themselves the most stable breadwinners in the family. Only rarely did the husband have a job so secure and profitable that the wife could, if she desired, leave the workplace permanently.

The movement of women back to work was further accelerated by employers who welcomed women because they could be paid less and because the job market had expanded in white-collar jobs defined as "women's work." The American democratic ethos that had a century before so troubled poor Mrs. Trollope because she could not find a willing servant anywhere continued through the twentieth century to deter white men from accepting many lower-level white-collar positions. Clerical work, while increasing its percentage of the total workforce through the 1950s and 1960s, remained women's work in part because, in addition to being a typist, file clerk, and receptionist, the secretary was expected to be her boss's personal servant.

All of these factors were more than enough to counteract the "homemaker" propaganda which urged women to return to their homes. According to Harry Braverman, the "labor force participation rate," which for men declined "from some 87 percent to only 80 percent between 1947 and 1971, increased for women from 31.8 percent to 43.4 percent.[6]

The increase of agricultural unemployment and the flight of the unemployed to the city, coupled with the return of women to the workplace, increased the number of those looking for work to dangerous levels. This danger to the social status quo was further aggravated by the fact that more and more women and men were not just looking for work but for "decent" work.

In the postwar decades more Americans than ever before believed themselves entitled to a share of the wealth, a piece of the American dream. Young men and women wanted jobs that promised upward mobility. Parents wanted the same for their children. They believed that each generation should start at least one step up the social ladder from where the previous generation had left off.[7]

Those who in postwar demanded entrance into the American middle class for their children, if not for themselves, were often second- and third-generation descendents of the "new immigrants" who had arrived in this country at the turn of the century. As Peter Schrag has argued so forcefully in *The Decline of the Wasp*, World War II for these working-class Americans had been the true "Americanizing" experience. The war had stretched the distance between here and there, making impossible, for Italians especially, the maintenance of any "dual allegiance." Forced to choose between allegiances and to seal that choice with the blood of their young, many Southern and Eastern Europeans cut the umbilical cords that united them with their roots across the sea. They now expected their children to be rewarded with title to the American dream, a secure middle-class existence with all the commodities and privileges it entailed. Unfortunately their demands for inclusion in the middle-class mainstream came at precisely that moment when the real opportunities for upward mobility were dwindling.[8]

According to David Riesman and Christopher Jencks, who surveyed in retrospect the postwar possibilities for upward mobility, there had been

> no significant change in the distribution of income [in the two decades following 1945].
>
> If the income distribution is taken as a crude index of the distribution of occupational skills, responsibilities, and prestige, it also seems fair to conclude that these latter have not been redistributed to any significant extent since 1945. In that case it also follows that the relative size of the various social classes has remained essentially unchanged for the past twenty years.[9]

To the men and women who constituted the still significant though now declining blue-collar sector of the working class, these conclusions would have come as no surprise. Still, there were enough exceptions to the social stasis and enough attention paid them to give faith to the discouraged.

For those who sought for their children a route into the middle classes, there was one cardinal rule to follow: keep them out of the factories and blue-collar jobs. As we have seen in the first two parts of this study, working people had recognized more than a century earlier that such employment had become—and would probably remain—a dead end as far as upward mobility was concerned. This perception had not changed much at all in the half-century since the National Association of Manufacturers had looked to industrial schooling to lure "Americans" back into the factory. Although the company literature painted a very different picture, for workers and public alike, Ely Chinoy in his 1955 study of automobile workers found that for the great majority "without special training or advanced education . . . there [were] sharp limits on the possibility of future advancement."[10]

Those who had not given up dreamed the dream as American as apple pie. They looked not to a future of wealth and leisure as much as to one where they could live comfortably as their own boss. Unfortunately, as they well knew, their chances of "making it" were not very great.[11]

The absence of possibility for advancement from within the factory—or into self-employment—in 1950 as in 1900 made white-collar work seem that much more appealing. Young men and women who looked with distaste at factory or blue-collar work were not nearly as distressed with the idea of office work. Neither were their parents, who believed that any shift from blue- to white-collar work was a step upward. Office work, even if it involved little more than filing papers or adding columns of figures, was considered an improvement on the alternatives, especially when the employer was one of the larger corporations with "room at the top" for the ambitious.

The corporate form of organization had become too powerful to ignore or compete with. Young men and women chose to don their gray flannel suits, to join the "organization," not simply because their generation was by nature unimaginative or conformist but because the opportunities available outside the organization were few and declining.[12]

Just as it had been assumed at the turn of the century that the path into the white-collar world ran through high school, it was now believed that a college degree was the route into those jobs that offered the greatest opportunity for further advancement. We have already seen how in Middletown parents anxious about their children's futures had pushed them towards college where they could, if nothing else, delay entrance into the work world while getting an education and making contacts. Ely Chinoy, interviewing auto workers in the middle 1950s, discovered among them even greater faith in schooling as the avenue to upward mobility. They too believed—or continued to hope—that the more schooling their children received, the better were their chances for success as adults.[13]

Postwar plans and planners: new goals for higher education

State and corporate policymakers were not unmindful of the increasing importance of college in the plans of those seeking a better life for their children. They were in fact quite in agreement that college was the best place for most young people to widen their employment horizons.

From the late 1940s through the 1960s, higher education planners at every level—from Washington, the state capitals, and the foundations—would argue for the expansion of access to higher education, not simply because that was what the people wanted but because that was what the economy needed.

Unemployment was rising and would continue to rise as farm employment decreased, automation increased, and millions of women entered the labor force. Prolonging schooling through the early twenties might not solve the problem; it would certainly make it more manageable.

The first and most prestigious postwar planning commission, established by President Truman and chaired by George Zook, president of the American Council on Education, declared in 1947 that the nation had to begin to enroll in its higher education institutions a much larger percentage of college-age youth. With an excess of candor not usually found in government reports, the President's Commission directly refuted "the old, comfortable idea that 'any boy can get a college education who has it in him.' . . . Low family income, together with the rising costs of education," the commission reported, constituted "an almost impassable barrier to college education for many young people."

It was these young people who had to be admitted, and quickly, to college, not only because their exclusion was giving "democracy" a bad name overseas but because they had to be trained and credentialed for the "semiprofessional" and technical jobs being created in the public and private sectors.

> Because of advancing technology, the occupational center of our economic system is shifting away from the major producing industries.
>
> One result of this development is a new and rapidly growing need for trained semiprofessional workers. . . . To meet the needs of the economy our schools must train many more young people for employment as medical secretaries, recreational leaders, hotel and restaurant managers, aviators, salesmen in fields like life insurance and real estate, photographers, automobile and electrical technicians, and so on through a long list of positions in the business and professional world.
>
> Education on the technician level—that is, the training of medical technicians, dental hygienists, nurses' aides, laboratory technicians—offers one practical solution for the acute shortage of professional personnel in medicine, dentistry, and nursing.[14]

The President's Commission was setting "new goals" for American higher education. In the past, the colleges and universities had in the broadest sense served as vocational training grounds for the upper echelon of the workplace pyramid: the professionals, the social, cultural, political, and corporate leaders. Now the commission was arguing that higher education had to accept the additional responsibility of training students for the lower-level white-collar, paraprofessional, and technical positions.

Referring directly to the postwar experience with the returning veterans and buttressing the argument with "scientific" data from G.I. intelligence testing, the commissioners argued that a great many of those denied postsecondary schooling for financial reasons, could profit from such schooling if given the chance. The nation, engaged in a Cold War struggle for global political, economic, and moral supremacy, could ill afford to squander any of its human resources.[15]

The commission called for "democratized" higher education but carefully circumscribed the meaning it gave this word. Democracy meant not equal opportunity for all or an equal education for all. The higher education planners were in basic agreement with President Russell of Teachers College, who had proclaimed in the context of the debate on high school expansion a half-century earlier that it was foolish and potentially dangerous to school "the masses in precisely the same manner as we do those who are to be our leaders." The postwar planners did not intend to "democratize" higher education by admitting the "masses" to the institutions now attended by their future "leaders." They made it quite clear that the expansion of higher education they envisioned would not be accomplished by requiring or requesting the private colleges and universities to enroll those traditionally excluded, but rather by enlarging existing public institutions and building new two-year "community colleges." While the commission argued that up to 49 percent of college-age youth should be in some post-secondary institution, they were not recommending that all of them attend four-year colleges. As was explained, "The same kind and content of higher education are [not] desirable for all."[16]

The "tidal wave" approaches

The 1947 President's Commission had ambitious plans for America's colleges and universities, especially the public ones. It recommended not only a doubling of enrollment by 1960 but proposed a doubling of the proportion of the GNP devoted to education to pay for it. Unfortunately, at the time the report was released in 1947, the federal government was already spending close to one billion dollars on veterans' education. It was not prepared to spend any more.[17]

There were, however, only a limited supply of veterans. By 1949 those who had enrolled were getting ready to graduate. Between 1949 and 1951 alone, the colleges lost over 440,000 veteran students along with the millions of dollars they had brought with them.[18]

Though higher education was able to rebound from the loss of veterans, there was through the early fifties no increase in

enrollments. Only towards the middle of the decade did enrollments begin to expand: by some 43 percent for the public institutions and by 25 percent for the private. The increase followed
directly on the termination of the Korean War. With the cessa-
tion of hostilities, college-age youth lost their social utility. In
the five-year period from 1953 to 1958, the number of men on
active duty decreased by almost a million and the unemployment rate more than doubled.[19]

Many high school graduates were pushed into college by the
absence of jobs; many more were pulled in by the promise of
better jobs after graduation. Though the hard data remained
ambiguous concerning the relationship between a college degree and increased earnings, there was, according to Riesman
and Jencks, "a trend towards more popular *awareness* of the
connection between education and adult success." As the Ford
Foundation, summarizing the results of a poll of high school
students, put it in 1959, the fact that 69 percent of eighteen-
year-olds were "expected by the parents to go to college . . .
demonstrates that a college education has come to be widely
regarded as *sine qua non* of personal success, just as the high
school diploma did earlier."[20]

More and more high school students were getting their diplomas and going on to college—and without the federal and
state assistance that the 1947 President's Commission had recommended. (The only new incentive for attending was the neg-
ative one contained in the 1950 Selective Service Act which offered college students temporary draft deferments.) For the
foreseeable future this upward trend in enrollments was expected to continue. Every sign pointed in this direction: unemployment for high school graduates would remain high; the
numbers of college-age youth would increase; and the need for
college-educated (or credentialed) workers would expand.[21]

The public institutions responded to the increase in applicants by expanding their entering classes to admit all who met
their standards. The private colleges and universities responded
in the opposite manner. They maintained a constant level of enrollment, but as the number of qualified applicants rose, raised
both their standards for admission and their tuition. Through

the early fifties, private tuition "had averaged between two and three times public tuition." From 1956 to 1964, "it rose to about four times the public level. Or to put it another way, having hovered around 12 percent of median family income from 1928 to 1956, mean private tuition rose to 18 percent of family income in the next eight years." [22]

The increasing costs of attending private colleges and universities, as much as the new admission standards, contributed to the upward spiral in public sector enrollments as a percentage of total enrollment. More and more students, without federal or state scholarships, were deciding to go on to college. Because the state systems were, in general, required by state law to accept all high school graduates, the size and rate of expansion of the public sector was being determined almost exclusively by the students themselves. The state education planners, while applauding the rapid expansion of enrollment, could not allow it to continue unplanned, uncoordinated, and uncontrolled. [23]

California had in the late 1940s taken the lead in formulating and implementing specific plans to control the influx of new students. Now, in 1955, it commissioned a restudy of the state's needs in higher education. Between 1956 and 1959 alone, twenty-seven other states also took "official legislative or gubernatorial action to have statewide studies of their higher education institutions and the problems faced." [24]

In 1962, T. R. McConnell, author of the 1955 California *Restudy*, published under a Carnegie Corporation grant, *A General Pattern for American Public Higher Education*. McConnell, whose *Restudy* recommendations had already been embodied in law as the 1960 California Master Plan, warned other educators of the dangers that would befall their public institutions if they did not begin at once to implement statewide plans for the "rising tide" of new students. As he explained, "Educators might as well face up to the fundamental fact that it will not be up to them alone to determine how many young people will go to college in the future. . . . Mass education is here to stay. American higher education will become more rather than less inclusive." [25]

As David Henry, author of a much later Carnegie Commission report, observed, the metaphors used by McConnell and the other state planners betrayed their anxiety. To characterize the new students as a "rising tide" that might "inundate" the public institutions was to put the matter in the worst possible light.[26]

The state planners were worried that this "rising tide" would bring them too many students who, though meeting the requirements for admission set by state legislators, did not, in their opinion, belong in college. As McConnell himself put it, "Robert M. Hutchins once insisted that under effective teaching all students could master the great books. The evidence is clearly to the contrary." (Yet McConnell himself gave no evidence whatsoever to either refute Hutchins' position or support his own.)[27]

McConnell was neither the first nor the most influential educator to voice such fears about the "rising tide," the "flood tide," the "tidal wave" of new students. James Conant, whose credentials included service as president of Harvard in prewar, as chairman of the National Defense Research Committee during World War II, and as high commissioner for Germany in postwar, expressed his fears for the future in *The Citadel of Learning*, published in 1956.[28]

John Gardner, as influential a public servant and educational spokesman, speaking as president of the Carnegie Foundation in 1955 and for himself in *Excellence*, published in 1961, confronted directly the "danger" posed by the "tidal wave." As Gardner explained, higher education's social task was not simply to educate but to "sort-out": "Those who receive the most education are going to move into virtually all the key jobs. Thus the question 'Who should go to college?' translates itself into the more compelling question 'Who is going to manage the society?'" Once higher education had become a mass institution, how would future leaders be "sorted-out" from their followers, the corporate executives from the functionaries, the professionals from their assistants. More importantly, how would those sorted into the lower reaches of the labor force be convinced that the process that put them there had been a fair one? Was there some method, some magic formula through which access could be increased without damage to the "sorting-out" role of the nation's colleges and universities?[29]

There was such a method. And it was precisely the one the high school reformers had employed a half-century earlier to protect the secondary schools from another "tidal wave" of students. Just as the high school reformers had attempted to preserve the sanctity of the high schools by funneling the "plain people" into industrial and vocational programs, the higher education planners intended to maintain the selectivity of their colleges and universities by diverting the "tidal wave" of new students to other postsecondary institutions.

McConnell in his 1962 book, *A General Pattern for American Public Higher Education*, pointed to the University of Minnesota as an example of a "mass" institution that had maintained its high "selectivity" by instituting a new "policy of selective admission of Freshmen." High school graduates in the state were guaranteed entrance to the university (the state legislature would have allowed no less), but *not* to any part of it they chose. The tidal wave of new students was, in Minnesota, diverted away from the traditional four-year courses of study to the two-year General College of the University.[30]

California had been the first state in the union to formulate such "selective admissions" policies. James Conant, in his 1964 book, *Shaping Educational Policy*, recommended directly that "other states follow suit."[31]

The California Master Plan, which would become the model for so many other states, protected the "selectivity" of the four-year universities and colleges by state law. All but the top 12.5 percent (by grade point average) of the state's high school graduates were barred from the four-year state universities. All but the top 33 percent were barred from the four-year state colleges. But, and this was for the educational planners the key to the system, the same law that kept the lower two-thirds of each high school class out of the four-year institutions guaranteed them a place in the two-year community colleges.[32]

Here was the magic formula for maintaining selectivity within a mass institution. State systems of higher education could remain selective and "open-access" (i.e., open enrollment or open admission) simultaneously if, as in Minnesota and California, they raised the admission requirements of their four-year schools but maintained "open admissions" in their two-year institutions.

Of plans and planners

There was no conscious conspiracy here, no veiled intention to restrict the opportunity for upward mobility through college attendance. The master plans that established the public education systems of the 1960s were debated and passed by state legislatures; they are now part of the public record. So too is the logic behind them.

Too much competition for too few good jobs can lead to disillusioned, frustrated, and potentially dangerous young women and men. Because the B.A. or B.S. degree carries with it specific vocational expectations, it has to be restricted to that percentage of the population that will, on graduation, secure the jobs earmarked for college graduates. If only x percent of the labor force can, at any given time, find positions in the upper reaches of the workplace hierarchy, then only x percent of college-age youth can be admitted to institutions awarding credentials that qualify one for these jobs. As Steven Zwerling, author of *Second-Best: The Crisis of the Community College,* suggests, it is surely not coincidental that the 1968 New York City master plan, which claimed that only 21 percent of future jobs would require a B.A. degree, also estimated that only 25 percent of high school graduates had "the ability to achieve a baccalaureate degree." [33]

Because higher education had, through the twentieth century, become the funnel through which workers were channeled into the different levels of the white-collar pyramid, the state planners were charged with the responsibility of adjusting the higher education system—as funnel—to the labor market—as receptacle. There were, unfortunately, not enough upper-level white-collar, managerial, and professional positions for all those who sought them, nor were there lower- and middle-level white-collar, technical, and paraprofessional positions for those who looked in this direction for employment. Though the supply of such jobs had increased dramatically in postwar, it had not expanded as rapidly as the demand, propelled upward as we have seen by the rising expectations of ethnic whites, of blacks, and Latins newly arrived in the cities, and women returning to the workplace.[34]

As Colin Greer has argued in *The Great School Legend*, the American schooling system has always functioned on a "scarcity" principle. Because there has been a scarcity of good jobs, the schools have manufactured a scarcity of workers schooled and credentialed enough to fill them. In the postwar period, it was the scarcity of professional and managerial positions on the one hand and paraprofessional and technical positions on the other that would regulate the number of B.A./B.S. and A.A./A.S. (Associate of Arts/Associate of Sciences) graduates.[35]

Like the high school reformers more than a half-century before, the higher education planners had to decide which of two masters to serve: the individual students or the social status quo. As we saw in the last section, the turn-of-the-century struggle between the rank-and-file educational community and the "establishment" represented at the NEA conventions concerned exactly this point: were the schools to meet the educational needs of their students (and the democratic ethos of the society at large) or the labor-power requirements of the social order as defined by the economic masters of that order, the corporate employers and their political representatives. In the case of the high schools, the considerable if informal power of the local school boards, principals, teachers, and students ultimately forced the state officials advocating industrial and vocational schooling to compromise their objectives and accept comprehensive rather than curricularly differentiated high schools.

There were not the same traditions of local control over higher education. Through the later fifties and sixties, master planners and commissions were established in almost every state capital to formulate and administer statewide higher education plans. "By 1969, twenty-three states had completed master plans; eight others were in the process of completing master plans, and an additional seven expected to develop such a plan." Where in 1940 thirty-three states had no coordinating or planning or consolidating mechanisms covering the entire public sector, [by 1975] none [were] without them." [36]

State planners, in order to satisfy their state's "manpower needs," adopted the same "principal of differential functions" that had been urged on the high schools at the turn of the century. Each tier of the higher education system was assigned a different function. The four-year colleges and universities were to provide students with an education that would train and credential them for professional and managerial positions or prepare them for a graduate school that would accomplish that end. The community colleges were made "primarily responsible for technical and semiprofessional training designed to provide enrollees with occupational competence in a wide variety of fields within a two-year period or less." [37]

It was the responsibility of the state planners and coordinators to "functionally differentiate" and regulate admissions to the higher education institutions in their states. No more students could be admitted to the four-year schools as freshman or as transfers from the community colleges than there were anticipated openings in the professional, managerial, and upper-level white-collar job categories. No more students could be granted two-year degrees than there were anticipated openings in the middle and lower levels of the technical and white-collar occupational pyramids.

Only state master planners and coordinators could be relied on to properly regulate local institutions in this manner. As Harold Hodgkinson, reviewing his own study of institutional change in the postwar period, observed, higher education institutions left on their own tended to be "upwardly mobile": two-year colleges begin to offer B.A. degrees; four-year colleges, graduate degrees. Such unplanned and uncontrolled "upward mobility," because it undermined the "functional differentiation" of the system as a whole, had to be—and was—curtailed. [38]

Through the later fifties and sixties, important policy decisions on admissions, budgeting, tuition, program, curricula, staffing, and articulation and transfer between two-year and four-year schools were removed from the local campuses to the state office buildings. Centralized, coordinated plans were formulated and administered by centralized, coordinating agencies. As a Carnegie Foundation report summarized the changes in 1975, "The free-standing campus, uncoordinated and unregulated and unconsolidated with other institutions, once the standard model, is increasingly a rarity in the public sector of higher education." Higher education had, in the words of the *Second Newman Report*, undergone a "revolution in decision-making." [39]

15

The "Tidal Wave" Contained—
Open Admissions

Through the later fifties and sixties, the California plan was adopted, with modifications, in state after state. The four-year colleges and universities were protected by a rapidly expanding network of community colleges, over 360 of which were established between 1958 and 1968. The national increase in public two-year enrollments approached 300 percent for the decade of the 1960s, close to triple that for overall higher education enrollments. In New York, two-year enrollments increased from 6 percent of total public enrollments in 1960 to nearly 50 percent in 1970. The increases in Massachusetts, New Jersey, and Connecticut were as dramatic, from 4 percent to 26 percent, 2 percent to 28 percent, and zero to 20 percent respectively. By 1976, more than one third of all college freshmen and nearly 50 percent of those in public institutions were enrolled in community colleges.[1]

Due in no small part to this rapid increase in the number and enrollment of the community colleges, higher education had come within reach of the 1947 President's Commission recommendations: nearly one-half of the college-age population was attending some institution of higher education. As the 1973 *Second Newman Report*—commissioned and funded by the Department of Health, Education, and Welfare—proudly proclaimed, American higher education "by the middle 1960s began moving into . . . [an] *egalitarian* [period]. Increasingly the American public has assumed that everyone should have a chance at a college education."[2]

Unfortunately for those offered that chance, the system, though opened at the bottom, remained as closed as ever on top. The new generation of students was not granted access to higher education in general but to particular institutions—the community colleges. And these colleges, though presented as transitional institutions to the four-year schools, were in fact designed to keep students away from the senior colleges. As Amitai Etzioni of Columbia University explained for the readers of the *Wall Street Journal*, "If we can no longer keep the floodgates closed at the admissions office, it at least seems wise to channel the general flow away from four-year colleges and toward two-year extensions of high school in the junior and community colleges."[3]

This function of the community college within the higher education system as a whole, characterized so snidely by Etzioni, was in fact the *raison d'etre* of the new two-year schools. As phrased in slightly more acceptable language by David Riesman and Christopher Jencks, the community college had become "an essential pillar of the academic revolution . . . not primarily [as] an alternative model for other colleges or [as] an alternative path to the top for individuals, but rather [as] a safety valve releasing pressures that might otherwise disrupt the dominant system."[4]

Open admissions: for whom?

Though the 1960s has too often been referred to as the decade of "open admissions," "open enrollment," and "open access," these phrases describe only half the situation and rather poorly at that. Open admissions was not invented in the 1960s but had been the standard operating procedure in many schools, private and public, long before then. The private colleges and universities, with some exceptions, had until the middle 1950s been open admissions for those who could afford the tuition. They accepted most of their applicants as a matter of course. In the public sector, open admissions had been not only the tradition but often the law.[5]

What was new to the 1960s was not the admission procedures but the population of students enrolled and the schools in which they were allowed to enroll.

According to K. Patricia Cross, a leading expert on the "new students": "The new clientele for higher education in the 1970s consists of everyone who wasn't there in the 1940s, 1950s, and 1960s." Although Cross believes that these "new learners" are best categorized in terms of low academic ability rather than class, race, or sex, the evidence shows that more students from poor families, more blacks and Latins, and more women attended college in the 1960s and 1970s than ever before.[6]

The studies that Cross uses to demonstrate the increase in "low academic achievers" going to college in the 1960s also demonstrate a quite extraordinary increase in the number of students from families of low socioeconomic-status (SES): a measure of comparative family occupation and education levels. (I hasten to add, like Cross, who makes use of these figures, that the two "sets of data were not designed to be comparable." Nonetheless, I believe, as she does, that they can be used to establish broad, long-term trends.)[7]

When we compare the college attendance rates for 1961 and 1967 high school seniors, we see that—whatever the "ability" group—the percentage increase in attendance was greater for the low socioeconomic-status students than for the high.[8]

For example, when we compare males in the upper "ability" quartile, we see that between 1961 and 1967 the increase in college attendance was 2 percent for those with high SES and 17 percent for those with low. When we compare females who ranked in the upper "ability" quartile, we see the same relationship: those with high SES were attending college in numbers greater by only 8 percent, while those with low SES increased their enrollment by 26 percent. Comparable figures for every other "ability" group show a greater increase for the low SES groups than for the high.[9]

The increase in enrollments for black and Latin students,

though smaller and later to develop than the increase in students of low SES, was also significant. Blacks in 1966 comprised about 12 percent of the total college-age population but accounted for less than 5 percent of college enrollments. By 1972, though enrollments were still not consistent with overall population, they had risen to 8.7 percent. There are no comparable nationwide figures for Latin students, though it is generally believed that their enrollment gains matched those for blacks.[10]

There is a third group that must be included in the "new student" population of the 1960s—women. While women have always performed better than men in high school, they have been much less likely to go on to college. In 1950 only 32 percent of all college students were female. By 1960 this percentage had risen to 37 percent; by 1970, to 42 percent.[11]

Taking all these figures together, we see that the college population of the 1960s, though not as "egalitarian" as had been proclaimed, included more working-class (as defined by low SES), black, Latin, and women students than a decade before. It appeared that, just as a half-century earlier the "plain people" had begun to enter the high schools, they were in the 1960s going on to college. Yet, as was the case with the high school movement at the turn of the century, the doors, though they had opened to admit students in greater numbers, were not opened wide enough to allow in all those previously excluded. Though access was expanded through the 1960s, it did not become universal.

The Presidential Commission, which had first called for "expanded access" in 1947, had carefully sidestepped all questions as to how far this access should be expanded. As a rough guideline, however, it did report that World War II military IQ tests indicated that "a minimum of 49 percent of the college-age population of this country has the ability to complete at least the first two years of college work, and at least 32 percent has the ability to complete additional years of higher education."[12]

It is important to note that this particular commission, along with the other commissions, committees, advisory boards, and master planners of the forties, fifties, and sixties, spoke of free or universal access but never of free or universal attendance. As

the enrollment figures pushed towards the 49 percent figure first
mentioned by the 1946–1948 commission report, the distinction
was underlined repeatedly.

A 1970 Carnegie Commission report emphasized the difference between the two concepts, arguing strongly for "universal access" but as strongly against "universal attendance":

> We do not believe that each young person should of neces-
> sity attend college. Quite the contrary. Many do not want and
> will not want to attend and it cannot be shown that all young
> persons will benefit sufficiently from attendance to justify
> their time and the expense involved. . . . We therefore op-
> pose universal attendance as a goal of American higher educa-
> tion.
>
> We favor, on the other hand, universal *access* for those who
> want to enter institutions, are able to make reasonable prog-
> ress after enrollment, and can benefit from attendance.[13]

In 1975 the Carnegie Foundation for the Advancement of
Teaching returned again to the question of universal access. It
prefaced its remarks by observing that "expanded" or "universal" access was not only "the major goal recommended by the
Carnegie Commission on Higher Education" but also "the
major policy basis for the Higher Education Amendments of
1972 . . . and . . . again endorsed as the first goal by the National Commission on the Financing of Postsecondary Education." Recognizing that no precise definition had yet been formulated, the Foundation in 1975 took the task upon itself. Its
conclusions:

> In our view, the concept of universal access does not mean
> . . . that enrollment rates of 18- to 24-year-olds from families
> in the lower half of the income distribution would be the same
> as those in the upper half. . . . There will be enrollment-rate
> differences across income groups under any likely universal-
> access policy.[14]

These tortured distinctions and definitions demonstrate
rather clearly that the state and foundation planners never intended to expand the higher education systems to the point
where equal educational opportunity would be available to all.

As we have seen throughout this study, the various schooling systems—common, secondary, and higher—have served the social order as much by keeping some students out as by inviting others in. The vocational and industrial schooling programs at the turn of the century were restricted to the "American" children who were able to stay out of work and in school through their teenage years. To have made these programs equally available to immigrant children would have destroyed their purpose: the channeling of "Americans" back into the factories at the supervisory and skilled levels.

If the intent and effect of the industrial schooling programs in the turn-of-the-century high schools had been to prepare the workplace division between the "American" and immigrant workers, the effect (though perhaps not the conscious intent) of the community college expansion has been to stretch the occupational and social distance between the second and third generation descendents of those immigrants and the latest arrivals in the metropolis, the blacks and Latins.

Though the conventional wisdom says otherwise, the community college movement of the 1960s was not conceived as a device for expanding access to blacks and Latins alone. Most of the new community colleges were not even built in the central cities, where the blacks and Latins resided, but in the suburbs and urban fringe areas where they remained more of a minority. Though the newly established two-year schools did increase by some 14 percent the percentage of blacks within commuting distance of a college, this was only 1 percent more than the increase for whites and was balanced out by an overall decrease for the Latin population.[15]

According to K. Patricia Cross, describing the "new learners" for *Change* magazine, "actually most . . . are the white sons and daughters of blue-collar workers. . . . Numerically it is whites, not blacks who have gained through open admissions."[16]

Although the percentage of blacks enrolled in higher education institutions increased greatly during the later sixties, it does not yet equal that for white students. Though blacks comprise some 12 percent of the college-age population, the 1976

American Council on Education report on enrollment shows that they account for only 7.3 percent of male enrollments and 9.6 percent of female enrollments nationwide.[17]

Even in California, the state with the most highly developed community college system and the greatest percentage of high school graduates attending college, the percentage of black and Latin students in college is below their proportion of the total state population. The California joint legislative committee, which in 1969 evaluated the state's Master Plan, found that while Latins comprised 14.4 percent of the elementary school population, they accounted for only 7.5 percent of the junior college enrollment. Comparable figures for blacks were 8.6 percent of the elementary school population and 6.1 percent of the junior college enrollment. Only for whites was the percentage of enrollment at every level of the higher education system greater than their proportion of the elementary school population.[18]

The "common knowledge" about the community college population is faulty not only as concerns the proportion of black and Latin students but also the number of poor students. As Charles Monroe, author of *Profile of the Community College: A Handbook*, has put it, the "emphasis on the 'poor-man' concept of the community college" has been "overdone":

> Community-college students are from the homes of neither the very rich nor the very poor. They tend to come from the lower-middle-income homes, definitely much lower than the homes of university students. Typical community college students in large urban centers are the children of third-generation Americans of European background who have become skilled laborers, low-level supervisors, and industrial managers, and who have aspirations that their children will become the first college graduates in their families. One would not expect to find many students from the lowest quarter of the income groups. Students tend to come from the middle group of families who find it difficult to send their children away to college but want them to join the white-collar and professional ranks.[19]

These figures and observations illustrate a point often overlooked in this modern age of open access. Many students are still denied access to college, and those excluded are more often than not poorer, with a greater chance of being black or Latin than those accepted.

Open admissions: to where? and why?

In the early decades of the century, working-class students enrolling in high school for the first time had been greeted with new industrial, vocational, and domestic science curricula designed with them in mind. In the 1960s, new college students would similarly be greeted with technical, vocational, and occupational curricula designed for them. The high school students had been differentiated into academic and vocational programs; the college students of the 1960s would be differentiated into four-year and two-year colleges.

When we examine the decade of open admissions, looking not only at who went to college but at the colleges they went to, we are led to the conclusion that the era of open admissions was in fact as much an era of closed admissions. In earlier periods, those high school graduates guaranteed a place in college were likely to be admitted directly to the four-year institutions. Though many would later drop out or be academically dismissed, those who did succeed graduated with four-year degrees that entitled them to the "better" jobs available. Open admissions students in the 1960s, on the other hand, were explicitly barred from institutions awarding the B.A./B.S., still, as we shall see, the most important undergraduate degree in terms of future earnings and job possibilities.

Between 1958 and 1968 alone, the percentage of open admission students admitted to four-year, as opposed to two-year, public colleges declined from 47 percent to 18 percent. In most every state of the union, it became more difficult for the high school graduate to be admitted to a four-year institution. In the West, "where in 1958 half of all public four-year colleges had been free-access [i.e., open admissions], by 1968 that ratio had been reduced to less than one out of three." In the Midwest, "where two thirds of . . . public four-year institutions were accessible in 1958, only one-fourth were in 1968." Nationwide, 88 four-year state colleges and universities that were open admissions in 1958 had by 1968 closed their admission procedures.[20]

Open admissions, it has been claimed, combines the best of all possible institutional worlds: it is "egalitarian" and "meritocratic" at the same time. All high school graduates are admitted to college, but merit alone, as determined by high school average, decides who shall get into what tier of the system. Differentiation takes place, but only by ability. Those not able to complete high school are denied admission to any college; those not able to complete high school with high averages are denied access to the four-year schools; those not able to graduate with the highest averages are denied access to the universities; those not able to meet the high admission standards and even higher fees are denied access to the private colleges and universities.[21]

Though the master planners do not profess that this system is without faults, most would agree that it is a meritocratic one, at least as far as the public sector is concerned. The evidence, however, points in another direction. Academic ability, as measured by high school grade point average or any of the standard achievement or aptitude tests, is directly (though not exactly) correlated with class background and family income. (For a detailed study of this relationship, though one which reaches different conclusions than presented here, see *Inequality: A Reassessment of the Effect of Family and Schooling in America* by Christopher Jencks et al.) Common sense would predict this. Because, as we have seen, the "plain people" from their first entrance into the public secondary schools, have been differentiated into nonacademic or less academically rigorous programs, their academic achievement has been less than that of students pursuing traditional academic programs. This practice of differentiating students has not decreased in recent years. The Sputnik scare gave new impetus to those who argued for segregating students by ability. Through the 1960s, not only were more students at the high school and junior high levels sorted, and into more "tracks"—vocational or general, and any number of "fast," "slow," and "medium" academic/college preparatory—but such differentiation was extended backwards into the elementary schools. By 1967 it was estimated that up to

70 percent of the nation's primary schools were "ability group-ing" all or some of their students.

Though these tracks are "by definition segregated in terms of academic ability, this almost inevitably means that they are also segregated, albeit to a lesser extent, in terms of social class and race."[22]

There are significant differences in the schooling students re-ceive not only within the different high school tracks but be-tween secondary schools. Schools that cater to middle-class stu-dents, not surprisingly, spend more money on their schooling, enroll more of them in college preparatory tracks, and send a greater proportion to college.[23]

Though the experts interpret the results differently, most studies of high school students and their achievement demon-strate a direct correlation between social class (as measured by parental occupation, income, or education) and academic achievement in high school. As K. Patricia Cross reports from perhaps the most extensive study of high school students and their grades, Project Talent, 83 percent of the tested high school seniors with low socioeconomic status scored low on academic achievement tests, while 79 percent of those with high status scored high.[24]

A study of New York City high school graduates in 1970 showed similar evidence that class background (as measured by family income) is directly related to high school average. Of those students from families with incomes over $15,000, 61.8 percent graduated with averages of 80 percent or better. In the same income group only 10 percent had averages below 70 per-cent. On the other hand, only 12.4 percent of the students with family incomes of $3700 or less had averages of 80 percent or better, while nearly a third had averages under 70 percent.[25]

Though the correlation between family income and grade point average is not exact, the state planners, by tying admission to the upper tiers of the public systems to performance in high school, have, intentionally or not, designed a class-stratified system. In California, for example, where high school average determines whether one shall be admitted to the state universi-ties, the state colleges, or the community colleges, there is a direct relationship between family income and the tier of the state system one is enrolled in. The higher the family income, the more likely one will be admitted to the four-year schools. The lower the income, the more likely one will be barred from the state universities and colleges and admitted only to the community colleges. According to Samuel Bowles and Herbert Gintis, authors of *Schooling in Capitalist America,* comparative income figures for all California college students in the middle 1960s demonstrate that:

> Over 18 percent of the students at the [upper tier] Universities of California . . . came from families earning $20,000 or more. Less than 7 percent of the students in community colleges, on the other hand, came from such families. . . . Similarly, while only 12.5 percent of the students attending the Universities of California came from families earning less than $6,000, 24 percent of the students attending community colleges . . . came from such families.[26]

Though the California system is perhaps the most efficient and thorough in its class tracking, the other state-coordinated systems (and there are such systems in forty-six other states) are beginning to function in the same way.[27]

Even in New York City, where active student and community opposition forced a restructuring of the original "open admissions" master plan away from the California model, students still appear to be "tracked" according to family income. In a study of the class of 1971, Ellen Trimberger found that while 39 percent of all city high school graduates were admitted to the four-year schools and 22.8 percent to the two-year, only 12 percent of those with family incomes over $15,000 were tracked into the two-year schools as opposed to 41.4 percent of those with family incomes under $3700.[28]

When we move from the rigidly structured California system and the more open New York City one to consider the nation as a whole, we see that the pattern of family income tracking holds firm. According to data compiled by the American Council on Education on the "estimated parental income" for Fall 1971 freshmen, 42 percent of two-year public college freshmen were from families with incomes under $10,000, compared to 26 percent in the public universities. At the other end of the spectrum, those families with incomes over $20,000 accounted for only 11.5 percent of two-year students but 22 percent of public university students. The percentage of students at two-year public colleges is greater than at four-year schools for every income grouping below $12,500 but less for every grouping above this figure.

This class stratification is demonstrated with greater clarity in a comparison of family income figures for public community college students and private university students. In 1971, 42 percent of private university freshmen came from families with incomes over $20,000, but only 11 percent came from families with incomes under $8000. The public community colleges, on the other hand, enrolled over 27 percent of their freshmen from families with incomes under $8000 but only 12 percent from families with incomes over $20,000.[29]

Even when comparing students of similar "ability groupings," there is a significant difference between the chances for success of students from high- and lower-income families. A 1970 study sponsored by the American Council on Education found that when "academic ability" is held constant, socioeconomic status is a significant determinant of college entrance and success. For every 100 students with "high socioeconomic status and high ability," 82 will enter a senior college and 63 will graduate. For every 100 students with "low socioeconomic status and high ability," only 52 will be admitted and 32 will graduate.[30]

College students today are tracked by race as well as by social class. Only in the South, where many of the black colleges are four-year institutions, are blacks as likely as whites to attend college in senior rather than junior colleges. As a 1970 study by the College Entrance Examination Board demonstrated, black male high school graduates with A or B+ averages "are more than twice as likely to enter a community college and less than two-thirds as likely to enter a [four-year] university as their white counterparts."[31]

Students are tracked by social class and race not only *into* the community colleges but *within* them as well. The most attractive programs within the community colleges (as determined by student preference) have been the transfer ones that prepare students for four-year schools where they may earn their B.A.'s or B.S.'s. The community colleges also offer—and widely publicize—their nontransfer, terminal, technical, and vocational programs. The technical programs provide students with specific skills for specific technician jobs, usually within or alongside the engineering or computer fields. The vocational, often called occupational, programs direct students into the lowest levels of the white-collar workplace, usually as para- or subprofessionals, assistants to those with B.A.'s.

Data compiled in 63 community colleges that offered all three programs—transfer, technical, and vocational—provide evidence that tracking within the community college is as class-stratified as tracking into it. Students with parental incomes over $10,000 accounted for 36 percent of all transfer program students, 28 percent of the technical students, and 21 percent of the vocational. For those students from families with incomes under $6000, the pattern is reversed: these students make up only 14 percent of the transfer and technical program students but 24 percent of the vocational.[32]

All these figures on family income and college attendance support the argument that public higher education has not yet closed the door to the class and race discrimination the 1947 President's Commission found so abhorrent and un-American.

Though the enrollment of working-class, black, and Latin students has increased considerably in the decade of "expanded access," we cannot overlook the fact that "expanded access" has not meant "expanded opportunity." As Jerome Karabel has suggested in his *Harvard Educational Review* article, "Community Colleges and Social Stratification," "The critical question is not who gains access to higher education, but rather what happens to people once they get there."[33]

What happens to most community college students is that they drop out or are academically dismissed. The percentage of students in the two-year schools who do not return for a second year is much higher than in the four-year schools.[34]

The reasons for the comparatively high drop-out rates at the community colleges are not difficult to locate. As we have seen, the two-year students are more likely than their senior college counterparts to have been prepared for college in poorer high schools, where they were enrolled in nonacademic or "slow" tracks and received lower grades. Simple common sense would dictate that the two-year schools, in order to compensate for the relative educational deprivation of their students, would have to spend more money on their college education.

This, however, has never been the case. According to figures compiled by D. Kent Halstead in his HEW-sponsored *Statewide Planning in Higher Education,* for the 1970–1971 academic year, the community colleges spent an average of $1294 per student for "student education expenditures," compared to $1759 in the four-year public colleges, $2151 in the private colleges, $2457 in the public universities, and $3252 in the private universities. Though some of the difference in costs can be attributed to the higher expense of schooling graduate students, the figures show rather conclusively that the community colleges spend much less to educate their students than do the four-year schools. Figures derived from a comparative study of education costs in the California higher education system confirm this point: according to this 1969 study, nearly twice as much money was spent on the first two years of college for those who enter the four-year colleges ($2700) and universities ($2970) than for those admitted to the community colleges ($1440). It appears then that, in terms of educational expenditures alone, the community college students are being shortchanged.[35]

In fact, when we look beyond what is spent by the schools to what the economic benefits to the students will be after graduation, their comparative deprivation actually becomes much worse. As we have seen throughout these chapters, one important reason for the increased college enrollments in the postwar period was the expectation—on the part of young people and their parents—that college "paid off" in better jobs and higher lifetime earnings. Unfortunately, this appears to be the case only for those who graduate with B.A.'s or B.S.'s. For all other students—no matter what school they enter or what degree they receive short of the B.A./B.S.—college attendance has a much smaller effect on future employment and earnings.

A study of educational attainment and income for college students in the late sixties demonstrated that while holders of the B.A. earned on the average 50 percent more than high school graduates, those who left college after three or four terms (with or without a degree) earned only 19 percent more. The average annual salary of community college graduates appears, from these figures, to be closer to that of high school graduates than senior college graduates. When we look at the relation between education and professional and/or managerial employment, the advantage of the four-year degree comes into even sharper focus. While over 82 percent of males who graduated with B.A. or graduate school degrees were employed in professional and managerial occupations in the latter 1960s, the comparable figures for those who completed only three or four terms of college was 28 percent.[36]

These figures seem to support the argument that, in terms of employment and earnings, the most substantial value of the community college lies not in its terminal two-year degrees but in its role as gateway to institutions that can award four-year degrees. Unfortunately, the vast majority of community college students will never attain their Bachelor's degrees. Though over 70 percent of all community college students have plans to continue in school until they receive their Bachelor's degree, the proportion who actually transfer to a senior institution is somewhere between 25 percent and 35 percent, and the percentage who attain the B.A./B.S. degree is even lower.[37]

Beginning one's education in a community college appears to be not just a detour but a barrier to attaining the B.A. degree. A 1970 study of comparative graduation rates for students entering two-year and four-year institutions demonstrates that no matter what their ability or family background (SES), those students who began their pursuit of the B.A./B.S. in a two-year rather than a four-year college were less likely to have attained it within five years.[38]

This is as it should be. For the higher education system to function properly, two-year students must somehow be diverted from the four-year schools. The scarcity of Bachelor's degrees must be protected. That the two-year schools serve effectively as "safety valves" to prevent a glut of overqualified, overcredentialed graduates can be vouched for by another set of statistics. Those states with the most students in community colleges award the smallest percentage of four-year degrees. California, for example, which ranks first among the states in percentage of students in community colleges ranks forty-ninth in percentage of B.A./B.S.'s per total enrollment. New York, which in 1960 ranked towards the middle in both measures, decreased its percentage of Bachelor's degree holders as it increased its proportion of two-year students. In the ten year period (1960–1970), in which New York rose from twentieth to third among the states in percentage of students in two-year schools, it fell from thirty-third to forty-eighth in the proportion of students who received four-year degrees.[39]

This diversionary role of the two-year schools is, again, not accidental but an intended, intrinsic function of these schools within the state systems. According to Charles Monroe, a former community college president and author of one of the more important texts on these colleges, the two-year schools have in the postwar period been assigned the role of social "switchman": it is their "distasteful task" to sort out or select "between the 'fit' and the 'unfit' " by, among other means, limiting access to the four-year schools and their degrees.

Regrettably, for Monroe and other community college officials, this theoretically simple and absolutely essential "sorting out" function has become complicated because "students at the college level have the freedom to choose their life patterns and college programs." In Europe students can be tested at an early age and channeled into their appropriate slots in the educational and workplace hierarchies. In America, conversely, it is "not easy, perhaps not proper, for a college to force students into compartments or educational tracks which they do not choose to enter."[40]

Because students cannot be forced into the programs the educational planners believe appropriate for them, they must be "persuaded" into them. In the community college this guidance role has become a major institutional function, so major that not only Monroe but Halstead, in his compendium of information on higher education in the 1970s, includes it among the primary "differential functions" of the two-year schools.[41]

Monroe refers to this community college guidance function as "goal-finding or cooling-out": "the process by which the faculty and counselors gently, through patience and persuasion, assist misdirected transfer students into realistic programs of general and occupational education." (The term, though not the function, was originated by Burton R. Clark in his 1960 book, *The Open Door College*.) Community college students are told that the path to senior college, and perhaps from there to graduate school, will be a long and hazardous one. They are counseled to lower their expectations to the point where they may be more realistically met.[42]

As we have seen already, and shall see again, if the schooling system is to function as a transmission belt into the workplace pyramid, there must be as little room at the top of the educational pyramid as at the top of the workplace one. Cooling-out, though it may also be a well-intentioned gesture by the individuals concerned, is the institutional response to the discrepancy between student aspirations for the better jobs and the proportion of those better jobs in the labor force. It is the process by which the community college attempts to structure the educational and employment expectations of its students by downgrading them until they mesh with the requirements of the labor market.

The higher education pyramid

Not all community college students are "cooled-out" of their attempt to transfer to a senior institution where they can attain a B.A. or B.S. degree. When those who do transfer receive their degrees, however, they may discover that their value in terms of landing a better job is not what it once was.

The higher education pyramid, if it is to serve as entrance into the workplace pyramid, must be as narrow at the top as it is wide at the bottom. What this means is that as more students succeed in attaining their four-year degrees, the value of these degrees must decrease. Where once the B.A./B.S. by itself might have opened doors to the better jobs, its value for many now rests even more in the doors it can open to the better graduate schools.[43]

As the graduate schools replace the undergraduate as the direct line into the upper reaches of the social and workplace hierarchy, they become more selective in student body and less generous in the offer of scholarships to those who cannot pay their own way. There are few "public" graduate schools with low cost tuition. There are no "free access' or "open admission" graduate schools.

Though the need for scientific researchers accentuated by the "Sputnik gap" in the late fifties pried loose some scholarship money for "hard science" graduate students, or those who could justify their graduate schooling as contributing to the national defense, many graduate students must pay their own way through graduate school or have families with incomes large enough to support them for three to seven years.[44]

The importance of family income in determining graduate and professional school attendance is demonstrated by comparing the family incomes of first year medical students with the national norms. While 36 percent of U.S. families in 1974 had incomes under $10,000, only 17 percent of first year medical students came from families at this income level. Though less than 40 percent of U.S. families had incomes over $15,000, over 65 percent of medical students came from families with incomes greater than this, including 37 percent with family incomes over $25,000.[45]

The figures on the enrollment of blacks and women in graduate and professional schools provide an even more dramatic illustration of the function of this top level of the higher education pyramid in screening out those considered unfit for the top levels of the workplace pyramid.

Blacks, though comprising 12 percent of the student-age population, accounted for only 6.3 percent of medical school enrollment and 4.4 percent of Ph.D. program enrollment in the 1973–1974 academic year.[46]

Women, though consistently better students than men in high school, received only 45 percent of the B.A.'s, 13 percent of the professional degrees, and 21 percent of the Ph.D.'s awarded in 1975.[47]

Women, though welcomed into the workplace in increasing numbers, are not supposed to make it to the top. They have become the new reserve army of the white-collar unemployed—the last to be hired, at the lowest wages, and the first to be let go. Keeping women out of graduate school, where they would gain the skills, credentials, and confidence to rise to the upper-employment levels, is but one of the ways of locking them into the lowest levels of the social and workplace hierarchies.

The higher education pyramid must narrow towards the top as dramatically as the white-collar one, if the status quo is to be maintained. As students progress from high school to graduate or professional school, more and more must be discarded along the way. If we trace the progress through the system of those male high school graduates who have demonstrated "high ability," we discover that, of those from high-income families, 91 of 100 begin college, 82 enroll at a senior college, 63 get their B.A.'s, and 36 continue on to graduate school. On the other hand, for males with "high ability" from low-income families, only 69 of 100 will even begin college, 52 will enroll at a senior college, 32 will get their B.A.'s, and 15 will continue on to graduate school.[48]

The higher education system has become more selective towards the top as it has allowed in more people at the bottom. We are told that, since we can't all be doctors, lawyers, corporation executives, or government officials, it is the task of the educational system, as Thomas Jefferson said two hundred years ago, to rake the rubbish for the genius, or as Charles Monroe put it a little more diplomatically, to select the "fit" from the "unfit."[49]

In times past, the schooling system has attempted to convince many of us that we were not among the best and therefore had to settle for a second-best education and the second-best jobs it led to. At the turn of the century, vocational tracks in high school were created for the second-best working-class students.

In the 1960s, community colleges were established for the same purpose: to divert the "plain people" from the schools traditionally reserved for the middle- and upper-middle-class children. These students newly admitted to secondary or post-secondary schooling were told to be thankful for the opportunity extended them to continue in school further than their parents had. They were also told that, for them, second-best was good enough: they were not the "academic" type, not really "college material."[50]

Just as the "American" working-class children at the turn of the century refused to accept the places prepared for them in vocational and industrial schooling tracks, so too did many of the students, newly admitted to higher education in mid-century, refuse to settle for the second-best schooling created for them.

According to Jerome Karabel, the struggle between the sponsors of community college vocational education and the students who are to be tracked into these programs can best be described as "submerged class conflict between [those] . . . who represent the interests and outlook of the more privileged sectors of society, and community college students, many of them working class." As Karabel demonstrates, this "submerged" struggle occasionally becomes "overt":

> At Seattle Community College in 1968-9, the Black Student Union vigorously opposed a recommendation to concentrate trade and technical programs in the central (Black) campus while the "higher" semiprofessional programs were allocated to the northern and southern (white) campuses. Rutgers (Newark) was the scene in 1969 of extensive demonstrations to gain open admissions to a branch of the state university. The import of the case of Rutgers (Newark) was that the protests took place in a city where students already had access to an open-door community college (Essex) and a mildly selective state college (Newark State). What the students were resisting here was not being tracked within the community college, but rather being channeled into the community college itself.

Further evidence of student resistance to the plans formulated with them in mind can be found in New York City where much of the protest resulting in the Open Admissions policy of the early 1970s came from black and Third World student demands not only for inclusion in the City University but for admission to the senior colleges.[51]

Charles Monroe emphasizes these points in retelling the story of his own ouster as president of a Chicago community college. According to Monroe, student leaders at this school "demanded that failing grades be abolished as well as other 'Establishment' impediments that had been placed in the road of a black student who wanted a 'real' education, namely a four-year degree." For our purposes the heart of this quotation is the students' desire for a "real" education, which they equated with a four-year degree.[52]

The students are not unaware that the lower tiers of the higher education system are designed to prepare and direct them into the lower levels of the workplace pyramid. Community college students become the technicians who test blood and urine for M.D.'s; the paraprofessional playground, cafeteria, and classroom assistants for M.A.T.'s (Master of Arts in Teaching); the case and office workers who report to M.S.W.'s (Master of Social Work); the administrative assistants, the computer programmers, the legal workers. In every job category they serve as the lower-level subordinates with less wages, less security, less responsiblity, and much less meaningful and creative work situations than their credentialed, professional associates.

The community colleges are having some difficulty channeling students into their "appropriate" educational slots. As Burton Clark had warned might occur, students, having discovered that the function of the community college is not so much to prepare them for transfer as to cool out their expectations, begin to abandon it, or resist being restricted to the nontransfer programs.[53]

The 1971 Carnegie Commission Report on the community colleges touched on this problem: "The resistance to occupational programs by many students who might profit from them has long disturbed community college leaders."[54]

Charles Monroe, in his 1972 *Profile of the Community College*,

pointed to the same phenomenon: "Studies of the attitudes of
. . . students reveal that the transfer courses hold a favored
position over other courses in the majority of cases." According
to Monroe, the situation had become so serious (with "almost
two-thirds" of the students enrolled in transfer programs where
the ideal percentage should have been nearer 25 percent) that
the colleges were going to have to begin "to limit the free choice
of students by denying them admission to college programs
which they will almost certainly drop out of." [55]

In New York City, where community college graduates were
once automatically admitted to the senior colleges, Monroe's
proposal is being implemented. Beginning (most probably)
with the 1978-79 academic year, community college graduates
will have to pass a new "competency" examination, designed
and administered not by their own teachers, but by a "centralized" Board of Higher Education staff. Students who once had
the option of transferring to four-year colleges on graduation from
two-year programs may discover this choice denied them. [56]

Because the community college, as Monroe puts it, includes
"a social class connotation as well as a geographic one," with a
majority of its students "from middle and upper lower-class
families," part of its social task has been the preparation of future subordinate workers for their subordinate roles within the
workplace. It is in the interests of the social status quo that
these workers not be too educated. The logic of the social order
indicates that social stability is best maintained if subordinates
are kept less informed than their supervisors. The social and
workplace hierarchies would be pulled apart by dissension if
the nurses and patients began to question the doctors; the
teaching assistants and parents, the teachers; the paraprofes-
sionals and clients, the professionals; the people, the government experts. [57]

This particular systemic objective is not always pursued by
the teachers themselves. They, for the most part, still believe in
education for all, though their own class, race, and sexual biases
shape the extent to which they believe all can be educated. Still,
most teachers want to be educators, not job trainers. Many be-

lieve that the task of higher education is to give students the tools of literacy, the self-confidence, the skills, and the intellectual training to think for themselves.[58]

It is because these educational goals are in direct conflict with the manpower training objectives of the system as a whole that the teachers at the classroom level, like the students themselves, have been divested of much of their control over the institutions in which they are employed.

The postwar higher education system has enlisted in the "national service" as defined by the state/corporate leadership. The private universities have entered the "knowledge for order" business, supplying the state/corporate alliance with the information and trained personnel it requires. The public university systems have been expanded and overhauled to provide the productive order with the lower- and middle-level white-collar and technical workers it requires.

Everyone is happy—except for many of the teachers and students. The overhaul of higher education has left some students from middle-class families and many more from working-class backgrounds with second-rate schools to prepare them for second-rate jobs. For the greatest number of these students, a college education not only fails as the promised road to the "better" job, it is as intellectually stifling, as morally inconsequential, and as great a waste of time as high school. College for too many has become no more and no less than "a high school with ashtrays."[59]

The students who are entering college because they want to develop their intellectual skills and learn to think for themselves have to fight for these goals every step of the way. It is not impossible to get an education in the community and state colleges. Though the schools to which the working-class students are now admitted are understaffed, underfunded, and almost devoid of serious remedial programs to compensate for high schools that have taught their students nothing but an abiding dislike of the classroom, there are still teachers at these schools who want to teach. Though the "mission" of the two-year and, increasingly, many of the four-year schools dictates a greater emphasis on the vocational than the liberal arts, the traditional courses of study have not yet been totally submerged.

As long as there are teachers who want to teach and students who want to learn, the educational mission of the colleges and universities, though subordinated to other tasks, will be preserved. And as long as the necessity remains for disguising the class-determined process of allocating work and social roles as a meritocratic one, the path leading out of the bottom through to the top of the educational and workplace pyramids, though barricaded, will remain open enough for some to follow it.

As it becomes clearer to students that the higher education system has been expanded, but not to meet their needs; that "education" is still possible, but no longer a priority; that some students will "make it," but only a relative few; the students themselves may force into the light the contradictions that lie at the heart of the schooling system.

They will perhaps even begin to expose the myth of the meritocracy by succeeding in higher education—despite the odds—and then demanding the jobs associated with academic success. The social order may in the future be forced to drop its meritocratic disguise or pay off those who have succeeded "on merit."

If higher education drops its meritocratic disguise, a crucial instrument in dividing the working class among itself, "new" immigrants from newer, black and Latin from white, women from men, will be destroyed. A most efficient tool in disguising structural unemployment will be blunted, and the illusion of social mobility fostered by the expansion of higher education will be broken.

On the other hand, if the higher education system remains as it is, providing access to all and the possibility of success to some, then the likelihood increases that more and more of the wrong people will succeed at all levels of higher education, ultimately exerting greater pressure on the society to reward their academic success with better positions in the workplace and social hierarchy.

This is a serious danger. No society can long endure a situation where a large part of its educated young people have grown dissatisfied with their possibilities for the future. As *The Second Newman Report* recognized, the dangers of an "accumulation of frustrated and unemployed college-trained individuals" has posed a serious dilemma to the social stability of developed and underdeveloped nations alike. This country, though so far immune, could be afflicted by the same social malady.[60]

Either way, then, whether access remains open or whether it becomes more limited, the social process by which one generation transmits its privileges to the next will likely undergo severe strain in the coming years. Perhaps, just perhaps, the system is not as foolproof as its master planners would have us believe.

Conclusion

The past century and a half has been a period of unparalleled expansion and reform in American public schooling.

In the two decades following the 1837 accession of Horace Mann to the secretaryship of the Massachusetts Board of Education, the foundation was laid for a state-mandated, state-coordinated, tax-supported system of common schools, open to the children of every community.[1]

At the turn of the century the high schools were transformed by the entrance of the "children of the plain people." In 1890 less than 4 percent of the nation's fourteen-to-seventeen-year-olds attended public high schools; thirty years later, the percentage approached 30 percent. In the interim, the high schools could proudly be proclaimed the new "people's colleges."[2]

In the post-World War II decades it was higher education that was expanded and reformed. The promise of a college education was offered first to the returning veterans and then to the majority of high school graduates. Where in 1940 under 15 percent of the eighteen-to-twenty-one-year-old population attended college, thirty years later the proportion approached 50 percent.[3]

In each period of reform, schooling systems were transformed from "elite" to "mass." But was this "massification" a "democratization"? Did the expansion of access indicate a corresponding increase in opportunity?[4]

Let us look first at the common school crusade. This period of reform, unlike later ones, did not result in a significant increase in the proportion of children in school. There was an increase in public school enrollment, but this increase reflected more a shift of students from private and parochial schools than an influx of newly enrolled students.

Those who had been excluded from schooling before the common school reform movement were not affected by its triumph. The poor and immigrant children of the factory towns and cities could not have attended school without child labor legislation and family income subsidies, neither of which were forthcoming. Girls, always expendable as far as formal schooling was concerned, remained no less so in the common schools. For blacks the period was one of diminishing opportunity. In the South, laws prohibiting the instruction of blacks were strengthened where they already existed, passed anew where they did not. In the North, tradition and public hostility accomplished the same end.

The guiding force behind the common school crusade was not so much the education of the children as the maintenance of social peace and prosperity. Because the republic and its private property were endangered more by "immoral" than by illiterate adults, the common schools' responsibility for character training and moral instruction overrode all others. Teachers would instruct their students in the three R's, but this was not to be the *raison d'etre* of an expanded and reformed public schooling system.

The reformers, educators, and industrialists who were in the forefront of the second schooling crusade had much the same objectives as their predecessors in the reform movement. The "children of the plain people" were now entering the secondary schools and demanding the education that had traditionally been offered there. The reformers were pleased that the new students chose to remain in school but most unhappy with their choice of curriculum. Latin, ancient history, and trigonometry might make sense for future professionals or corporate executives but not so for students from families that had never before had the resources to support anyone beyond the primary grades.

The high schools, though enormously expanded in this period, were never democratized. They remained closed to blacks and to the majority of "new immigrants" who could not afford to postpone wage earning to attend school through adolescence. Class and race determined not only who got in but what happened to them after admission. The "traditional" middle-class students were offered the traditional academic program, from this point on labeled "college-preparatory" to distinguish it from courses of study for those students who could not afford college. The new students, "the children of the plain people," were "differentiated" into vocational programs to prepare them for their future lives within factory, workshop, or working-class household.

That the reform proposals could not be fully implemented, in part because they were so blatantly antidemocratic, did not deter a new generation of educational planners from re-creating them in slightly different form a half-century later. The "democratization" of higher education followed the pattern set by the "democratization" of secondary schooling. Class, race, and sex remained a significant determinant not only of who got into college but where they were accepted and the nature of their studies once admitted.

The postwar expansion of higher education was as little concerned with the educational needs of its students as previous reform movements. The first significant enrollment increase was spurred by a G.I. bill designed more to combat unemployment than to assist higher education. The same could be said of the postwar increase in federal funding for university research and development. The funds funneled into the nation's more prestigious colleges and universities were spent to sustain corporate profits, not to improve the educational opportunities for college students.

There is cause both for celebration and for lament in the history of American public schooling. We can celebrate the expansion and triumph of the public institutions or lament the lost opportunities for democratization and the failure of students to receive the type of education they sought. In either case, we are avoiding the obvious: that the public schools are social institutions dedicated *not* to meeting the self-perceived needs of their students but to preserving social peace and prosperity within the context of private property and the governmental structures that safeguard it.

This is not to say that the history of public schooling has been no more than a history of public victimization. Ours is a society dedicated, in principle, to the proposition that the people shall have some say in their governance, at least as concerns their public schools. As the reformers and their opponents were well aware, this was not Prussia, where state officials could with the wave of a proclamation bring their reforms to life. In the United States, the local citizens or their representatives had to be coaxed, cajoled, "educated" to accept the proposals. And the proposals themselves had to be properly packaged to appeal to the local communities without whose acquiescence they could not be implemented. Too often, for the reformers at least, not even the most attractive packages could conceal the class-biased contents of the reform proposals. The poor parents who withheld their children from the charity schools in the 1820s and 1830s; the communities who resisted the institution of industrial schooling programs at the turn of the century; those students who insisted on taking Latin in the 1900s as well as those who matriculated to four-year colleges in the 1960s and 1970s were exercising their power to compromise the more blatantly antidemocratic aspects of public school reform.

The "nontraditional" students invited into the public schools during each period of expansion and reform had minds of their own. Many knew and pursued the education they wanted: the same type that had been offered to the middle- and upper-class students before the entrance of the "masses." Though a number of high school students in the early 1900s and college students in the 1960s and 1970s were diverted and "differentiated," some managed to steer their way through the institutional mazes, emerging in the end with the education required for the upward mobility they sought.

Reformers and persons of wealth, social standing, and power have in each of the periods we have examined attempted to remake the public schools. But their plans, though never entirely defeated, have not been fully implemented. Because the local taxpayers objected, the common schools could not be supported exclusively by local taxes in the antebellum decades. Because local school boards refused, separately administered and funded industrial schools were not established alongside public high schools at the turn of this century. Because students have their own educational and career objectives, the community colleges have not succeeded in "cooling out" all their "nontraditional" students.

The public schools emerge in the end compromised by reform and resistance. They do not belong to the corporations and the state, but neither do they belong to their communities. They remain "contested" institutions with several agendas and several purposes. The reformers have not in the past and will not in the future succeed in making them into efficient agencies for social channeling and control. Their opponents will not, on the other hand, turn them into truly egalitarian educational institutions without at the same time effecting radical changes in the state and society that support them. The public schools will, in short, continue to be the social arena where the tension is reflected and the contest played out between the promise of democracy and the reality of class division.

Notes

Introduction

1. Fred M. Hechinger, "Murder in Academe: The Demise of Education," *Saturday Review* 3, no. 12 (March 20, 1976), pp. 10–12; *Time* 108, no. 14 (October 4, 1976), p. 58; *Newsweek* 88, no. 10 (September 6, 1976), p. 51; *ibid.*, 90, no. 18 (October 31, 1977), p. 111.

2. Edward A. Krug, *The Shaping of the American High School: 1880–1920*, 2 vols. (Madison: University of Wisconsin Press, 1969), 1:169; David D. Henry, *Challenges Past, Challenges Present: An Analysis of American Higher Education Since 1930* (San Francisco: Jossey-Bass, 1975), p. 99.

Chapter One

1. Frances Trollope, *Domestic Manners of the Americans* (New York: Knopf, 1949), p. 213.

2. Eneas Mackenzie, quoted in George R. Clay, "Children of the Young Republic," *American Heritage* 11 (April 1960), p. 49.

3. Robert Bremner, ed., *Children and Youth in America: A Documentary History*, 3 vols. (Cambridge, Mass.: Harvard University Press, 1970), 1:344.

4. Clay, "Children of the Young Republic," p. 46.

5. Harriet Martineau, *Society in America*, ed. Seymour Martin Lipset (Gloucester, Mass.: Peter Smith, 1968), pp. 310–311.

6. Alexis de Tocqueville, *Democracy in America*, trans. Phillips Bradley, 2 vols. (New York: Random House, Vintage Books, 1945), 2:206–210.

7. *Ibid.*, pp. 212–215; Rowland Berthoff, *An Unsettled People: Social Order and Disorder in American History* (New York: Harper and Row, 1971), pp. 97, 212–213.

8. Berthoff, *Unsettled People* pp. 96–97; Clifton Johnson, *Old-Time Schools and Schoolbooks* (1904; reprint ed., New York: Dover Books, 1963), pp. 1–3; Bernard Bailyn, *Education in the Forming of American Society* (New York: Norton, 1972), pp. 15–21.

9. Bailyn, *Education*, p. 31; David Rothman, *The Discovery of the Asylum* (Boston: Little Brown, 1971), p. 14.

10. Rothman, *Discovery*, pp. 169–71, 210–220; Stanley K. Schultz, *The Culture Factory: Boston Public Schools, 1789–1860* (New York: Oxford University Press, 1973), pp. 261–263.

11. Rothman, *Discovery*, pp. 221–224; Schultz, *Culture Factory*, pp. 243–246.

12. Newton Edwards and Herman G. Richey, *The School in the American Social Order*, 2nd ed. (Boston: Houghton Mifflin, 1963), pp.

221–225; Frank Tracy Carlton, *Economic Influences Upon Educational Progress in the United States, 1820–1850* (1908; reprint ed., New York: Teachers College Press, 1965), pp. 27–28; Rush Welter, *Popular Education and Democratic Thought* (New York: Columbia University Press, 1962), pp. 31, 34.

13. Rothman, *Discovery*, pp. 155–161.

14. Carl Russell Fish, *The Rise of the Common Man: 1830–1850* (Chicago: Quadrangle Paperbacks, 1971), p. 66.

15. Schultz, *Culture Factory*, p. 211; Rothman, *Discovery*, p. 57.

16. John F. Kasson, *Civilizing the Machine: Technology and Republican Values in America, 1776–1900* (New York: Viking Press, Grossman Publishers, 1976), pp. 55–60; Rothman, *Discovery*, p. 159.

17. Douglass C. North, *The Economic Growth of the United States, 1790–1860* (New York: Norton, 1966), pp. 66–70.

18. Sam Bass Warner, Jr., *The Private City: Philadelphia in Three Periods of Its Growth* (Philadelphia: University of Pennsylvania Press, 1968), pp. 63–72; Norman Ware, *The Industrial Worker: 1840–1860* (Chicago: Quadrangle Paperback, 1964), pp. 55–56.

19. Warner, *Private City*, pp. 72–78; Ware, *Industrial Worker*, pp. 44–48, 56–61.

20. Ware, *Industrial Worker*, p. xiv.

21. *Ibid.*, p. 27.

22. *Ibid.*, p. 36.

23. Andrew Jackson, quoted in Richard Hofstadter, *The American Political Tradition and the Men Who Made It* (New York: Random House, Vintage Books, 1948), p. 51.

24. Arthur M. Schlesinger, Jr., *The Age of Jackson* (Boston: Little, Brown and Co., 1945), pp. 132–209; Sidney Jackson, *America's Struggle for Free Schools* (New York: Russell & Russell, 1965), p. 13.

25. Schultz, *Culture Factory*, pp. 57–59; Bernard Wishy, *The Child and the Republic: The Dawn of Modern American Child Nurture* (Philadelphia: University of Pennsylvania Press, 1972), pp. 26–28.

26. Rothman, *Discovery*, pp. 216–221; Wishy, *Child and Republic*, pp. 17–19; Schultz, *Culture Factory*, pp. 51–5.

27. Wishy, *Child and Republic*, pp. 28–29.

28. Schultz, *Culture Factory*, pp. 25–30; Paul Monroe, *Founding of the American Public School System* (New York: Macmillan Company, 1940), pp. 299–304; Carl F. Kaestle, *The Evolution of an Urban School System: New York City, 1750–1850* (Cambridge, Mass.: Harvard University Press, 1973), pp. 80–84; Ellwood P. Cubberley, *Public Education in the United States*, rev. ed. (Boston: Houghton Mifflin, 1934), pp. 120–128.

29. Schultz, *Culture Factory*, pp. 47, 60–66; Kaestle, *Urban School System*, p. 78.

30. Edwards and Richey, *School in Social Order*, pp. 237–238.

31. Kaestle, *Urban School System*, pp. 80–84.

32. Diane Ravitch, *The Great School Wars: New York City, 1805–1973* (New York: Basic Books, Harper Colophon, 1974), pp. 15–16, 14.

33. Ravitch, *Great School Wars*, p. 12; Lancaster, quoted in Cubberley, *Public Education*, p. 131.

34. Edwards and Richey, *School in Social Order*, p. 242.

35. Schultz, *Culture Factory*, pp. 117–119; Monroe, *Founding*, pp. 469–471.

36. Schultz, *Culture Factory*, p. 272.

37. Vera M. Butler, *Education as Revealed by New England Newspapers Prior to 1850* (1935; reprint ed., New York: Arno Press, 1969), pp. 263, 261.

38. Butler, *Education as Revealed*, pp. 263–264.

39. Schultz, *Culture Factory*, p. 27.

40. Butler, *Education as Revealed*, pp. 250, 261, 262, 267, 338, 339, 341.

41. Leon F. Litwack, *North of Slavery: The Negro in the Free States* (Chicago: University of Chicago Press, 1961), p. 115; Howard K. Beale, "The Education of Negroes Before the Civil War," in *The American Experience in Education*, ed. John Barnard and David Burner (New York: Franklin Watts, 1975), pp. 88–90.

42. Beale, "Education of Negroes," p. 93; Litwack, *North of Slavery*, pp. 113–117.

43. Litwack, *North of Slavery*, pp. 113–152; Eugene D. Genovese, *Roll, Jordan, Roll: The World the Slaves Made* (New York: Random House, Vintage Books, 1976), pp. 561–566; Frederick Douglass, *Narrative of the Life of Frederick Douglass* (New York: Signet, 1968).

44. Robert F. Berkhofer, Jr., "Model Zions for the American Indian," Barnard and Burner, *American Experience in Education*, pp. 105–106.

45. Monroe, *Founding*, pp. 297–299; Cubberley, *Public Education*, pp. 187–189.

46. Schultz, *Culture Factory*, pp. 227–228.

47. Kaestle, *Urban School System*, pp. 85–88; Ravitch, *Great School Wars*, pp. 20–24; Cubberley, *Public Education*, pp. 187–189.

Chapter Two

1. Irvin G. Wyllie, *The Self-Made Man in America* (New York: Macmillan, Free Press, 1966), pp. 8–54.

2. Frederick M. Binder, *The Age of the Common School, 1830–1865* (New York: John Wiley & Sons, 1974), p. 13.

3. Clifton Johnson, *Old-Time Schools and School-books* (1904; reprint ed., New York: Dover Books, 1963), p. 108.

4. Newton Edwards and Herman G. Richey, *The School in the American Social Order*, 2nd ed. (Boston: Houghton Mifflin, 1963), pp. 310–319; Jonathan Messerli, *Horace Mann* (New York: Knopf, 1972), pp. 260–267, 272.

5. Binder, *Age of Common School*, pp. 40–44, 53–54.

6. Messerli, *Horace Mann*, pp. 6–8.

7. *Ibid.*, p. 16.

8. *Ibid.*, pp. 23–27.

9. *Ibid.*, pp. 74–91.

10. Merle Curti, *The Social Ideas of American Educators* (Totowa, New Jersey: Littlefield, Adams & Co., 1974), pp. 117–135, 194–200.

11. *Ibid.*, pp. 104–105, 139.

12. Messerli, *Horace Mann*, p. 249.

13. Alexis de Tocqueville, *Democracy in America*, trans. Phillips Bradley, 2 vols. (New York: Random House, Vintage Books, 1945), 1:95.

14. Frances Trollope, *Domestic Manners of the Americans* (New York: Knopf, 1949), pp. 327–329.

15. Michel Chevalier, *Society, Manners, and Politics in the United States*, trans. and ed. John William Ward (Ithaca, New York: Cornell University Press, Cornell Paperbacks, 1969), pp. 170–171, 187.

16. Carl F. Kaestle, *The Evolution of an Urban School System: New York City, 1750–1850* (Cambridge, Mass.: Harvard University Press, 1973), pp. 88–91.

17. Sam Bass Warner, Jr., *The Private City: Philadelphia in Three Periods of Its Growth* (Philadelphia: University of Pennsylvania Press, 1968), pp. 111–112; Kaestle, *Urban School System*, p. 93.

18. Kaestle, *Urban School System*, p. 89; Henry Barnard, *Third Annual Report of the Secretary of the Board* (1841), in *Henry Barnard: American Educator*, ed. Vincent P. Lannie (New York: Teachers College Press, 1974), p. 120.

19. Albert Fishlow, "The American Common School Revival: Fact or Fancy?" in *Industrialization in Two Systems*, ed. Henry Rosovsky (New York: John Wiley & Sons, 1966), pp. 49–50, 53.

20. Curti, *Social Ideas*, pp. 75–77; Messerli, *Horace Mann*, pp. 248–249; Henry Barnard, *Sixth Annual Report of the Superintendent of Common Schools* (1851), in *School Reform: Past and Present*, ed. Michael Katz (Boston: Little Brown, 1971), p. 10.

21. Barnard, *Sixth Annual Report*, in *School Reform*, ed. Katz, pp. 10, 17.
22. Herbert G. Gutman, "Work, Culture, and Society in Industrializing America, 1815–1919," in *Work, Culture, and Society* (New York: Random House, Vintage Books, 1977), pp. 3–78.
23. Horace Mann, *Twelfth Annual Report of the Secretary of the Board* (1848), in *The Republic and the School: Horace Mann on The Education of Free Men*, ed. Lawrence A. Cremin (New York: Teachers College Press, 1957), p. 100.
24. Lawrence A. Cremin, *The American Common School* (New York: Teachers College Press, 1951), pp. 58–59.
25. *Ibid.*, p. 59; Kaestle, *Urban School System*, p. 85; Horace Mann, *First Annual Report of the Secretary of the Board*, in *Republic and School*, ed. Cremin, pp. 31–32.
26. Mann, *Twelfth Annual Report*, in *Republic and School*, ed. Cremin, p. 80.
27. Stanley K. Schultz, *The Culture Factory: Boston Public Schools, 1789–1860* (New York: Oxford University Press, 1973), p. 78; Messerli, *Horace Mann*, pp. 252–253.
28. Horace Mann, *Fourth Annual Report of the Secretary of the Board*, in *Republic and School*, ed. Cremin, pp. 51–52.
29. Mann, *Twelfth Annual Report*, in *Republic and School*, ed. Cremin, p. 80.
30. Rush Welter, *Popular Education and Democratic Thought in America* (New York: Columbia University Press, 1962), pp. 82–90; Binder, *Age of Common School*, pp. 39–41; Curti, *Social Ideas*, pp. 55–63, 75–87.
31. Mann, *Twelfth Annual Report*, in *Republic and School*, ed. Cremin, p. 92.
32. *Ibid.*, pp. 94–97.
33. Ruth Miller Elson, *Guardians of Tradition* (Lincoln: University of Nebraska Press, 1964), pp. 8–11.
34. *Ibid.*, pp. 3–4.
35. Richard D. Mosier, *Making the American Mind* (New York: King's College Press, 1947), pp. 1–32.
36. Elson, *Guardians of Tradition*, pp. 208–211.
37. *Ibid.*, pp. 194, 208–209, 295.
38. *Ibid.*, pp. 289–293.
39. Mann, *Twelfth Annual Report*, in *Republic and School*, ed. Cremin, pp. 95–96.
40. *Ibid.*, pp. 103–105, 108–109.
41. Cremin, *American Common School*, p. 193.

42. Messerli, *Horace Mann*, pp. 309–310.

43. Welter, *Popular Education*, pp. 105–106.

44. Timothy L. Smith, *Revivalism and Social Reform in Mid-Nineteenth Century America* (New York: Abingdon Press, 1957), p. 32.

Chapter Three

1. Alexander James Field, "Educational Expansion in Mid-Nineteenth Century Massachusetts: Human-Capital Formation or Structural Reinforcement?," *Harvard Educational Review* 46, no. 4 (November 1976):547.

2. *Ibid.*, p. 548.

3. Jonathan Messerli, *Horace Mann* (New York: Knopf, 1972), p. 272; Merle Curti, *The Social Ideas of American Educators* (Totowa, New Jersey: Littlefield, Adams, & Co., 1974), p. 113.

4. Maris Vinovskis, "Horace Mann on the Economic Productivity of Education," *New England Quarterly* 43 (1970):560–565; Curti, *Social Ideas*, p. 113.

5. Horace Mann, *Fifth Annual Report of the Secretary of the Board* (Boston: Dutton and Wentworth, State Printers, 1842), p. 83.

6. *Ibid.*, pp. 87–89.

7. *Ibid.*, p. 94.

8. *Ibid.*, pp. 90, 92.

9. *Ibid.*, pp. 108–112.

10. Caleb Mills, "An Address to the Legislature of Indiana at the Commencement of its Session," (1846) in *Caleb Mills and the Indiana School System*, ed. Charles W. Moones (Indianapolis: The Wood-Weaver Printing Co., 1905), pp. 409–414.

11. Curti, *Social Ideas*, pp. 72–75.

12. Rowland Berthoff, *An Unsettled People: Social Order and Disorder in American History* (New York: Harper and Row, 1971), p. 263.

13. Jay Marvin Pawa, "The Attitude of Labor Organizations in New York State toward Public Education, 1829–1890," (Ph.D. diss., Teachers College, Columbia University, 1964), p. 117.

14. Sidney Jackson, *America's Struggle for Free Schools* (New York: Russell and Russell, 1965), p. 165.

15. Pawa, "Attitude of Labor Organizations," pp. 75–86.

16. Jackson, *America's Struggle for Free Schools*, p. 167.

17. Ellwood P. Cubberley, *Public Education in the United States*, rev. ed. (Boston: Houghton Mifflin, 1934), pp. 179–180.

18. Cubberley, *Public Education*, pp. 180–183; Newton Edwards and

Herman G. Richey, *The School in the American Social Order*, 2nd ed. (Boston: Houghton Mifflin, 1963), pp. 328–330.

19. Messerli, *Horace Mann*, pp. 258–279; Nelson Barr, *Education in New Jersey: 1630–1871* (Princeton: Princeton University Press, 1942), pp. 214–215, 259–270.

20. Horace Mann, *First Annual Report of the Secretary of the Board* (1837), in *The Republic and the School: Horace Mann on The Education of Free Men*, ed. Lawrence A. Cremin (New York: Teachers College Press, 1957), pp. 29–30.

21. James G. Carter, *Letters on the Free Schools of New England* (1826; reprint ed., New York: Arno Press, 1969) p. 48; Messerli, *Horace Mann*, p. 373.

22. Mills, "An Address to the Legislature of Indiana," pp. 409–414.

23. Cubberley, *Public Education*, pp. 180–187.

24. Frank Tracy Carlton, *Economic Influences upon Educational Progress in the United States, 1820–50* (1908; reprint ed., New York: Teachers College Press, 1965), pp. 65–82; Paul Monroe, *Founding of the American Public School System* (New York: Macmillan, 1940), pp. 334–335.

25. Horace Mann, *Tenth Annual Report of the Secretary of the Board*, in *Republic and School*, ed. Cremin, pp. 59–78.

26. Carlton, *Economic Influences*, p. 66.

27. James Pyle Wickersham, *A History of Education in Pennsylvania* (Lancaster, Penn.: Inquirer Publishing Co., 1886), pp. 319–320.

28. Wickersham, *History of Education*, pp. 317–319, 323–331.

29. Cubberley, *Public Education*, pp. 181, 183–187.

30. Thomas E. Finegan, *Free Schools: A Documentary History of Free School Movement in New York State* (Albany: University of the State of New York, 1921), pp. 136–139, 171–172.

31. Thomas E. Finegan, *The Establishment and Development of the School System of the State of New York* (Syracuse: C. W. Brandon, 1913), pp. 38–41.

32. New York State Legislature, *Documents of the Assembly of the State of New York*, 73rd Session, vol. 6, Document no. 150, 26 March 1850, pp. 12–13.

33. *Ibid.*, pp. 13–14, 16.

34. *Ibid.*, Document no. 166, 30 March 1850, pp. 25–26.

35. Finegan, *Establishment and Development*, pp. 40–45; Cubberley, *Public Education*, pp. 200–202.

36. Alexis de Tocqueville, *Democracy in America*, trans. Phillips Bradley, 2 vols. (New York: Random House, Vintage Books, 1945), 1:60–66; Messerli, *Horace Mann*, p. 328.

37. Messerli, *Horace Mann*, p. 329.

38. *Ibid.*, p. 331; Vincent P. Lannie, ed., *Henry Barnard: American Educator* (New York: Teachers College Press, 1974), pp. 12–13.

39. Cubberley, *Public Education*, pp. 214–216; Frederick M. Binder, *The Age of the Common School, 1830–1865* (New York: John Wiley and Sons, 1974), p. 92.

40. Messerli, *Horace Mann*, p. 290.

41. Mann, *Fourth Annual Report of the Secretary of the School*, in *Republic and School*, ed. Cremin, pp. 51–52.

42. Cubberley, *Public Education*, pp. 359–360; Edwards and Richey, *School in Social Order*, pp. 307–309.

43. Messerli, *Horace Mann*, p. 403.

44. Orestes Brownson, "In opposition to centralization" (1839), in *School Reform: Past and Present*, ed. Michael B. Katz (Boston: Little, Brown, 1971), p. 284.

45. Messerli, *Horace Mann*, pp. 298–301, 329.

46. Cubberley, *Public Education*, p. 383.

47. Henry Barnard, *Third Annual Report of the Secretary of the Board* (1841), in *Henry Barnard: American Educator*, ed. Vincent P. Lannie (New York: Teachers College, 1974), p. 110.

48. Maris A. Vinovskis and Richard M. Bernard, *Women in Education in Ante-Bellum America* (Madison: University of Wisconsin Center for Demography & Ecology, 1973), p. 20.

49. Barnard, *Third Annual Report*, in *Henry Barnard*, ed. Lannie, p. 111.

50. Clifton Johnson, *Old-Time Schools and School-books* (1904; reprint ed., New York: Dover Books, 1963), pp. 119–134.

51. Brownson, "In opposition," in *School Reform*, ed. Katz, pp. 281–282.

52. *Ibid.*, p. 286.

53. *Ibid.*, pp. 277–278.

Chapter Four

1. Oscar Handlin, *Boston's Immigrants* (New York: Atheneum, 1974), pp. 43–51; Philip Taylor, *The Distant Magnet: European Emigration to U.S.A.* (New York: Harper Torchbooks, 1972), pp. 35–37.

2. Taylor, *The Distant Magnet*, pp. 174–175; Carl Russell Fish, *The Rise of the Common Man* (Chicago: Quadrangle Paperbacks, 1971), pp. 112–113.

3. Stephan Thernstrom, *Poverty and Progress: Social Mobility in a Nineteenth Century City* (New York: Atheneum, 1974), p. 27; Handlin, *Boston's Immigrants*, pp. 60, 250–251.

4. Frances Trollope, *Domestic Manners of the Americans* (New York: Knopf, 1949), pp. 52–55; Handlin, *Boston's Immigrants*, pp. 250–251.

5. Handlin, *Boston's Immigrants*, pp. 74–78.

6. *Ibid.*, pp. 78–80.

7. *Ibid.*, pp. 88–115; Rowland Berthoff, *An Unsettled People: Social Order and Disorder in American History* (New York: Harper and Row, 1971), pp. 226–227.

8. Handlin, *Boston's Immigrants*, pp. 151–175.

9. Carl F. Kaestle, *The Evolution of an Urban School System: New York City, 1750–1850* (Cambridge, Mass.: Harvard University Press, 1973), pp. 145–148.

10. Handlin, *Boston's Immigrants*, pp. 135–136; Kaestle, *Urban School System*, pp. 151–154; Thernstrom, *Poverty and Progress*, p. 24.

11. Ruth Miller Elson, *Guardians of Tradition* (Lincoln: University of Nebraska Press, 1964), pp. 125, 47–51.

12. Kaestle, *Urban School System*, pp. 154–156.

13. *Ibid.*, p. 86; Diane Ravitch, *The Great School Wars: New York City, 1805–1973* (New York: Basic Books, Harper Colophon, 1974), pp. 20–21, 26.

14. Ravitch, *The Great School Wars*, pp. 37–41.

15. Francis X. Curran, *The Churches and the Schools* (Chicago: Loyola University Press, 1954), pp. 85–86, 100–101.

16. Frederick M. Binder, *The Age of the Common School, 1830–1865* (New York: John Wiley & Sons, 1974), pp. 67–70.

17. Sam Bass Warner, Jr., *The Private City: Philadelphia in Three Periods of Its Growth* (Philadelphia: University of Pennsylvania Press, 1968), pp. 76–78, 137–140; John R. Commons, et al., *History of Labour in the United States*, 4 vols. (New York: Macmillan, 1918–1935), 1: 188–192.

18. Binder, *The Age of the Common School*, p. 63; Fish, *The Rise of the Common Man*, p. 115; Warner, *The Private City*, pp. 143–151.

19. Kaestle, *Urban School System*, p. 143.

20. Ravitch, *The Great School Wars*, p. 32.

21. Thernstrom, *Poverty and Progress*, pp. 24–25; Merle Curti, *The Social Ideas of American Educators* (Totowa, New Jersey: Littlefield, Adams, 1974), pp. 119–120.

22. Sherman Smith, *The Relation of the State to Religious Education in Massachusetts* (Syracuse, N.Y.: Syracuse University Book Store, 1926), p. 191–197.

23. George Stewart, Jr., *A History of Religious Education in Connecticut* (New Haven: Yale University Press, 1924), pp. 290–292.

24. Rush Welter, *Popular Education and Democratic Thought in America* (New York: Teachers College Press, 1962), pp. 106–107.
25. Handlin, *Boston's Immigrants*, p. 117.
26. Stanley K. Schultz, *The Culture Factory* (New York: Oxford University Press, 1973), pp. 298–300.
27. *Ibid.*, pp. 300–302.
28. *Ibid.*, pp. 299–301.
29. David Rothman, *The Discovery of the Asylum* (Boston: Little, Brown, 1971), p. 262.
30. Michael B. Katz, *The Irony of Early School Reform* (Boston: Beacon Press, 1968), pp. 41–42.
31. Schultz, *The Culture Factory*, p. 306.
32. *Ibid.*, p. 304.
33. Michael B. Katz, ed., *School Reform: Past and Present* (Boston: Little Brown & Co., 1971), p. 170.
34. Schultz, *The Culture Factory*, p. 302; Handlin, *Boston's Immigrants*, p. 135.

Chapter Five

1. Stephan Thernstrom, *Poverty and Progress: Social Mobility in a Nineteenth Century City* (New York: Atheneum, 1974), p. 24.
2. Jonathan Messerli, *Horace Mann* (New York: Knopf, 1972), p. 373.
3. Horace Mann, *Twelfth Annual Report of the Secretary of the Board* (1848), in *The Republic and the School: Horace Mann on The Education of Free Men*, ed. Lawrence A. Cremin (New York: Teachers College Press, 1957), p. 80.
4. Carl F. Kaestle, *The Evolution of an Urban School System: New York City, 1750–1850* (Cambridge, Mass.: Harvard University Press, 1973), pp. 92, 89.
5. Alexander James Field, "Educational Expansion in Mid-Nineteenth Century Massachusetts: Human-Capital Formation or Structural Reinforcement?," *Harvard Educational Review* 46, no. 4 (November 1976):526–528; Albert Fishlow, "The American Common School Revival: Fact or Fancy?," in *Industrialization in Two Systems*, ed. Henry Rosovsky (New York: John Wiley & Sons, 1966), p. 54.

Chapter Six

1. Arthur Schlesinger, *The Rise of the City* (New York: Macmillan Co., 1933), p. 192.

2. Joseph F. Kett, *Rites of Passage: Adolescence in America, 1790 to the Present* (New York: Basic Books, 1977), pp. 5–6, 243–244.

3. G. Stanley Hall, *Adolescence: Its Psychology and Its Relations to Physiology, Anthropology, Sociology, Sex, Crime, Religion and Education*, 2 vols. (New York: D. Appleton & Co., 1905).

4. *Ibid.*, 1:x, 333, 349.

5. *Ibid.*, p. xiv.

6. *Ibid.*, pp. xvi, xv.

7. *Ibid.*, p. 468; G. Stanley Hall, "How and When to Be Frank with Boys," *Ladies' Home Journal* 24 (September 1907): 26.

8. *Nineteenth Century Reader's Guide to Periodical Literature*, (1890–1899), 2 vols. (New York: H. W. Wilson, 1944), 1:312–313, 1463; *Reader's Guide to Periodical Literature* (1900–1904), 1:167; *Reader's Guide* (1905–1909), 2:260–262, 1205–1206.

9. *Reader's Guide* (1905–1909), 2:261.

10. Bernard Wishy, *The Child and the Republic: The Dawn of Modern American Child Nurture* (Philadelphia: University of Penn. Press, 1972), pp. 131–132.

11. Thomas C. Cochran and William Miller, *The Age of Enterprise: A Social History of Industrial America*, rev. ed. (New York: Harper Torchbooks, 1961), pp. 211–227.

12. Schlesinger, *The Rise of the City*, pp. 67, 68–69.

13. *Ibid.*, pp. 67–68.

14. Philip Taylor, *The Distant Magnet: European Emigration to U.S.A.* (New York: Harper Torchbooks, 1972), pp. 66–90.

15. *Ibid.*, p. 71.

16. David Brody, *Steelworkers in America: The Nonunion Era* (New York: Harper Torchbooks, 1969), pp. 27–49.

17. Taylor, *The Distant Magnet*, p. 196.

18. Jane Addams, *The Spirit of Youth and the City Streets* (1909; reprint ed., Urbana, Illinois: University of Illinois Press, 1972), pp. 3–21.

19. Anthony Platt, *The Child Savers: The Invention of Delinquency* (Chicago: University of Chicago Press, 1969), pp. 98–100, 137–145.

20. Joseph M. Hawes, *Children in Urban Society: Juvenile Delinquency in Nineteenth-Century America* (New York: Oxford University Press, 1971), pp. 171, 246.

21. Platt, *The Child Savers*, p. 140; Hawes, *Children in Urban Society*, pp. 179–186.

22. Platt, *The Child Savers*, p. 139.

23. Hall, *Adolescence*, 1:238; Addams, *Spirit of Youth*, p. 80.

24. Jane Addams, *Twenty Years at Hull-House* (1910; reprint ed., New York: Macmillan, Signet, 1960), pp. 227–228.

25. John Dewey, *The School and Society*, rev. ed. (Chicago: University of Chicago Press, 1915), p. 9.

26. *Ibid.*, pp. 9–12.

27. Robert H. Wiebe, *The Search for Order: 1877–1920* (New York: Hill and Wang, 1967), pp. 168–169.

28. Addams, *Twenty Years*, pp. 221, 227; Moses Rischin, *The Promised City: New York's Jews, 1870–1914* (New York: Harper Torchbooks, 1970), p. 206.

29. Wiebe, *The Search for Order*, pp. 168–171; Rischin, *The Promised City*, pp. 207–208.

30. Christopher Lasch, *The New Radicalism in America [1889–1963]: The Intellectual as a Social Type* (New York: Knopf, 1965), pp. 3–15; George E. Mowry, *The Era of Theodore Roosevelt and the Birth of Modern America: 1900–1912* (New York: Harper Torchbooks, 1962), pp. 86–87, 90–92; Dewey, *The School and Society*, pp. 9–12.

31. William Appleman Williams, *The Contours of American History* (New York: Franklin Watts, 1973), p. 333; Frank Luther Mott, *A History of American Magazines*, 5 vols. (Cambridge: Harvard University Press, 1938–1957), 4:173, 215.

32. Matthew Josephson, *The Politicos: 1865–1896* (New York: Harcourt, Brace & World, Harvest Books, 1963), pp. 508–509; Ray Ginger, *Altgeld's America: The Lincoln Ideal Versus Changing Realities* (New York: Franklin Watts, 1974), pp. 157–163, 177–179.

33. Walter Feinberg and Henry Rosemont, Jr., "Training for the Welfare State: The Progressive Education Movement," in *Work, Technology, and Education: Dissenting Essays in the Intellectual Foundations of American Education*, ed. Walter Feinberg and Henry Rosemont, Jr. (Urbana: University of Illinois Press, 1975), pp. 70–73.

34. Herbert G. Gutman, *Work, Culture, and Society in Industrializing America* (New York: Random House, Vintage Books, 1977), p. 33; Cochran and Miller, *The Age of Enterprise*, p. 136; Edward Chase Kirkland, *Industry Comes of Age: Business, Labor, and Public Policy, 1860–1897* (Chicago: Quadrangle Paperbacks, 1967), p. 171, 165.

35. Lewis Corey, *The Decline of American Capitalism* (New York: Covici Friede, 1934), pp. 27, 32.

36. Frederick Jackson Turner, *The Frontier in American History* (New York: Holt, 1920).

37. Dewey, *School and Society*, pp. 23–24; John Dewey, "A Policy of Industrial Education," *New Republic* 1, no. 7 (December 19, 1914): 12; Jane Addams, *Democracy and Social Ethics* (Cambridge, Mass.: Harvard University Press, Belknap Press, 1964), pp. 205–220.

38. Dewey, *School and Society*, p. 29.

39. John Dewey, *Democracy and Education: An Introduction to the Philosophy of Education* (New York: Macmillan, 1916), pp. 15, 16–17.

40. *Ibid.*, p. 231; Dewey, *School and Society*, pp. 14–18.

Chapter Seven

1. George E. Mowry, *The Era of Theodore Roosevelt and the Birth of Modern America: 1900–1912* (New York: Harper Torchbooks, 1962), pp. 78, 92–93.

2. *Ibid.*, pp. 59–60; Robert Wiebe, *The Search for Order: 1877–1920* (New York: Hill and Wang, 1967), pp. 159–163, 168, 174–175; Lincoln Steffens, *The Shame of the Cities* (1904; reprint ed., New York: Hill and Wang, 1957), pp. 1–12.

3. David Tyack, *The One Best System: A History of American Urban Education* (Cambridge, Mass.: Harvard University Press, 1974), pp. 78–80, 129–132.

4. *Ibid.*, pp. 79–80; Joseph M. Cronin, *The Control of Urban Schools: Perspective on the Power of Educational Reformers* (New York: Free Press, 1973), p. 57.

5. Raymond E. Callahan, *Education and the Cult of Efficiency: A Study of the Social Forces That Have Shaped the Administration of the Public Schools* (Chicago: University of Chicago Press, 1962), pp. 3–5, 14–15; Tyack, *One Best System*, pp. 100–101, 151–152; Lawrence A. Cremin, *The Transformation of the School: Progressivism in American Education: 1876–1957* (New York: Random House, Vintage Books, 1964), pp. 3–8.

6. Diane Ravitch, *The Great School Wars: New York City, 1805–1973* (New York: Basic Books, Harper Colophon, 1974), pp. 122–123; Tyack, *One Best System*, pp. 68, 151.

7. James Weinstein, *The Corporate Ideal in the Liberal State: 1900–1918* (Boston: Beacon Press, 1968), pp. 92–116; Wiebe, *Search for Order*, pp. 174–177.

8. Samuel P. Hays, "The Politics of Reform in Municipal Government in the Progressive Era," *Pacific Northwest Quarterly* 55 (October 1964): 159; Tyack, *One Best System*, p. 137.

9. William Issel, "Modernization in Philadelphia School Reform, 1882–1905," in *Education in American History: Readings on the Social Issues*, ed. Michael B. Katz (New York: Praeger, 1973), p. 182; David C. Hammack, "The Centralization of New York City's Public School System" (M.A. thesis, Columbia University, 1969), p. 344.

10. Hays, "Politics of Reform," p. 160; Hammack, "Centralization," pp. 343, 345–346, 365.

11. Tyack, *One Best System*, pp. 129–132, 150–152; Cronin, *Control of Urban Schools*, p. 84.

12. Tyack, *One Best System*, pp. 148, 139–140; Cronin, *Control of Urban Schools*, pp. 79, 82.

13. Tyack, *One Best System*, pp. 150–153; Issel, "Modernization," pp. 189–191; Hammack, "Centralization," pp. 372–375, 388–389.

14. Sol Cohen, *Progressives and Urban School Reform* (New York: Teachers College Press, 1964), p. 40; Tyack, *One Best System*, p. 143.

15. Tyack, *One Best System*, pp. 140–145; Callahan, *Education*, p. 6.

16. Tyack, *One Best System*, pp. 21–27.

17. Elwood P. Cubberley, *Public Education in the United States*, rev. ed. (Boston: Houghton Mifflin, 1934), p. 722.

18. Cronin, *Control of Urban Schools*, pp. 116–119.

19. *Ibid.*, p. 72.

20. Tyack, *One Best System*, pp. 157–158.

21. Issel, "Modernization," pp. 181–198.

22. Tyack, *One Best System*, p. 169.

23. Cronin, *Control of Urban Schools*, pp. 125–127; Tyack, *One Best System*, p. 141.

Chapter Eight

1. Colin Greer, *The Great School Legend: A Revisionist Interpretation of American Public Education* (New York: Viking Press, 1973), p. 118; David Tyack, *The One Best System: A History of American Urban Education* (Cambridge, Mass.: Harvard University Press, 1974), p. 230.

2. Greer, *Great School Legend*, p. 108.

3. United States Office of Education, *Digest of Educational Statistics* (Washington, D.C.: Government Printing Office, 1970), pp. 27, 28.

4. Michael B. Katz, *The Irony of Early School Reform: Educational Innovation in Mid-Nineteenth Century Massachusetts* (Boston: Beacon Press, 1968), pp. 35–40.

5. *Ibid.*, pp. 28–29, 36–37, 48–50.
6. Edward Chase Kirkland, *Dream and Thought in the Business Community, 1860–1900* (Chicago: Quadrangle Paperbacks, 1964), pp. 69–70.
7. *Ibid.*, pp. 75–80; Lawrence A. Cremin, *The Transformation of the School: Progressivism in American Education: 1876–1957* (New York: Random House, Vintage Books, 1964), pp. 32–34; Berenice M. Fisher, *Industrial Education: American Ideals and Institutions* (Madison: University of Wisconsin Press, 1967), pp. 72–77.
8. Marvin Lazerson, *Origins of the Urban School: Public Education in Massachusetts, 1870–1915* (Cambridge, Mass.: Harvard University Press, 1971), pp. 92–96.
9. Fisher, *Industrial Education*, pp. 78–82; Cremin, *Transformation of the School*, pp. 29–32; Lazerson, *Origins of the Urban School*, pp. 125–131.
10. Cremin, *Transformation of the School*, p. 36.
11. Fisher, *Industrial Education*, p. 76; U.S. Office of Education, *Digest of Educational Statistics*, p. 27.
12. Alba M. Edwards, *Sixteenth Census Reports: Comparative Occupation Statistics for the United States, 1870–1940* (Washington, D.C.: Government Printing Office, 1943), pp. 100, 110.
13. Harry Braverman, *Labor and Monopoly Capital: The Degradation of Work in the Twentieth Century* (New York: Monthly Review Press, 1974), p. 297.
14. C. Wright Mills, *White Collar: The American Middle Classes* (New York: Oxford University Press, 1956), pp. 5, 63–70.
15. David Brody, *Steelworkers in America: The Nonunion Era* (New York: Harper Torchbooks, 1969), p. 96; Philip Taylor, *The Distant Magnet: European Emigration to the U.S.A.* (New York: Harper Torchbooks, 1972), pp. 195–199.
16. Harold C. Livesay, *Andrew Carnegie and the Rise of Big Business* (Boston: Little, Brown, 1975, p. 134); NAM (1905) in *American Education and Vocationalism: A Documentary History, 1870–1970*, ed. Marvin Lazerson and W. Norton Grubb (New York: Teachers College Press, 1974), pp. 90–91.
17. U.S. Office of Education, *Digest of Educational Statistics*, p. 27.
18. Edward A. Krug, *The Shaping of the American High School: 1880–1920*, 2 vols. (Madison: University of Wisconsin Press, 1969), 1:169–171, 178; Patricia Albjerg Graham, *Community and Class in American Education, 1865–1918* (New York: John Wiley & Sons, 1974), pp. 18–19.

19. NEA (1897), p. 53.
20. Edward Chase Kirkland, *Industry Comes of Age: Business, Labor, and Public Policy, 1860–1897* (Chicago: Quadrangle Paperbacks, 1967), p. 281.
21. William Appleman Williams, *The Tragedy of American Diplomacy*, 2nd rev. ed. (New York: Delta, 1972), pp. 28–49.
22. Krug, *American High School*, 1:66; James Weinstein, *The Corporate Ideal in the Liberal State: 1900–1918* (Boston: Beacon Press, 1968), pp. 3–10.
23. Cremin, *Transformation of the School*, pp. 38–39; NSPIE, *Bulletin No. 1* (January 1907), p. 10.
24. NAM (1905), in *American Education*, ed. Lazerson and Grubb, pp. 88–89, 91–92; Weinstein, *Corporate Ideal*, pp. 13–17.
25. NEA (1905), p. 142.
26. NAM (1905), in *American Education*, ed. Lazerson and Grubb, pp. 91–92.
27. *Ibid.*, pp. 90–91.
28. NSPIE, *Bulletin No. 3* (September 1907), pp. 16–17.
29. *Ibid.*, pp. 34–35.
30. *Ibid.*, p. 28.
31. *Ibid.*, p. 53.
32. Fisher, *Industrial Education*, pp. 120, 124–126.
33. Lazerson, *Origins of the Urban School*, p. 181.
34. *Ibid.*, pp. 172–173; Massachusetts Commission on Industrial and Technical Education, *Report of the Sub-Committee on the Relation of Children to the Industries* (1906), in *American Education*, ed. Lazerson and Grubb, p. 78.

Chapter Nine

1. NEA (1898), p. 761.
2. Edward A. Krug, *The Shaping of the American High School: 1880–1920*, 2 vols. (Madison: University of Wisconsin Press, 1969), 1:280.
3. NAM (1912), in *American Education and Vocationalism: A Documentary History, 1870–1970*, ed. Marvin Lazerson and W. Norton Grubb (New York: Teachers College Press, 1974), p. 97.
4. *Ibid.*, pp. 97–99.
5. NEA (1895), pp. 731–732.

6. NEA (1903), p. 65; NEA (1907), p. 778; NEA (1909), pp. 49, v–ix.
7. David Tyack, *The One Best System: A History of American Urban Education* (Cambridge, Mass.: Harvard University Press, 1974), pp. 264–265.
8. *Ibid.*, pp. 188–189.
9. NEA (1908), p. 157.
10. *Ibid.*, (1908), p. 158.
11. *Ibid.*, (1908), pp. 754–755.
12. *Ibid.*, (1910), p. 203.
13. *Ibid.*, (1910), pp. v–vi.
14. *Ibid.*, (1905), pp. 436–444.
15. *Ibid.*, (1897), p. 53; Commissioner (1910), 2:1139.
16. Krug, *American High School*, 1:176–177, 286–287.
17. Commissioner (1916), p. 487.
18. Krug, *American High School*, 1:176–177, 278–283.
19. Patricia Albjerg Graham, *Community and Class in American Education, 1865–1918* (New York: John Wiley & Sons, 1974), pp. 79–81.
20. Robert S. Lynd and Helen Merrell Lynd, *Middletown: A Study in American Culture* (1929; reprint ed., New York: Harcourt, Brace & World, Harvest Books, 1956), p. 192.
21. Graham, *Community and Class*, p. 59.
22. John Dewey, *The School and Society*, rev. ed. (Chicago: University of Chicago Press, 1915), p. 27; Krug, *American High School*, 1:200–203.
23. Edgar B. Gumbert and Joel H. Spring, *The Superschool and the Superstate: American Education in the Twentieth Century, 1918–1970* (New York: John Wiley & Sons, 1974), pp. 87–112.
24. Krug, *American High School*, 1:278–282, 191–195.
25. NSPIE, *Bulletin No. 5* (April 1908), pp. 12–13.
26. Henry Allen Bullock, *A History of Negro Education in the South: From 1619 to the Present* (New York: Praeger, 1970), p. 149; Newton Edwards and Herman G. Richey, *The School in the American Social Order*, rev. ed. (Boston: Houghton Mifflin, 1963), pp. 491–493, 496–497; Graham, *Community and Class*, pp. 101–102, 105–107.
27. Graham, *Community and Class*, pp. 107–109.
28. James D. Anderson, "Education as a Vehicle for the Manipulation of Black Workers," in *Work, Technology, and Education: Dissenting Essays in the Intellectual Foundations of American Education*, ed. Walter Feinberg and Henry Rosemont, Jr. (Urbana: University of Illinois Press, 1975), pp. 33–34.
29. Berenice M. Fisher, *Industrial Education: American Ideals and Institu-*

tions (Madison: University of Wisconsin Press, 1967), pp. 163–164.

30. Krug, *American High School*, 1: 171–172; Graham, *Community and Class*, p. 23.

31. Krug, *American High School*, 1: 347, 279.

32. *Ibid.*, pp. 279, 281–282.

33. Lynd and Lynd, *Middletown*, p. 196.

34. NEA (1910), p. 128.

35. *Ibid.*, p. 131.

36. Krug, *American High School*, 1: 278, 309.

37. *Ibid.*, pp. 308, 357–358.

38. Lynd and Lynd, *Middletown*, p. 197.

39. *Ibid.*, p. 193; President's Research Committee on Social Trends, *Recent Social Trends in the United States* (New York: McGraw-Hill, 1933), p. 331.

40. Commissioner (1916), p. 487; President's Research Committee, *Recent Social Trends*, p. 331.

Chapter Ten

1. American Federation of Labor, *Labor and Education: A Brief Outline of the Resolutions and Pronouncements Adopted by the A. F. of L.* (Washington, D.C.: A. F. of L., 1939), p. 12.

2. AFL (1915), pp. 322–323.

3. NSPIE, *Bulletin No. 5* (April 1908), pp. 49–50.

4. AFL (1915), pp. 322–323.

5. Edward A. Krug, *The Shaping of the American High School: 1880–1920*, 2 vols. (Madison: University of Wisconsin Press, 1969), 1: 247–248.

6. U.S. Bureau of Education, "Vocational Secondary Education," *Bulletin No. 21* (1916), pp. 72–76.

7. NEA (1915), pp. 728–729.

8. *Ibid.*, (1895), pp. 731–732.

9. *Ibid.*, (1908), pp. 74–75.

10. David Tyack, *The One Best System: A History of American Urban Education* (Cambridge, Mass.: Harvard University Press, 1974), pp. 267–268; Robert Wiebe, *The Search for Order: 1877–1920* (New York: Hill and Wang, 1967), pp. 117–120.

11. NEA (1908), pp. 74–75.

12. Krug, *American High School*, 1: 230–231, 235, 243.

13. NEA (1914), p. 160.

14. Marvin Lazerson, *Origins of the Urban School: Public Education in Massachusetts, 1870–1915* (Cambridge, Mass.: Harvard University Press, 1971), p. 166.

15. Krug, *American High School*, 1: 235.

16. Mary J. Herrick, *The Chicago Schools: A Social and Political History* (Beverly Hills, Calif.: Sage Publications, 1971), p. 118; George S. Counts, *School and Society in Chicago* (New York: Harcourt, Brace, and World, 1928), pp. 138–139.

17. Herrick, *Chicago Schools*, pp. 118–119; Counts, *School and Society*, pp. 137–139.

18. NEA (1914), p. 170.

19. "Educational News and Editorial Comment: Types of Leadership," *School Review* 12 (April 1914):262.

20. John Dewey, "An Undemocratic Proposal" (1912), in Robert Bremner, ed., *Children and Youth in America: A Documentary History*, 3 vols. (Cambridge, Mass.: Harvard University Press, 1970), 2:1418.

21. NEA (1914), p. 170.

22. Berenice M. Fisher, *Industrial Education: American Ideals and Institutions* (Madison: University of Wisconsin Press, 1967), pp. 133–136.

23. Marvin Lazerson and W. Norton Grubb, "Introduction," in *American Education and Vocationalism: A Documentary History, 1870–1970*, ed. Lazerson and Grubb (New York: Teachers College Press, 1974), pp. 31–32.

24. August B. Hollingshead, *Elmtown's Youth: The Impact of Social Classes on Adolescents* (New York: John Wiley & Sons, 1949), pp. 163–203.

25. Willis Rudy, *Schools in an Age of Mass Culture: An Exploration of Selected Themes in the History of Twentieth-Century American Education* (Englewood Cliffs, N.J.: Prentice-Hall, 1965), pp. 164–188.

Chapter Eleven

1. C. Wright Mills, *White Collar: The American Middle Classes* (New York: Oxford University Press, 1956), pp. 3–9, 63–70; President's Research Committee on Social Trends, *Recent Social Trends in the United States* (New York: McGraw-Hill, 1933), pp. 284–292.

2. Robert S. Lynd and Helen Merrell Lynd, *Middletown: A Study in American Culture* (1929; reprint ed., New York: Harcourt, Brace, and World, Harvest Books, 1956), p. 45.

3. Mills, *White Collar*, p. 16.

4. Lynd and Lynd, *Middletown*, p. 49.

5. Edward A. Krug, *The Shaping of the American High School:* 2 vols. (Madison: University of Wisconsin Press, 1972), 2:44–45.

6. Krug, *American High School*, 2: 310; U.S. Office of Education, *Digest of Educational Statistics* (Washington, D.C.: Government Printing Office, 1970), p. 27.

7. Stuart Ewen, *Captains of Consciousness: Advertising and the Social Roots of the Consumer Culture* (New York: McGraw-Hill, 1976), pp. 31–102.

8. Thomas C. Cochran, *American Business in the Twentieth Century* (Cambridge, Mass.: Harvard University Press, 1972), p. 85.

9. Lynd and Lynd, *Middletown*, p. 44.

10. *Ibid.*, pp. 186–187.

11. CFAT, *The States and Higher Education: A Proud Past and a Vital Future* (San Francisco: Jossey-Bass, 1976), p. 30.

12. Christopher Jencks and David Riesman, *The Academic Revolution* (Garden City, New York: Doubleday, Anchor Books, 1969), p. 94.

13. Jencks and Riesman, *The Academic Revolution*, p. 279; Burton J. Bledstein, *The Culture of Professionalism: The Middle Class and the Development of Higher Education in America* (New York: Norton, 1976), pp. 121–128.

14. Frederick Rudolph, *The American College and University: A History* (New York: Random House, Vintage Books, 1962), pp. 257–259; Jencks and Riesman, *The Academic Revolution*, pp. 225–227.

15. C. Wright Mills, *The Power Elite* (New York: Oxford University Press, 1957), pp. 128–129.

16. CFAT, *More than Survival: Prospects for Higher Education in a Period of Uncertainty* (San Francisco: Jossey-Bass, 1975), p. 27.

17. Lynd and Lynd, *Middletown*, p. 30; Edgar B. Gumbert and Joel H. Spring, *The Superschool and the Superstate: American Education in the Twentieth Century, 1918–1970* (New York: John Wiley & Sons, 1974), p. 128; U.S. Office of Education, *Digest of Educational Statistics*, p. 27.

18. Gumbert and Spring, *The Superschool*, p. 128.

19. Lynd and Lynd, *Middletown*, pp. 30–35.

20. *Ibid.*, pp. 55–63.

21. U.S. Bureau of the Census, *Historical Statistics of the U.S.—Colonial Times to 1970* (Washington, D.C.: Government Printing Office, 1975), p. 135.

Chapter Twelve

1. U.S. Bureau of the Census, *Historical Statistics of the U.S.—Colonial Times to 1970* (Washington, D.C.: Government Printing Office, 1975), p. 135.

2. Robert Lekachman, *The Age of Keynes* (New York: Random House, Vintage Books, 1966), pp. 112–116, 104.

3. *Ibid.*, p. 153; John Morton Blum, *V Was For Victory: Politics and American Culture During World War II* (New York: Harcourt Brace Jovanovich, 1976), p. 91.

4. Blum, *V Was For Victory*, p. 122.

5. *Ibid.*, pp. 124–131; David W. Eakins, "Business Planners and America's Postwar Expansion," in *Corporations and the Cold War*, ed. David Horowitz (New York: Monthly Review Press, 1969), pp. 143–169.

6. Gabriel Kolko, *The Politics of War: The World and U.S. Foreign Policy, 1943–1945* (New York: Random House, 1968), pp. 242–247; Gabriel Kolko and Joyce Kolko, *The Limits of Power: The World and U.S. Foreign Policy, 1945–1954* (New York: Harper & Row, 1972), pp. 11–16, 20–27.

7. David R. B. Ross, *Preparing for Ulysses: Politics and Veterans During World War II* (New York: Columbia University Press, 1969), p. 34.

8. Keith W. Olson, *The G.I. Bill, the Veterans, and the Colleges* (Lexington, Kentucky: The University Press of Kentucky, 1974), p. 20.

9. Eric F. Goldman, *The Crucial Decade—And After: America, 1945–1960* (New York: Random House, Vintage Books, 1960), p. 6.

10. Ross, *Preparing for Ulysses*, pp. 36–37; Olson, *The G.I. Bill*, pp. 3–6.

11. Olson, *The G.I. Bill*, p. 8; Ross, *Preparing for Ulysses*, pp. 55–56, 61, 64.

12. Olson, *The G.I. Bill*, pp. 18–24; Blum, *V Was For Victory*, pp. 249–250.

13. Olson, *The G.I. Bill*, p. 23.

14. Blum, *V Was For Victory*, pp. 142–145.

15. Olson, *The G.I. Bill*, pp. 33–34, 25.

16. *Ibid.*, pp. 45, 72–74, 88, 43.

17. *Ibid.*, pp. 45–57, 55, 50–51.

18. *Ibid.*, pp. 74–75.

Chapter Thirteen

1. John Morton Blum, *V Was For Victory: Politics and American Culture During World War II* (New York: Harcourt Brace Jovanovich, 1976), pp. 100–105.

2. Eric F. Goldman, *The Crucial Decade—And After: America, 1945–1960* (New York: Random House, Vintage Books, 1960), pp. 80–81; William Appleman Williams, *The Tragedy of American Diplomacy*, 2nd ed. (New York: Delta, 1972), pp. 267–268, 273.

3. Gabriel Kolko and Joyce Kolko, *The Limits of Power: The World and U.S. Foreign Policy, 1945–1954* (New York: Harper & Row, 1972), pp. 11–15.

4. Williams, *American Diplomacy*, pp. 270–273; Thomas G. Paterson, "The Quest for Peace and Prosperity: International Trade, Communism, and the Marshall Plan," in *Politics and Policies of the Truman Administration*, ed. Barton J. Bernstein (Chicago: Quadrangle Books, 1972), pp. 102–105.

5. Paul A. Baran and Paul M. Sweezy, *Monopoly Capital: An Essay on the American Economic and Social Order* (New York: Modern Reader Paperbacks, 1966), p. 212; Rowland Berthoff, *An Unsettled People: Social Order and Disorder in American History* (New York: Harper & Row, 1971), p. 457.

6. Baran and Sweezy, *Monopoly Capital*, p. 176; James O'Connor, *The Fiscal Crisis of the State* (New York: St. Martin's Press, 1973), p. 97.

7. Thomas C. Cochran, *American Business in the Twentieth Century* (Cambridge, Mass.: Harvard University Press, 1972), p. 172; Goldman, *The Crucial Decade*, p. 239.

8. Goldman, *The Crucial Decade*, pp. 239–242.

9. Godfrey Hodgson, *America in Our Time* (New York: Random House, Vintage Books, 1978), pp. 80–81.

10. O'Connor, *The Fiscal Crisis*, pp. 23–24, 97–99, 101–107.

11. Alain Touraine, *The Academic System in American Society* (New York: McGraw-Hill, 1974), p. 45.

12. J. L. Penick, *The Politics of American Science—1939 to the Present* (Chicago: Rand-McNally, 1965), p. 42.

13. Daniel Bell, *The Coming of Post-Industrial Society: A Venture in Social Forecasting* (New York: Basic Books, Harper Colophon, 1976), pp. 252, 259; Fritz Machlup, *The Production and Distribution of Knowledge in the United States* (Princeton, N.J.: Princeton University Press, 1962), p. 156.

14. Bell, *Coming of Post-Industrial Society*, pp. 254–258; Frank Newman, et al., *The Second Newman Report: National Policy and Higher Education* (Cambridge, Mass.: The MIT Press, 1973), p. 165.

15. Don K. Price, *The Scientific Estate* (Cambridge, Mass.: Harvard University Press, 1965), p. 40; J. R. Killian, Jr., "University Research," in *The Corporation and the Campus*, ed. Robert H. Connery (New York: Praeger, 1970), p. 40.

16. Seymour Melman, *Our Depleted Society* (New York: Delta Books, 1965), pp. 92–94; O'Connor, *The Fiscal Crisis*, pp. 166–167.

17. Bell, *Coming of Post-Industrial Society*, p. 254.

18. Henry Jackson, quoted in Goldman, *The Crucial Decade*, p. 308; Joel Spring, *The Sorting Machine: National Educational Policy Since 1945* (New York: McKay, 1976), pp. 96–99; David D. Henry, *Challenges Past, Challenges Present: An Analysis of American Higher Education Since 1930* (San Francisco: Jossey-Bass, 1975), pp. 117–121.

19. Robert Bendiner, *Obstacle Course on Capitol Hill* (New York: McGraw-Hill, 1965); Spring, *The Sorting Machine*, pp. 98–102; Henry, *Challenges Past, Challenges Present*, pp. 121–122.

20. Henry, *Challenges Past, Challenges Present*, pp. 121–126; Alice M. Rivlin, *The Role of the Federal Government in Financing Higher Education* (Washington, D.C.: Brookings Institution, 1961), pp. 61–62; Bell, *Coming of Post-Industrial Society*, p. 234.

21. Henry, *Challenges Past, Challenges Present*, p. 85–98.

22. Melman, *Our Depleted Society*, p. 85.

23. Machlup, *Production and Distribution*, pp. 83, 152; Rivlin, *Financing Higher Education*, p. 38.

24. Rivlin, *Financing Higher Education*, p. 59.

25. *Ibid.*, p. 59; Clark Kerr, *The Uses of the University* (New York: Harper & Row, Harper Torchbooks, 1966), p. 55.

26. Rivlin, *Financing Higher Education*, p. 59.

27. Harold Hodgkinson, *Institutions in Transition: A Profile of Change in Higher Education* (New York: McGraw-Hill, 1971), pp. 16–18; Touraine, *Academic System*, p. 159.

28. Kerr, *The Uses of the University*, p. 59.

29. Touraine, *Academic System*, pp. 134, 260.

30. Merle Curti and Roderick Nash, *Philanthropy in the Shaping of American Higher Education* (New Brunswick, N.J.: Rutgers University Press, 1965), p. 227.

31. Edward Chase Kirkland, *Dream and Thought in the Business Community, 1860–1900* (Chicago: Quadrangle Paperbacks, 1964), pp. 95–101; Curti and Nash, *Philanthropy*, pp. 231, 226, 233–234.

32. Curti and Nash, *Philanthropy*, p. 250.

33. *Ibid.*, pp. 242–243, 251.

34. Hayden W. Smith, "Prospects for Voluntary Support," in *The Corporation and the Campus*, ed. Connery, p. 135.

35. Curti and Nash, *Philanthropy*, pp. 235–237.

36. Bell, *Coming of Post-Industrial Society*, pp. 245–246.

Chapter Fourteen

1. U.S. Bureau of the Census, *Historical Statistics of the U.S.—Colonial Times to 1970* (Washington, D.C.: Government Printing Office, 1975), p. 135.

2. Robert Lekachman, *The Age of Keynes* (New York: Random House, Vintage Books, 1966), p. 175.

3. James O'Connor, *The Fiscal Crisis of the State* (New York: St. Martin's Press, 1973), pp. 25–29, 22–23.

4. Harry Braverman, *Labor and Monopoly Capital: The Degradation of Work in the Twentieth Century* (New York: Monthly Review Press, 1974), p. 238.

5. Frances Fox Piven and Richard A. Cloward, *Regulating the Poor: The Functions of Public Welfare* (New York: Random House, Vintage Books, 1971), pp. 200–201, 214–215.

6. Braverman, *Labor and Monopoly Capital*, pp. 385–386, 390–391; Godfrey Hodgson, *America in Our Time* (New York: Random House, Vintage Books, 1978), pp. 480–481.

7. Ely Chinoy, *Automobile Workers and the American Dream* (Boston: Beacon Press, 1965), pp. 126–127.

8. Peter Schrag, *The Decline of the Wasp* (New York: Simon and Schuster, 1971), pp. 47–56.

9. Christopher Jencks and David Riesman, *The Academic Revolution* (Garden City, N.Y.: Doubleday, Anchor Books, 1969), pp. 71–72.

10. Chinoy, *Automobile Workers*, p. 6.

11. *Ibid.*, pp. 4–6.

12. William H. Whyte, Jr., *The Organization Man* (New York: Simon and Schuster, Clarion Books, 1972), pp. 63–78.

13. Chinoy, *Automobile Workers*, p. 127.

14. President's Commission on Higher Education, *Higher Education for American Democracy*, 6 vols. (Washington, D.C.: Government Printing Office, 1947), vol. 1, *Establishing the Goals*, pp. 28, 68–69.

15. *Ibid.*, vol. 2, *Equalizing and Expanding Individual Opportunity*, pp. 6–9.

16. NEA (1908), p. 157; President's Commission, *Higher Education for American Democracy*, 1:67–69; *Ibid.*, 2:7.

17. President's Commission, *Higher Education for American Democracy*, 1:39; *Ibid.*, vol. 5, *Financing Higher Education*, p. 26; Frank Newman et al., *The Second Newman Report: National Policy and Higher Education* (Cambridge, Mass.: The MIT Press, 1973), p. 165.

18. Keith W. Olson, *The G.I. Bill, the Veterans, and the Colleges* (Lexington: The University Press of Kentucky, 1974), p. 44; Alice M. Rivlin, *The Role of the Federal Government in Financing Higher Education* (Washington, D.C.: Brookings Institution, 1961), p. 70.

19. Harold L. Hodgkinson, *Institutions in Transition: A Profile of Change in Higher Education* (New York: McGraw-Hill, 1971), p. 51; Bureau of the Census, *Historical Statistics*, pp. 1141, 135.

20. Jencks and Riesman, *The Academic Revolution*, p. 98; T. R. McConnell, *A General Pattern for American Public Higher Education* (New York: McGraw-Hill, 1962), p. 1.

21. David D. Henry, *Challenges Past, Challenges Present: An Analysis of American Higher Education Since 1930* (San Francisco: Jossey-Bass, 1975), pp. 99–103; Martin Trow, "Reflections on the Transition from Mass to Universal Higher Education," in *The Embattled University*, ed. Stephen R. Graubard and Geno A. Ballotti (New York: Braziller, 1970), pp. 3–4.

22. Jencks and Riesman, *The Academic Revolution*, pp. 279–286, 272–273.

23. Newman et al., *The Second Newman Report*, pp. 51–158.

24. McConnell, *American Public Higher Education*, p. 113; S. V. Martorana and Ernest V. Hollis, *State Boards Responsible for Higher Education* (Washington, D.C.: Department of Health, Education, and Welfare, 1960), p. 3.

25. McConnell, *American Public Higher Education*, p. 18.

26. Henry, *Challenges Past, Challenges Present*, p. 99.

27. McConnell, *American Public Higher Education*, p. 20.

28. James Bryant Conant, *The Citadel of Learning* (New Haven: Yale University Press, 1956), pp. 70–79.

29. John W. Gardner, *Excellence: Can We Be Equal and Excellent Too?* (New York: Harper & Row, Perennial Library, 1971), p. 83.

30. McConnell, *American Public Higher Education*, p. 97.

31. James Bryant Conant, *Shaping Educational Policy* (New York: McGraw-Hill, 1964), p. 103.

32. *Ibid.*, pp. 99–100.

33. Newman et al., *The Second Newman Report*, pp. 18–27, 33–35;

L. Steven Zwerling, *Second Best: The Crisis of the Community College* (New York: McGraw-Hill, 1976), pp. 72–73.

34. Newman et al., *The Second Newman Report*, pp. 20–25, 27–35; Jencks and Riesman, *The Academic Revolution*, pp. 99–100.

35. Colin Greer, *The Great School Legend: A Revisionist Interpretation of American Public Education* (New York: Viking, 1973), p. 59; Newman et al., *The Second Newman Report*, pp. 20–25.

36. D. Kent Halstead, *Statewide Planning in Higher Education* (Washington, D.C.: Department of Health, Education, and Welfare, 1974), p. 10; CFAT, *The States and Higher Education: A Proud Past and a Vital Future* (San Francisco: Jossey-Bass, 1976), p. 85.

37. Council for Higher Education, *Master Plan for Higher Education in Maryland* (Baltimore: Maryland Council For Higher Education, 1968), pp. 5–7; Halstead, *Statewide Planning*, pp. 192–208.

38. Hodgkinson, *Institutions in Transition*, pp. 48–50.

39. CFAT, *The States and Higher Education*, p. 85; Newman et al., *The Second Newman Report*, p. 50.

Chapter Fifteen

1. Richard I. Ferrin, *A Decade of Change in Free-Access Higher Education* (New York: College Entrance Examination Board, 1971), p. 41; American Council on Education, *A Fact Book on Higher Education, 1976* (Washington, D.C.: American Council on Education, 1976) pp. 103, 111; D. Kent Halstead, *Statewide Planning in Higher Education* (Washington, D.C.: Department of Health, Education and Welfare, 1974), pp. 88, 108–109.

2. Frank Newman et al., *The Second Newman Report: National Policy and Higher Education* (Cambridge, Mass.: The MIT Press, 1973), pp. 2, 3.

3. Amitai Etzioni, *Wall Street Journal* (March 17, 1970), quoted in Samuel Bowles and Herbert Gintis, *Schooling in Capitalist America: Educational Reform and the Contradictions of Economic Life* (New York: Basic Books, 1976), p. 203.

4. Christopher Jencks and David Riesman, *The Academic Revolution* (Garden City, N.Y.: Doubleday, Anchor Books, 1969), pp. 491–492.

5. *Ibid.*, pp. 264–265, 279–283.

6. K. Patricia Cross, "The New Learners," in *On Learning and Change*, eds. *Change Magazine* (New Rochelle, N.Y.: *Change*, 1973), pp. 68, 73; Newman et al., *The Second Newman Report*, pp. 3, 28–33; Fred

Pincus, "Tracking in Community Colleges," *Insurgent Sociologist* 4, no. 3 (Spring 1974):23–27.

7. K. Patricia Cross, *Beyond the Open Door* (San Francisco: Jossey-Bass, 1971), pp. 6–7, 175–182.

8. *Ibid.*, p. 7.

9. *Ibid.*

10. Newman et al., *The Second Newman Report*, pp. 28, 143.

11. American Council on Education, *A Fact Book, 1976*, p. 80.

12. President's Commission on Higher Education, *Higher Education for American Democracy*, 6 vols. (Washington, D.C.: Government Printing Office, 1947), vol. 2, *Equalizing and Expanding Individual Opportunity*, p. 7.

13. Carnegie Commission on Higher Education, *A Chance to Learn* (New York: McGraw-Hill, 1970), p. 11.

14. CFAT, *More than Survival: Prospects for Higher Education in a Period of Uncertainty* (San Francisco: Jossey-Bass, 1975), pp. 114–115.

15. Ferrin, *A Decade of Change*, p. 27.

16. Cross, "The New Learners," in *On Learning and Change*, pp. 68–69.

17. American Council on Education, *A Fact Book, 1976*, p. 192.

18. A. J. Jaffe and W. Adams, "Two Models of Open Enrollment," in *Universal Higher Education*, ed. L. Wilson and O. Mills (Washington, D.C.: American Council on Education, 1972), p. 232.

19. Charles R. Monroe, *Profile of the Community College: A Handbook* (San Francisco: Jossey-Bass, 1976), pp. 185–186.

20. Ferrin, *A Decade of Change*, pp. 17, 19, 61, 59.

21. Newman et al., *The Second Newman Report*, pp. 2–4.

22. Christopher Jencks et al., *Inequality: A Reassessment of the Effect of Family and Schooling in America* (New York: Harper & Row, Harper Colophon, 1973), pp. 33–34.

23. *Ibid.*, pp. 149–150, 156–159.

24. Cross, *Beyond*, p. 6.

25. Ellen Kay Trimberger, "Open Admissions: A New Form of Tracking?" *Insurgent Sociologist* 4, no. 1 (Fall 1973):37.

26. Bowles and Gintis, *Schooling in Capitalist America*, p. 210.

27. Eugene C. Lee and Frank M. Bowen, *The Multicampus University* (New York: McGraw-Hill, 1971), p. 4.

28. Trimberger, "Open Admissions," p. 37.

29. American Council on Education, "The American Freshman," A.C.E. Research Reports 6, no. 6 (1971), p. 39.

30. Alain Touraine, *The Academic System in American Society* (New York: McGraw-Hill, 1974), p. 94.

31. Newman et al., *The Second Newman Report*, p. 30.
32. Jerome Karabel, "Community Colleges and Social Stratification," *Harvard Educational Review* 42, no. 4 (November 1972):541.
33. *Ibid.*, p. 530.
34. *Ibid.*, p. 533.
35. Halstead, *Statewide Planning*, p. 543; Karabel, "Community Colleges," p. 552.
36. Jaffe and Adams, "Two Models of Open Enrollment," p. 249.
37. Karabel, "Community Colleges," p. 532.
38. *Ibid.*, pp. 534–535.
39. Jencks and Riesman, *The Academic Revolution*, pp. 491–492; Halstead, *Statewide Planning*, pp. 88–89, 108–109.
40. Monroe, *Profile of the Community College*, pp. 37, 39.
41. Halstead, *Statewide Planning*, p. 209.
42. Monroe, *Profile of the Community College*, p. 39; Burton R. Clark, *The Open Door College* (New York: McGraw-Hill, 1960).
43. Jencks and Riesman, *The Academic Revolution*, pp. 19–24.
44. *Ibid.*, pp. 120–121, 218.
45. Association of American Medical Colleges, *Descriptive Study of Enrolled Medical Students* (Washington, D.C.: Association of American Medical Colleges, 1975), p. 24; American Council on Education, *A Fact Book on Higher Education, 1975* (Washington, D.C.: American Council on Education, 1975), p. 27.
46. James E. Blackwell, *Access of Black Students to Graduate and Professional Schools* (Atlanta: Southern Education Foundation, 1975), pp. 40, 38.
47. American Council on Education, *A Fact Book, 1975*, p. 204.
48. Touraine, *The Academic System*, p. 94.
49. Merle Curti, *The Social Ideas of American Educators* (Totowa, New Jersey: Littlefield, Adams & Co., 1974), p. 41; Monroe, *Profile of the Community College*, p. 37.
50. L. Steven Zwerling, *Second Best: The Crisis of the Community College* (New York: McGraw-Hill, 1976), pp. xviii–xxi, 75–103.
51. Karabel, "Community Colleges," pp. 549–550; *Idem.*, "Open Admissions: Towards Meritocracy or Democracy?" in *On Learning and Change*, ed. *Change Magazine* (New Rochelle N.Y.: *Change*, 1973), p. 86.
52. Monroe, *Profile of the Community College*, p. 235.
53. Karabel, "Community Colleges," p. 538.
54. Leland L. Medsker and Dale Tillery, *Breaking the Access Barriers: A Profile of Two-Year Colleges* (New York: McGraw-Hill, 1971), p. 60.

55. Monroe, *Profile of the Community College*, pp. 60, 186.
56. *New York Times*, "City U. Students Face Cut in Rolls," 5 March 1976, p. 23.
57. Monroe, *Profile of the Community College*, p. 30.
58. Jencks and Riesman, *The Academic Revolution*, pp. 487–488.
59. Zwerling, *Second Best*, pp. 17–25.
60. Newman et al., *The Second Newman Report*, pp. 33–34.

Conclusion

1. Frederick M. Binder, *The Age of the Common School, 1830–1865* (New York: John Wiley and Sons, 1974), pp. 22–54.
2. U.S. Office of Education, *Digest of Educational Statistics* (Washington, D.C.: Government Printing Office, 1970), p. 27; Edward A. Krug, *The Shaping of the American High School: 1880–1920*, 2 vols. (Madison: University of Wisconsin Press, 1969), 1: 178.
3. CFAT, *More than Survival: Prospects for Higher Education in a Period of Uncertainty* (San Francisco: Jossey-Bass, 1975), p. 27.
4. Martin Trow, "Reflections on the Transition from Mass to Universal Higher Education," in *The Embattled University*, ed. Stephen R. Graubard and Geno A. Ballotti (New York: George Braziller, 1970), pp. 1–4; Alain Touraine, *The Academic System in American Society* (New York: McGraw-Hill, 1974), pp. 83–84.

Bibliography

General

Barnard, John and David Burner. *The American Experience in Education.* New York: Franklin Watts, 1975.

Bernstein, Barton J., ed. *Towards a New Past: Dissenting Essays in American History.* New York: Random House, Vintage Books, 1969.

Berthoff, Rowland. *An Unsettled People: Social Order and Disorder in American History.* New York: Harper and Row, 1971.

Boorstin, Daniel J. *The Americans.* 3 vols. New York: Random House, Vintage Books, 1958.

Bowles, Samuel and Herbert Gintis. *Schooling in Capitalist America: Educational Reform and The Contradictions of Economic Life.* New York: Basic Books, 1976.

Bremner, Robert, ed. *Children and Youth in America: A Documentary History.* 3 vols. Cambridge, Mass.: Harvard University Press, 1970.

Bullock, Henry Allen. *A History of Negro Education in the South: From 1619 to the Present.* New York: Praeger, 1970.

Butts, R. Freeman and Lawrence A. Cremin. *A History of Education in American Culture.* New York: Holt, 1953.

Calhoun, Arthur. *A Social History of the American Family.* 3 vols. Cleveland: Arthur H. Clark, 1917–1919.

Calhoun, Daniel, ed. *The Educating of Americans: A Documentary History.* Boston: Houghton Mifflin, 1969.

Cremin, Lawrence A. *The Genius of American Education.* New York: Random House, Vintage Books, 1965.

Edwards, Newton and Herman G. Richey. *The School in the American Social Order*. 2d ed. Boston: Houghton Mifflin, 1963.

Greer, Colin. *The Great School Legend: A Revisionist Interpretation of American Public Education*. New York: Viking, 1973.

Hofstadter, Richard. *Anti-intellectualism in American Life*. New York: Knopf, 1963.

Hofstadter, Richard and Walter P. Metzger. *The Development of Academic Freedom in the United States*. New York: Columbia University Press, 1955.

Katz, Michael B. *Education in American History: Readings on the Social Issues*. New York: Praeger, 1973.

————, ed. *School Reform: Past and Present*. Boston: Little, Brown, 1971.

Kett, Joseph F. *Rites of Passage: Adolescence in America, 1790 to the Present*. New York: Basic Books, 1977.

Kuczynski, Jurgen. *A Short History of Labour Conditions Under Industrial Capitalism. Vol. 2: The United States of America, 1789–1946*. New York: Barnes and Noble, 1973.

Mott, Frank Luther. *A History of American Magazines*. 5 vols. Cambridge, Mass.: Harvard University Press, 1938–1957.

Perkinson, Henry J. *The Imperfect Panacea: American Faith in Education, 1865–1965*. New York: Random House, 1968.

Ravitch, Diane. *The Great School Wars: New York City, 1805–1973*. New York: Basic Books, Harper Colophon, 1974.

Robertson, Ross M. *History of the American Economy*. 3d ed. New York: Harcourt Brace Jovanovich, 1973.

Tyack, David. *The One Best System: A History of American Education*. Cambridge, Mass.: Harvard University Press, 1974.

Wiebe, Robert H. *The Segmented Society: An Introduction to the Meaning of America*. New York: Oxford University Press, 1975.

Williams, William Appleman. *The Contours of American History*. New York: Franklin Watts, 1973.

Part I

Bailyn, Bernard. *Education in the Forming of American Society*. New York: Norton, 1972.

Barr, Nelson. *Education in New Jersey: 1630–1871*. Princeton, N.J.: Princeton University Press, 1942.

Benson, Lee. *The Concept of Jacksonian Democracy: New York as a Test Case*. Princeton, N.J.: Princeton University Press, 1961.

Berrol, Selma Cantor. "The Schools of New York in Transition, 1898–1914." *Urban Review* 1:15–20.

———. "William Henry Maxwell and a New Educational New York." *History of Education Quarterly* 8:215–228.

Billington, Ray. *The Protestant Crusade, 1800–1860: A Study of the Origins of American Nativism.* New York: Macmillan, 1938.

Binder, Frederick M. *The Age of the Common School, 1830–1865.* New York: John Wiley and Sons, 1974.

Branch, Douglas. *The Sentimental Years, 1830–1860.* New York: Appleton-Century, 1934.

Burns, J. A. *The Growth and Development of the Catholic School System in the United States.* New York: Benziger Brothers, 1912.

Butler, Vera M. *Education as Revealed by New England Newspapers Prior to 1850.* 1935. Reprint. New York: Arno Press, 1969.

Calhoun, Daniel. *The Intelligence of a People.* Princeton, N.J.: Princeton University Press, 1973.

Carlton, Frank Tracy. *Economic Influences Upon Educational Progress in the United States, 1820–1850.* 1908. Reprint. New York: Teachers College Press, 1965.

Carter, James G. *Letters on the Free Schools of New England.* 1826. Reprint. New York: Teachers College Press, 1965.

Chevalier, Michel. *Society, Manners, and Politics in the United States.* trans. and ed., John William Ward. Ithaca, N.Y.: Cornell University Press, Cornell Paperbacks, 1969.

Clay, George R. "Children of the Young Republic." *American Heritage* 11:46–52.

Cochran, Thomas C. and William Miller. *The Age of Enterprise: A Social History of Industrial America.* rev. ed. New York: Harper Torchbooks, 1961.

Cole, Arthur C. *The Irrepressible Conflict, 1850–1865.* New York: Macmillan, 1934.

Commons, John R. et al. *The History of Labour in the United States.* Vol. 1. New York: Macmillan, 1918.

Cremin, Lawrence A. *The American Common School: An Historic Conception.* New York: Teachers College Press, 1951.

———. *American Education: The Colonial Experience, 1607–1783.* New York: Harper Torchbooks, 1970.

———, ed. *The Republic and the School: Horace Mann on The Education of Free Men.* New York: Teachers College Press, 1957.

Cubberley, Ellwood P. *Public Education in the United States.* 2d. ed., rev. Boston: Houghton Mifflin, 1934.

Curti, Merle. *The Social Ideas of American Educators.* Totowa, N.J.: Littlefield, Adams, 1974.

Demos, John. *A Little Commonwealth: Family Life in Plymouth Colony.* New York: Oxford University Press, 1970.

Douglass, Frederick. *Narrative of the Life of Frederick Douglass.* New York: Signet, 1968.

Eggleston, Edward. *The Hoosier School-Master.* 1871. Reprint. New York: Hill and Wang, 1965.

Elson, Ruth Miller. *Guardians of Tradition.* Lincoln, Neb.: University of Nebraska Press, 1964.

Feinberg, Walter and Henry Rosemont, Jr., eds. *Work, Technology, and Education: Dissenting Essays in the Intellectual Foundations of American Education.* Urbana, Ill.: University of Illinois Press, 1975.

Field, Alexander James. "Educational Expansion in Mid-Nineteenth Century Massachusetts: Human-Capital Formation or Structural Reinforcement?" *Harvard Educational Review* 46:521–552.

Finegan, Thomas E. *The Establishment and Development of the School System of the State of New York.* Syracuse, N.Y.: C. W. Brandon, 1913.

———. *Free Schools: A Documentary History of Free School Movement in New York State.* Albany: University of the State of New York, 1921.

Fish, Carl Russell. *The Rise of the Common Man.* Chicago: Quadrangle Paperbacks, 1971.

Foner, Eric. *Free Soil, Free Labor, Free Men: The Ideology of the Republican Party Before the Civil War.* New York: Oxford University Press, 1970.

Genovese, Eugene D. *Roll, Jordan, Roll: The World the Slaves Made.* New York: Random House, Vintage Books, 1976.

Gutman, Herbert G. *Work, Culture, and Society in Industrializing America.* New York: Random House, Vintage Books, 1977.

Habakkuk, H. J. *American and British Technology in the Nineteenth Century: The Search for Labour-Saving Inventions.* London: Cambridge University Press, 1962.

Handlin, Oscar. *Boston's Immigrants.* New York: Atheneum, 1974.

Hartz, Louis. *Economic Policy and Democratic Thought: Pennsylvania, 1776–1860.* Cambridge, Mass.: Harvard University Press, 1948.

Hoyt, Charles and R. Clyde Ford. *John D. Pierce: Founder of the Michigan School System.* Ypsilanti, Michigan: Scharf Tag, Label and Book, 1905.

Hugins, Walter, ed. *The Reform Impulse, 1825–1850.* New York: Harper and Row, 1972.

Jackson, Sidney. *America's Struggle for Free Schools.* New York: Russell and Russell, 1965.

Johnson, Clifton. *Old-Time Schools and School-books*. 1904. Reprint. New York: Dover Books, 1963.

Jorgenson, L. *The Founding of Public Education in Wisconsin*. Madison: State Historical Society of Wisconsin, 1956.

Kaestle, Carl F. *The Evolution of an Urban School System: New York City, 1750–1850*. Cambridge, Mass.: Harvard University Press, 1973.

Kasson, John F. *Civilizing the Machine: Technology and Republican Values in America, 1776–1900*. New York: Viking Press, 1976.

Katz, Michael B. *The Irony of Early School Reform: Educational Innovation in Mid-Nineteenth Century Massachusetts*. Boston: Beacon Press, 1968.

Lannie, Vincent P., ed. *Henry Barnard: American Educator*. New York: Teachers College Press, 1974.

———. *Public Money and Parochial Education: Bishop Hughes, Governor Seward, and the New York School Controversy*. Cleveland: Press of Case Western Reserve University, 1968.

Litwack, Leon F. *North of Slavery: The Negro in the Free States*. Chicago: University of Chicago Press, 1961.

McCadden, Joseph J. *Education in Pennsylvania, 1801–1835, and its Debt to Robert Vaux*. Philadelphia: University of Pennsylvania Press, 1937.

Mann, Horace. *Fifth Annual Report of the Secretary of the Board*. Boston: Dutton and Wentworth, State Printers, 1842.

Martineau, Harriet. *Society in America*. Gloucester, Mass.: Peter Smith, 1968.

May, Henry F. *Protestant Churches and Industrial America*. New York: Harper and Row, 1949.

Messerli, Jonathan. *Horace Mann*. New York: Knopf, 1972.

Meyers, Marvin. *The Jacksonian Persuasian: Politics and Belief*. Stanford, Ca.: Stanford University Press, 1957.

Michigan Department of Public Instruction. *Report of the Superintendent of Public Instruction*. Detroit: John S. Bagg, 1837.

Monroe, Paul. *Founding of the American Public School System*. New York: Macmillan, 1940.

Moones, Charles W., ed. *Caleb Mills and the Indiana School System*. Indianapolis: The Wood-Weaver Printing Co., 1905.

Morgan, Edmund S. *The Puritan Family: Religion and Domestic Relations in Seventeenth Century New England*. 2d ed., rev. New York: Harper Torchbooks, 1966.

Mosier, Richard D. *Making the American Mind*. New York: King's College Press, 1947.

New York State Legislature. *Documents of the Assembly of the State of New York*. 73rd Session. Vol. 6, no. 150, pp. 12–13.

————. Vol. 6, no. 166, pp. 25–26.

North, Douglass C. *The Economic Growth of the United States, 1790–1860.* New York: Norton, 1966.

Ohio Department of Education. *Annual Report of the State Commissioner of Common Schools for 1854.* Columbus: Statesman Steam Press, 1855.

Pawa, Jay Marvin. *The Attitude of Labor Organizations in New York State Toward Public Education, 1829–1890.* Ph.D. dissertation, Teachers College, Columbia University, 1964.

Pessen, Edward. *Riches, Class, and Power Before the Civil War.* Lexington, Mass.: D. C. Heath, 1973.

Randall, S. S. *History of the Common School System of the State of New York, from its Origin in 1795, to the Present Time: Including the Various City and Other Special Organizations, and the Religious Controversies of 1821, 1822, and 1840.* New York: Ivison, Blakeman, Taylor and Co., 1871.

Rosovsky, Henry, ed. *Industrialization in Two Systems.* New York: John Wiley and Sons, 1966.

Rothman, David. *The Discovery of the Asylum.* Boston: Little, Brown, 1971.

Schlesinger, Arthur. *The Rise of the City.* New York: Macmillan, 1933.

Schlesinger, Arthur M., Jr. *The Age of Jackson.* Boston: Little, Brown, 1945.

Schultz, Stanley K. *The Culture Factory: Boston Public Schools, 1789–1860.* New York: Oxford University Press, 1973.

Smith, Sherman. *The Relation of the State to Religious Education in Massachusetts.* Syracuse, N.Y.: Syracuse University Bookstore, 1926.

Smith, Timothy L. "Protestant Schooling and American Nationality, 1800–1850." *Journal of American History* 53:679–695.

————. *Revivalism and Social Reform in the Mid-Nineteenth Century.* New York: Abingdon Press, 1957.

Stewart, George, Jr. *A History of Religious Education in Connecticut.* New Haven: Yale University Press, 1924.

Taylor, George. *The Transportation Revolution.* New York: Rinehart, 1951.

Taylor, Philip. *The Distant Magnet: European Emigration to U.S.A.* New York: Harper Torchbooks, 1972.

Thernstrom, Stephan. *Poverty and Progress: Social Mobility in a Nineteenth Century City.* New York: Atheneum, 1974.

Tocqueville, Alexis de. *Democracy in America.* Translated by Phillips Bradley. 2 vols. New York: Random House, Vintage Books, 1945.

Trollope, Frances. *Domestic Manners of the Americans.* New York: Knopf, 1949.

Tyack, David B. "The Kingdom of God and the Common School: Protestant Ministers and the Educational Awakening in the West." *Harvard Educational Review* 31: 447–469.

Van Deusen, Glyndon G. *The Jacksonian Era: 1828–1848.* New York:
Harper Torchbooks, 1963.

Vinovskis, Maris A. "Horace Mann on the Economic Productivity of
Education." *New England Quarterly* 43:560–565.

———. "Trends in Massachusetts Education, 1826–1860." *History of
Education Quarterly* 12:501–529.

Vinovskis, Maris A. and Carl F. Kaestle. "Quantification, Urbanization
and the History of Education: An Analysis of the Determinants of
School Attendance in New York State in 1845." Madison: University
of Wisconsin Center For Demography and Ecology, 1973.

Vinovskis, Maris A. and Richard M. Bernard. "Women in Education in
Ante-Bellum America." Madison: University of Wisconsin Center for
Demography and Ecology, 1973.

Wade, Richard C. *The Urban Frontier: The Rise of Western Cities,
1790–1830.* Cambridge, Mass.: Harvard University Press, 1959.

Ware, Norman. *The Industrial Worker: 1840–1860.* Chicago: Quadrangle
Paperbacks, 1964.

Warner, Sam Bass, Jr. *The Private City: Philadelphia in Three Periods of
Its Growth.* Philadelphia: University of Pennsylvania Press, 1968.

Welter, Rush. *Popular Education and Democratic Thought in America.*
New York: Teachers College Press, 1962.

Wickersham, James Pyle. *A History of Education in Pennsylvania.* Lancaster, Pa.: Inquirer Publishing Co., 1886.

Wishy, Bernard. *The Child and The Republic: The Dawn of Modern American Child Nurture.* Philadelphia: University of Pennsylvania Press,
1972.

Wright, Louis B. *Culture on the Moving Frontier.* New York: Harper
Torchbooks, 1961.

Wyllie, Irvin G. *The Self-Made Man in America.* New York: Macmillan,
Free Press, 1966.

Part II

Adams, Henry. *The Education of Henry Adams: An Autobiography.* Boston: Houghton Mifflin, 1961.

Addams, Jane. *Democracy and Social Ethics.* Cambridge, Mass.: Harvard University Press, Belknap Press, 1964.

———. *The Spirit of Youth and the City Streets.* 1909. Reprint. Urbana,
Ill.: University of Illinois Press, 1972.

————. *Twenty Years at Hull-House.* 1910. Reprint. New York: Macmillan, Signet, 1960.

American Federation of Labor. *Labor and Education: A Brief Outline of Resolutions and Pronouncements Adopted by the A. F. of L.* Washington, D.C.: A. F. of L., 1939.

American Federation of Labor. *Report of Proceedings.* 1906–1915.

Braverman, Harry. *Labor and Monopoly Capital: The Degradation of Work in the Twentieth Century.* New York: Monthly Review Press, 1974.

Bremner, Robert. *American Philanthropy.* Chicago: University of Chicago, 1960.

————. *From the Depths: The Discovery of Poverty in the United States.* New York: New York University Press, 1956.

Brody, David. *Steelworkers in America: The Nonunion Era.* New York: Harper Torchbooks, 1969.

Brown, Elmer Ellsworth. *The Making of Our Middle Schools.* New York: Longmans, Green, 1914.

Callahan, Raymond E. *Education and the Cult of Efficiency: A Study of the Social Forces That Have Shaped the Administration of the Public Schools.* Chicago: University of Chicago Press, 1962.

Carlson, Robert A. *The Quest for Conformity: Americanization Through Education.* New York: John Wiley and Sons, 1975.

Carnoy, Martin. *Education as Cultural Imperialism.* New York: David McKay, 1974.

Cochran, Thomas C. *American Business in the Twentieth Century.* Cambridge, Mass.: Harvard University Press, 1972.

Cohen, David K. and Marvin Lazerson. "Education and the Corporate Order." *Socialist Revolution* 2:47–72.

Cohen, Sol. "The Industrial Education Movement, 1906–17." *American Quarterly* 20:95–110.

————. *Progressives and Urban School Reform.* New York: Teachers College Press, 1964.

Conant, James Bryant. *The Comprehensive High School.* New York: McGraw-Hill, 1967.

Counts, George S. *School and Society in Chicago.* New York: Harcourt, Brace and World, 1928.

Cremin, Lawrence A. *The Transformation of the School: Progressivism in American Education, 1876–1957.* New York: Random House, Vintage Books, 1964.

Cronin, Joseph M. *The Control of Urban Schools: Perspective on the Power of Educational Reformers.* New York: Free Press, 1973.

Curoe, Philip R. V. *Educational Attitudes and Policies of Organized Labor in the United States*. New York: Teachers College Press, 1926.

Curran, Francis X. *The Churches and the Schools*. Chicago: Loyola University Press, 1954.

Curti, Merle. *The Social Ideas of American Educators*. Totowa, N.J.: Littlefield, Adams, 1974.

Dewey, John. *Democracy and Education: An Introduction to the Philosophy of Education*. New York: Macmillan, 1916.

————. *Experience and Education*. New York: Collier, 1963.

————. "A Policy of Industrial Education." *New Republic* 1: 11–12.

————. *The School and Society*. Rev. ed. Chicago: University of Chicago Press, 1915.

————. "Splitting Up the School System." *New Republic* 2:283–284.

Drinnon, Richard. *Rebel in Paradise: A Biography of Emma Goldman*. Boston: Beacon, 1970.

Ensign, Forest. *Compulsory School Attendance and Child Labor*. Iowa City: Athens Press, 1921.

Ewen, Stuart. *Captains of Consciousness: Advertising and the Social Roots of the Consumer Culture*. New York: McGraw-Hill, 1976.

Fisher, Berenice M. *Industrial Education: American Ideals and Institutions*. Madison, Wis.: University of Wisconsin Press, 1967.

Gersman, Elinor M. "Progressive Reform of the St. Louis School Board, 1897." *History of Education Quarterly* 10:3–21.

Ginger, Ray. *Altgeld's America: The Lincoln Ideal Versus Changing Realities*. New York: Franklin Watts, 1974.

————. *Eugene V. Debs: A Biography*. New York: Collier, 1962.

Graham, Patricia Albjerg. *Community and Class in American Education, 1865–1918*. New York: John Wiley and Sons, 1974.

Hall, G. Stanley. *Adolescence: Its Psychology and Its Relations to Physiology, Anthropology, Sociology, Sex, Crime, Religion and Education*. 2 vols. New York: D. Appleton, 1905.

————. "How and When to be Frank with Boys." *Ladies Home Journal* 24:26.

Hammack, David C. "The Centralization of New York City's Public School System." M.A. thesis, Columbia University, 1969.

Handlin, Oscar. *The Uprooted*. 2d ed. Boston: Little, Brown, 1973.

Hawes, Joseph M. *Children in Urban Society: Juvenile Delinquency in Nineteenth Century America*. New York: Oxford University Press, 1971.

Hays, Samuel P. "The Politics of Reform in Municipal Government in the Progressive Era." *Pacific Northwest Quarterly* 55: 157–169.

———. *The Response to Industrialism*. Chicago: University of Chicago Press, 1957.

Henry, Jules. *Culture Against Man*. New York: Random House, Vintage Books, 1963.

Herrick, Mary J. *The Chicago Schools: A Social and Political History*. Beverly Hills, Ca.: Sage Publications, 1971.

Higham, John. *Strangers in the Land: Patterns of American Nativism, 1860–1925*. New York: Atheneum, 1966.

Hofstadter, Richard. *The Age of Reform*. New York: Random House, 1955.

———. *Social Darwinism in American Thought*. Rev. ed. Boston: Beacon, 1955.

Hollingshead, August B. *Elmtown's Youth: The Impact of Social Classes on Adolescents*. New York: John Wiley and Sons, 1949.

Howe, Irving. *World of Our Fathers*. New York: Simon and Schuster, Touchstone Books, 1976.

Josephson, Matthew. *The Politicos: 1865–1896*. New York: Harcourt, Brace and World, Harvest Books, 1963.

———. *The Robber Barons: The Great American Capitalists, 1861–1901*. New York: Harcourt, Brace and World, Harvest Books, 1962.

Karier, Clarence J., Paul Violas, and Joel Spring. *Roots of Crisis: American Education in the Twentieth Century*. Chicago: Rand McNally, 1973.

Katz, Michael B. *Class, Bureaucracy, and Schools: The Illusion of Educational Change in America*. New York: Praeger, 1971.

———. "The Emergence of Bureaucracy in Urban Education: The Boston Case, 1850–1884." *History of Education Quarterly* 8:155–188, 319–357.

———. *The Irony of Early School Reform: Educational Innovation in Mid-Nineteenth Century Massachusetts*. Boston: Beacon, 1968.

Kazin, Alfred. *A Walker in the City*. New York: Harcourt, Brace and World, 1951.

Kessner, Thomas. *The Golden Door: Italian and Jewish Immigrant Mobility in New York City, 1880–1915*. New York: Oxford University Press, 1977.

Kirkland, Edward Chase. *Dream and Thought in the Business Community, 1860–1900*. Chicago: Quadrangle Paperbacks, 1964.

———. *Industry Comes of Age: Business, Labor, and Public Policy, 1860–1897*. Chicago: Quadrangle Paperbacks, 1967.

Kolko, Gabriel. *Railroads and Regulation, 1877–1916*. Princeton, N.J.: Princeton University Press, 1965.

———. *The Triumph of Conservatism: A Reinterpretation of American History, 1900–1916*. New York: Macmillan, 1963.

Korman, Gerd. *Industrialization, Immigrants, and Americanizers*. Madison, Wis.: State Historical Society of Wisconsin, 1967.

Krug, Edward A. *The Shaping of the American High School: 1880–1941*. 2 vols. Madison, Wis.: University of Wisconsin Press, 1969.

Lacour-Gayet, Robert. *Everyday Life in the United States Before the Civil War: 1830–1860*. New York: Fredrick Ungar, 1969.

Lasch, Christopher. *The New Radicalism in America* [1889–1963]: *The Intellectual as a Social Type*. New York: Knopf, 1965.

Lazerson, Marvin. *Origins of the Urban School: Public Education in Massachusetts, 1870–1915*. Cambridge, Mass.: Harvard University Press, 1971.

Lazerson, Marvin and W. Norton Grubb, eds. *American Education and Vocationalism: A Documentary History, 1870–1970*. New York: Teachers College Press, 1974.

Livesay, Harold C. *Andrew Carnegie and the Rise of Big Business*. Boston: Little, Brown, 1975.

Lubove, Roy. *The Professional Altruist: The Emergence of Social Work as a Career*. Cambridge, Mass.: Harvard University Press, 1965.

Lynd, Robert S. and Helen Merrell Lynd. *Middletown: A Study in American Culture*. 1929. Reprint. New York: Harcourt, Brace and World, Harvest Books, 1956.

Massachusetts Commission on Industrial and Technical Education. *Report*. Boston: n.p., 1906.

Mennel, Robert M. *Thorns and Thistles: Juvenile Delinquents in the United States, 1825–1940*. Hanover, N.H.: University Press of New England, 1973.

Mills, C. Wright. *White Collar: The American Middle Classes*. New York: Oxford University Press, Galaxy Books, 1956.

Morgan, H. Wayne. *Unity and Culture: The United States, 1877–1900*. Baltimore: Penguin Books, 1971.

Mowry, George E. *The Era of Theodore Roosevelt and the Birth of Modern America: 1900–1912*. New York: Harper Torchbooks, 1962.

National Association of Manufacturers. *Proceedings of the Annual Convention*. 1905, 1912.

National Education Association. *Journal of Proceedings and Addresses*. 1880–1920.

National Society for the Promotion of Industrial Education. *Bulletins*. 1907–1915.

New York City Board of Education. *Annual Reports of the City Superintendent of Schools*. 1898–1899.

Osofsky, Gilbert. *Harlem: The Making of a Ghetto: Negro New York, 1890–1930*. New York: Harper Torchbooks, 1968.

Ostrander, Gilman M. *American Civilization in the First Machine Age,
1890–1940*. New York: Harper Torchbooks, 1972.

Platt, Anthony. *The Child Savers: The Invention of Delinquency*. Chicago:
University of Chicago Press, 1969.

President's Research Committee on Social Trends in the United States.
Recent Social Trends in the United States. New York: McGraw-Hill,
1933.

Riis, Jacob A. *How the Other Half Lives: Studies Among the Tenements of
New York*. 1890. Reprint. New York: Hill and Wang, 1957.

Rischin, Moses. *The Promised City: New York's Jews, 1870–1914*. Cambridge, Mass.: Harvard University Press, 1962.

Rosenberg, Nathan. *Technology and American Economic Growth*. New
York: Harper Torchbooks, 1972.

Rudolph, Fredrick. *The American College and University*. New York:
Random House, Vintage Books, 1962.

Rudy, Willis. *Schools in an Age of Mass Culture: An Exploration of Selected Themes in the History of Twentieth-Century American Education*.
Englewood Cliffs, N.J.: Prentice-Hall, 1965.

Schlesinger, Arthur. *The Rise of the City*. New York: Macmillan, 1933.

School Review, eds. "Educational News and Editorial Comment: Types
of Leadership." *School Review* 22:262.

Smith, Timothy L. "Immigrant Social Aspirations and American Education, 1880–1930." *American Quarterly* 21:523–543.

Spring, Joel H. *Education and the Rise of the Corporate State*. Boston:
Beacon, 1972.

Steffens, Lincoln. *The Shame of the Cities*. 1904. Reprint. New York: Hill
and Wang, American Century, 1957.

Swift, David. *Ideology and Change in the Public Schools: Latent Functions
of Progressive Education*. Columbus, Ohio: Merrill, 1971.

Symes, Lilian and Clement Travers. *Rebel America: The Story of Social
Revolt in the United States*. New York: Harper and Row, 1934.

Taylor, Philip. *The Distant Magnet: European Emigration to the U.S.A.*
New York: Harper Torchbooks, 1972.

Troen, Selwyn. "Popular Education in Nineteenth Century St. Louis."
History of Education Quarterly 13:23–40.

Turner, Fredrick Jackson. *The Frontier in American History*. New York:
Holt, 1920.

Tyack, David B. "Bureaucracy and the Common School: The Example
of Portland, Oregon, 1851–1913." *American Quarterly* 19:475–498.

U.S. Bureau of Education. "Vocational Secondary Education." *Bulletin
no. 21*. Washington, D.C.: Government Printing Office, 1916.

U.S. Department of the Interior, Commissioner of Education. *Annual Reports*. 1888/9–1916/17.

U.S. Office of Education. *Digest of Educational Statistics*. Washington, D.C.: Government Printing Office, 1970.

Venn, Grant. *Man, Education, and Work*. Washington, D.C.: American Council on Education, 1964.

Warner, Sam Bass, Jr. *The Private City: Philadelphia in Three Periods of its Growth*. Philadelphia: University of Pennsylvania Press, 1968.

Weinstein, James. *The Corporate Ideal in the Liberal State: 1900–1918*. Boston: Beacon, 1968.

Wiebe, Robert. *The Search for Order: 1877–1920*. New York: Hill and Wang, 1967.

———. "The Social Functions of Public Education." *American Quarterly* 21: 147–164.

Williams, William Appleman. *The Roots of the Modern American Empire: A Study of the Growth and Shaping of Social Consciousness in a Marketplace Society*. New York: Random House, 1969.

———. *The Tragedy of American Diplomacy*. 2nd rev. ed. New York: Delta, 1972.

Part III

American Council on Education. "The American Freshman: National Norms for Fall, 1971." *A.C.E. Research Reports*. Vol. 6, no. 6.

———. *A Fact Book on Higher Education, 1974–1976*. Washington, D.C.: American Council on Education, 1974–1976.

Aptheker, Bettina. *The Academic Rebellion in the United States*. Secaucus, N.J.: Citadel Press, 1972.

Aronowitz, Stanley. *False Promises*. New York: McGraw-Hill, 1973.

———. *Food, Shelter, and the American Dream*. New York: Seabury, 1974.

Ashby, Eric. *Any Person, Any Study: An Essay on American Higher Education*. New York: McGraw-Hill, 1971.

Association of American Medical Colleges. *Descriptive Study of Enrolled Medical Students*. Washington, D.C.: Association of American Medical Colleges, 1975.

Baran, Paul A. and Paul M. Sweezy. *Monopoly Capital: An Essay on the American Economic and Social Order*. New York: Modern Reader Paperbacks, 1966.

Bell, Daniel. *The Coming of Post-Industrial Society: A Venture in Social Forecasting*. New York: Basic Books, Harper Colophon, 1976.

Ben-David, J. *American Higher Education: Directions Old and New*. New York: McGraw-Hill, 1972.

Bendiner, Robert. *Obstacle Course on Capitol Hill*. New York: McGraw-Hill, 1965.

Bensman, Joseph and Arthur J. Vidich. *The New American Society: The Revolution of the Middle Class*. Chicago: Quadrangle Books, 1971.

Bernstein, Barton J., ed. *Politics and Policies of the Truman Administration*. Chicago: Quadrangle Books, 1972.

Bird, Caroline. *The Case Against College*. New York: David McKay, 1975.

Blackwell, James E. *Access of Black Students to Graduate and Professional Schools*. Atlanta: Southern Education Foundation, 1975.

Bledstein, Burton J. *The Culture of Professionalism: The Middle Class and the Development of Higher Education in America*. New York: Norton, 1976.

Blum, John Morton. *V Was For Victory: Politics and American Culture During World War II*. New York: Harcourt, Brace and Jovanovich, 1976.

Bowles, Frank H. "The Evolution of Admissions Requirements." *College Admissions*. Princeton, N.J.: College Entrance Examination Board, 1956.

Braverman, Harry. *Labor and Monopoly Capital: The Degradation of Work in the Twentieth Century*. New York: Monthly Review Press, 1974.

Carnegie Commission on Higher Education. *The Campus and the City*. New York: McGraw-Hill, 1972.

———. *The Capitol and the Campus: State Responsibility and Higher Education*. New York: McGraw-Hill, 1971.

———. *A Chance to Learn: An Action Agenda for Equal Opportunity in Higher Education*. New York: McGraw-Hill, 1970.

———. *Higher Education: Who Pays? Who Benefits? Who Should Pay?* New York: McGraw-Hill, 1973.

———. *New Students and New Places: Policies for the Future Growth and Development of Higher Education*. New York: McGraw-Hill, 1971.

———. *The Open-Door Colleges: Policies for the Community Colleges*. New York: McGraw-Hill, 1970.

———. *Priorities for Action: Final Report*. New York: McGraw-Hill, 1973.

Carnegie Foundation for the Advancement of Teaching. *More Than Survival*. San Francisco: Jossey-Bass, 1975.

————. *The States and Higher Education*. San Francisco: Jossey-Bass, 1976.

Catton, Bruce. *The War Lords of Washington*. New York: Harcourt, Brace, 1948.

Change Magazine, eds. *On Learning and Change*. New Rochelle, N.Y.: *Change Magazine*, 1973.

Chinoy, Ely. *Automobile Workers and The American Dream*. Boston: Beacon, 1965.

Cloward, Richard A. and Frances Fox Piven. *The Politics of Turmoil*. New York: Random House, Vintage Books, 1975.

Cochran, Thomas C. *American Business in the Twentieth Century*. Cambridge, Mass.: Harvard University Press, 1972.

Conant, James Bryant. *The Citadel of Learning*. New Haven: Yale University Press, 1956.

————. *Shaping Educational Policy*. New York: McGraw-Hill, 1964.

————. *Slums and Suburbs*. New York: McGraw-Hill, 1961.

Connery, Robert H., ed. *The Corporation and the Campus*. New York: Praeger, 1970.

Corey, Lewis. *The Decline of American Capitalism*. New York: Covici Friede, 1934.

Cross, K. Patrica. *Beyond the Open Door*. San Francisco: Jossey-Bass, 1971.

Curti, Merle and Roderick Nash. *Philanthropy in the Shaping of American Higher Education*. New Brunswick, N.J.: Rutgers University Press, 1965.

Educational Policies Commission. *Higher Education in a Decade of Decision*. Washington, D.C.: National Education Association, 1957.

Ferrin, Richard I. *A Decade of Change in Free-Access Higher Education*. New York: College Entrance Examination Board, 1971.

Freeland, Richard M. *The Truman Doctrine and the Origins of McCarthyism: Foreign Policy, Domestic Politics, and Internal Security, 1946–48*. New York: Knopf, 1972.

Galbraith, John Kenneth. *The New Industrial State*. 2d ed., rev. New York: New American Library, 1972.

Gans, Herbert J. *The Urban Villagers: Group and Class in the Life of Italian-Americans*. New York: Free Press, 1962.

Gardner, John W. *Excellence: Can We Be Equal and Excellent Too?* New York: Harper and Row, Perennial Library, 1971.

Gartner, Alan, Colin Greer, and Frank Riessman. *The New Assault on Equality: IQ and Social Stratification*. New York: Harper and Row, 1974.

Goldman, Eric F. *The Crucial Decade—And After: America, 1945–1960*. New York: Random House, Vintage Books, 1960.

Goodman, Paul. *Growing Up Absurd: Problems of Youth in the Organized Society*. New York: Random House, Vintage Books, 1960.

Graubard, Stephen R. and Geno A. Ballotti, eds. *The Embattled University*. New York: Braziller, 1970.

Gumbert, Edgar B. and Joel H. Spring. *The Superschool and the Superstate: American Education in the Twentieth Century, 1918–1970*. New York: John Wiley and Sons, 1974.

Halstead, D. Kent. *Statewide Planning in Higher Education*. Washington, D.C.: Department of Health, Education and Welfare, 1974.

Handlin, Oscar and Mary F. Handlin. *The American College and American Culture: Socialization as a Function of Higher Education*. New York: McGraw-Hill, 1970.

Harris, Seymour E. *A Statistical Portrait of Higher Education*. New York: McGraw-Hill, 1972.

Henry, David D. *Challenges Past, Challenges Present: An Analysis of American Higher Education Since 1930*. San Francisco: Jossey-Bass, 1975.

Hodgkinson, Harold. *Institutions in Transition: A Profile of Change in Higher Education*. New York: McGraw-Hill, 1971.

Hodgson, Godfrey. *America in Our Time*. New York: Random House, Vintage Books, 1978.

Horowitz, David, ed. *Corporations and the Cold War*. New York: Monthly Review Press, 1969.

Jencks, Christopher and David Riesman. *The Academic Revolution*. Garden City, N.Y.: Doubleday, Anchor Books, 1969.

Jencks, Christopher, et al. *Inequality: A Reassessment of the Effect of Family and Schooling in America*. New York: Harper and Row, Harper Colophon, 1973.

Karabel, Jerome. "Community Colleges and Social Stratification." *Harvard Educational Review* 42: 521–561.

Keniston, Kenneth. *Young Radicals: Notes on Committed Youth*. New York: Harcourt, Brace and World, 1968.

———. *Youth and Dissent: The Rise of a New Opposition*. New York: Harcourt, Brace and Jovanovich, Harvest Books, 1971.

Kerr, Clark. *The Uses of the University*. New York: Harper and Row, Harper Torchbooks, 1966.

Kolko, Gabriel. *The Politics of War: the World and U.S. Foreign Policy, 1943–1945*. New York: Random House, 1968.

———. *Wealth and Power in America: An Analysis of Social Class and Income Distribution*. New York: Praeger, 1962.

Kolko, Gabriel and Joyce Kolko. *The Limits of Power: the World and U.S. Foreign Policy, 1945–1954.* New York: Harper and Row, 1972.

Lauter, Paul and Florence Howe. *The Conspiracy of the Young.* New York: World, 1971.

Lee, Eugene C. and Frank M. Bowen. *The Multicampus University.* New York: McGraw-Hill, 1971.

Lekachman, Robert. *The Age of Keynes.* New York: Random House, Vintage Books, 1966.

Lynd, Robert S. and Helen Merrell Lynd. *Middleton: A Study in American Culture.* 1929. Reprint. New York: Harcourt, Brace and World, Harvest Books, 1956.

McConnell, T. R. *A General Pattern for American Public Higher Education.* New York: McGraw-Hill, 1962.

Machlup, Fritz. *The Production and Distribution of Knowledge in the United States.* Princeton, N.J.: Princeton University Press, 1962.

Magdoff, Harry. *The Age of Imperialism: The Economics of U.S. Foreign Policy.* New York: Modern Reader, 1969.

Marcuse, Herbert. *One-Dimensional Man.* Boston: Beacon, 1964.

Martorana, S. V. and Ernest V. Hollis. *State Boards Responsible for Higher Education.* Washington, D.C.: Department of Health, Education and Welfare, 1960.

Medsker, Leland L. and Dale Tillery. *Breaking the Access Barriers: A Profile of Two-Year Colleges.* New York: McGraw-Hill, 1971.

Melman, Seymour. *Our Depleted Society.* New York: Delta Books, 1965.

Mills, C. Wright. *The Power Elite.* New York: Oxford University Press, 1957.

———. *White Collar: The American Middle Classes.* New York: Oxford University Press, 1956.

Monroe, Charles R. *Profile of the Community College.* San Francisco: Jossey-Bass, 1976.

Newman, Frank, et al. *Report on Higher Education.* Washington, D.C.: Government Printing Office, 1971.

———. *The Second Newman Report: National Policy and Higher Education.* Cambridge, Mass.: The MIT Press, 1973.

Newt Davidson Collective. *Crisis at CUNY.* New York: n.p., 1974.

Novak, Michael. *The Rise of the Unmeltable Ethnics.* New York: Macmillan, 1972.

O'Conner, James. *The Fiscal Crisis of the State.* New York: St. Martin's Press, 1973.

Olson, Keith W. *The G.I. Bill, the Veterans, and the Colleges.* Lexington, Ky.: University Press of Kentucky, 1974.

O'Neill, William L. *Coming Apart: An Informal History of America in the 1960's*. New York: Quadrangle, 1971.

Orlans, Harold, ed. *Science Policy and the University*. Washington, D.C.: Brookings Institution, 1968.

Parker, Richard. *The Myth of the Middle Class*. New York: Harper Colophon, 1972.

Penick, J. L. *The Politics of American Science—1939 to the Present*. Chicago: Rand-McNally, 1965.

Pincus, Fred. "Tracking in Community Colleges." *Insurgent Sociologist* 4:17–35.

Piven, Frances Fox and Richard A. Cloward. *Regulating the Poor: The Functions of Public Welfare*. New York: Random House, Vintage Books, 1971.

President's Commission on Higher Education. *Higher Education for American Democracy*. 6 vols. Washington, D.C.: Government Printing Office, 1947.

President's Committee on Education Beyond the High School. *First Interim Report to the President*. Washington, D.C.: Government Printing Office, 1956.

Price, Don K. *The Scientific Estate*. Cambridge, Mass.: Harvard University Press, Belknap, 1965.

Reagan, Michael D. *Science and the Federal Patron*. New York: Oxford University Press, 1969.

Riesman, David. *The Lonely Crowd*. New Haven: Yale University Press, 1974.

Riesman, David and Verne A. Stadtman, eds. *Academic Transformation: Seventeen Institutions Under Pressure*. New York: McGraw-Hill, 1973.

Riesman, David, Joseph Gusfield, and Zelda Gamson. *Academic Values and Mass Education*. Garden City, N.Y.: Doubleday, 1970.

Rivlin, Alice M. *The Role of the Federal Government in Financing Higher Education*. Washington, D.C.: Brookings Institution, 1961.

Ross, David R.B. *Preparing for Ulysses: Politics and Veterans During World War II*. New York: Columbia University Press, 1969.

Rudolph, Fredrick. *The American College and University: A History*. New York: Random House, Vintage Books, 1962.

Schrag, Peter. *The Decline of the Wasp*. New York: Simon and Schuster, 1971.

Sklar, Martin J. "On the Proletarian Revolution and the End of Political-Economic Society." *Radical America* 3:1–41.

Smith, David N. *Who Rules the Universities?* New York: Monthly Review Press, 1973.

Spring, Joel. *The Sorting Machine: National Educational Policy Since 1945.* New York: McKay, 1976.

Touraine, Alain. *The Academic System in American Society.* New York: McGraw-Hill, 1974.

Trimberger, Ellen Kay. "Open Admissions: A New Form of Tracking?" *Insurgent Sociologist* 4:29–43.

U.S. Bureau of Census. *Historical Statistics of the U.S.—Colonial Times to 1970.* Washington, D.C.: Government Printing Office, 1975.

U.S. Office of Education. *Digest of Educational Statistics.* Washington, D.C.: Government Printing Office, 1970.

Veysey, Laurence R. *The Emergence of the American University.* Chicago: University of Chicago Press, 1965.

Wheeler, Thomas C., ed. *The Immigrant Experience: The Anguish of Becoming American.* New York: Penguin Books, 1971.

Whyte, William, Jr. *The Organization Man.* New York: Simon and Schuster, Clarion Books, 1972.

Willingham, Warren W. *Free-Access Higher Education.* New York: College Entrance Examination Board, 1970.

Wilthey, Stephen B. *A Degree and What Else? Correlates and Consequences of a College Education.* New York: McGraw-Hill, 1971.

Woodring, Paul. *The Higher Learning in America: A Reassessment.* New York: McGraw-Hill, 1968.

Zwerling, L. Steven. *Second Best: The Crisis of the Community College.* New York: McGraw-Hill, 1976.

Index

74
LH

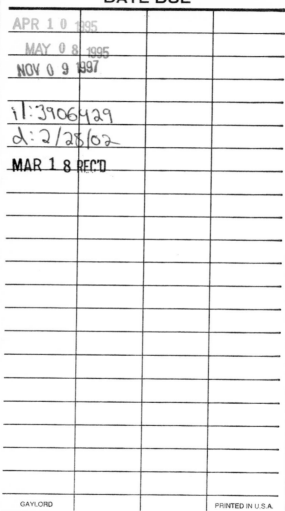

DATE DUE